Praise for
SEALING THE DEAL

"With deep wisdom and compassion, Diana Kirschner provides a powerful blueprint for any woman struggling to find an enduring relationship. Kirschner writes with the authority of a therapist with thousands of hours in the trenches, helping real-life women get out of their own way and into happy partnerships. Read this book: some of these insights might just change your life."

—Evan Marc Katz, author of *Why You're Still Single*

"Dr. Diana has done it again with her fantastic book, SEALING THE DEAL: *The Love Mentor's Guide to Lasting Love*! Her knowledge and teachings are second to none! Definitely read this book, take the quizzes, and find out for sure if he's really the One."

—Julie Spira, bestselling author, *The Perils of Cyber-Dating: Confessions of a Hopeful Romantic Looking for Love Online*

"SEALING THE DEAL is a must-read and a necessary addition to any woman's self-help shelf. It is filled with timeless advice for finding and keeping the One."

—Tamsen Fadal, WPIX-TV morning news anchor
and author of *Why Hasn't He Called?*

"A superlative successor to the smash *Love in 90 Days*. Dr. Diana outlines a thorough and achievable blueprint for creating a nurturing relationship."

—Sherry Amatenstein, author of
The Complete Marriage Counselor

"With a successful 25-year marriage and decades as a therapist to her credit, Diana Kirschner is a relationship expert worth taking seriously. Her book SEALING THE DEAL offers practical, empowering and solid advice for those ready to find and keep the love of a lifetime."

—Arielle Ford, author of *The Soulmate Secret*

"SEALING THE DEAL is a sharp, psychologically astute, hands-on guide to getting and keeping good love in your life. It's like having an older sister whisper the real story in your ear to combat all the relationship lies and myths we learn from Hollywood movies and dating Web sites. My favorite part is when Dr. Diana opens up about her own struggles from the past, proving the wisdom she's sharing is deep and hard-won."

—Susan Shapiro, author of *Secrets of a Fix-up Fanatic* and *Overexposed*

"Fantastic! Bang on! A must read for any woman (or man) who truly wants to have a loving, strong, lasting relationship and is ready to be honest enough to do the work and make the necessary changes."

—Gloria MacDonald, author of *Perfect Partners*

Sealing *The* Deal

The Love Mentor's Guide to Lasting Love

DIANA KIRSCHNER, Ph.D.

CENTER
STREET

NEW YORK BOSTON NASHVILLE

"Love after Love" from COLLECTED POEMS 1948–1984 by Derek Walcott.
Copyright © 1986 by Derek Walcott. Reprinted by permission of Farrar,
Straus and Giroux, LLC.

"Unconditional" from POEMS FOR THE PATH by Jennifer Paine Welwood.
Copyright © 1998 by Jennifer Paine Welwood. Reprinted by permission
of Jennifer Paine Welwood.

"Why Marriage?" Copyright © 1996 by Mari Nichols-Haining. Reprinted
by permission of Mari Nichols-Haining.

"Your Desperation" from THE TAO OF A WOMAN by Michele Ritterman.
Copyright © 2009 by Michele Ritterman. Reprinted by permission
of Skipping Stones Editions.

Center Street
Hachette Book Group
237 Park Avenue
New York, NY 10017
www.centerstreet.com

Center Street is a division of Hachette Book Group, Inc.
The Center Street name and logo are trademarks of Hachette Book Group, Inc.

Printed in the United States of America

First Edition: February 2011

10   9   8   7   6   5   4   3   2   1

Library of Congress Cataloging-in-Publication Data
Kirschner, Diana Adile
Sealing the deal : the love mentor's guide to
lasting love / by Diana Kirschner.—1st ed.
p. cm.
ISBN 978-1-59995-120-1
1. Man-woman relationships.   2. Love.   3. Commitment (Psychology)
4. Single women—Psychology.   I. Title.
HQ801.K5647 2011
646.7'7—dc22
2010032785

*To my husband and love partner, Sam, whose unseen hand
lifts and lights my soul and all that I do.*

*To my great son, Jason, a true-heart warrior, and his beloved
bride, Rachel, who radiates inner grace and outer beauty,
on the occasion of their marriage. May you forever find
love in each other's eyes, blessings in each other's care,
and together create a life rich with unfolding
wonders and new delights.*

CONTENTS

MY LASTING LOVE GRATITUDE LIST

As I expanded out of a childhood chrysalis of great fear and ignorance, I was blessed to learn how to make love itself take seed and grow; doubly blessed to experience such magic in my own marriage; and triply blessed to help many other couples find their own shared path of dreams. With all that I learned, I have longed to write a book about the secrets for making passionate love last. Now that great dream has come true!

First I want to acknowledge all my clients, Love Mentees, and students, who were absolutely instrumental in helping refine the work.

Very special thanks also to: Bel Grubert; Carol and Nolan Grubert; Beth Grubert; Stan and Dr. Hildy Richelson; Beth Coltoff Koren and Dr. Tedd Koren; Michele Ritterman, Ph.D.; Terry Barak; Joey Avniel; and our superb online strategist, Steve Paul, for their ideas, support, and belief in me and the project.

A big shout-out to my first group of brilliant, loving, and magically helpful Love Mentors who work with me, helping women all over the world find their own true love: Lori Hammel, Betts Mayer, Claudia

Braun-Cole, Jim Delpino, and Alec Satin. As I write these words I am thrilled to say that a second, much larger group of talented men and women have joined me as expert Love Mentors to help meet the many requests I receive daily.

Greatest thanks to my wise, dear, and super-supportive friends: the brilliant and generous author Susan Shapiro, the ever-helpful Melanie Gorman from Yourtango.com, Laura Marini, Cathy Kadets, Nanci Deutsch, Deb Kalas, Susan Davies, Alexandra Desbrow, Sandra Park, Sherri Tennant, Mitchell and Liz Rigie, Anna Garduno, Susan Rosbrow-Reich, Ph.D., and Connie Bennett.

My incredible son, Jason Kirschner, was terrifically encouraging, especially when he rescued me from shoulder problems with new mouse gadgets. His amazing wife, Rachel, was always steady and fully supportive.

My dearest soul mate sister, Sandra Robertson, supported me, as ever, with complete and unwavering belief in me and my mission of spreading love.

And thanks to the incredible team at Center Street, whose mission married mine: Rolf Zettersten, Andrea Glickson, Shannon Stowe PR maven, Jody Waldrup, and the whole Hachette Book Group sales force. And most especially, visionary Harry Helm and the dynamo sales goddess Gina Wynn. Heartfelt thanks for believing in me and doing such a fantastic job on the book and its promotion. Thanks to Shauna Toh for her work on the endnotes and to Veronica Sepe for editorial assistance.

I am thrilled and blessed to once again have the brilliant editor Sarah Sper McLellan to shape my manuscript! She is thoughtful, incredibly savvy, and—most important—cares deeply about you finding lasting love! Plus I have been doubly blessed with the gift of very helpful input from my new editor and champion, Kate Hartson.

My PR Angel, Barb Burg, has been a wonder as she has worked her special magic!

My agent, Wendy Sherman, is the best goddess charioteer in the world. She has continued to clear the way for me no matter what, handles all problems, and carries my work to the world. I love her dearly and will be eternally grateful.

My beloved mentor, Dr. Arthur Stein, laid the foundation for this book as well as *Love in 90 Days*, long ago. He is a gifted genius who has graced and transformed my life.

I am also grateful to the many other magnificent and truly inspiring mentors, teachers, and role models who generously gave of themselves, informing and enriching all that I may have to offer.

Finally, I am most grateful to my darling partner in sublime, who taught me the meaning of love in every way, my husband of more than twenty-five amazing years, Dr. Sam Kirschner. What a long, strange, blessed trip it's been!

Wishing you great and lasting love,
Dr. Diana

INTRODUCTION

If you've ever dreamed of lasting love with a powerful and exciting man who is your true match—a real partner with whom you feel secure, held, nourished, and appreciated for who you are—then this could be the *most* life-changing book you will ever read: an experience that will turbocharge your love life faster and more effectively than anything you have tried before.

You may have met a wonderful man, fallen head-over-Jimmy-Choos for him, and two months into the relationship had him tell you he's not ready for anything serious. Maybe you're stuck in feelings for a guy you've known for some time: You are sure that he's the One, although he never seems to get it. Or maybe you have been disappointed, cheated on, and let down by guys who come on so strong in the beginning, only to fizzle out when it's time to move from casual to committed. Perhaps you are caught in a stormy relationship where you're living together or married and you know it is bad for you, yet you can't seem to move forward or get out.

After all you've been through, you may feel hurt, untrusting, hopeless, or even bitter about ever having the security of true love. Not to worry. Your anxious days of uncertainty, insecurity, and disappointment can be over—*for good*. I am going to show you how to free yourself from hurt, worry, and all the leftover baggage from the past. How to banish the worrisome feeling that you'll never have the relationship you want.

This is the moment to leave it all behind, to decide that you will learn how to change things and create the relationship that is just right for you, to find the security, the certainty, the deep fulfillment of committed love that works. As you take this journey with me, you'll discover exactly how a man decides to commit, learn how to ask for what you want, and feel more confident, sexy, and worthy. Welcome to the beginning of the love life of your dreams.

So Who Should Read This Book?

If you...

- Want a great guy you are dating casually to commit to you exclusively
- Are in love with a man who is scared and a commitment-phobe
- Feel uncertain, nervous, and needy once a relationship gets too serious, even if he seems like a great guy
- Don't know how to talk to your man about commitment because you've been together awhile and he never brings it up
- Wonder why an accomplished, clever woman like you does not have a great partner who is committed to her
- Are living together or even married but losing the closeness and connection you really want
- Feel like you are dealing with a Peter Pan
- Are gearing up to give your man an ultimatum about making the decision to move forward or break up
- Notice other women—women who have as much going for them as you do, or even less—married to good men and think, *What gives?*

- Run hot and cold with your guy in terms of emotional connection and commitment
- Feel stuck in a relationship that disappoints and wounds you
- Are shy about asking your man for what you really need and want
- Never get beyond a few months of dating before it fizzles
- Find it hard to keep a man's interest and attraction to you
- Are worried that he may be cheating on you
- Have been betrayed or devastated by a nasty divorce or breakup and now find it hard to open up to the man you are dating
- Have great relationships where you help the guy grow and develop, only to have him leave you and marry the next woman he meets

…then this book was meant for you! It will give you powerful new information that will help you take a rapid 180-degree turn in your love life. This book will guide you through the maze of questions that come up in dealing with the difficult and challenging yet most important aspect of your life: love. It will show you exactly how to resolve a relationship filled with ups and downs and plagued by the anxiety of not knowing where things are going and that leaves you wondering if you are with Mr. Right. Instead, you will learn how to create the security of a deeply fulfilling and committed relationship, either with your current partner or with a new, better match for you.

> The mystery of love is greater than the mystery of death.
> —*Oscar Wilde*

Who Am I?

The professional side: I am a psychologist who is a frequent guest on the *Today* show; I successfully ran the 90 Day Love Challenge on the Fox *Morning Show*; and I'm the star of a PBS TV special, *Finding Your Own True Love*, based on my best-selling dating advice book

Love in 90 Days. More important for you, I have helped thousands of women of all ages find lasting love.

The personal side: I haven't always understood love. In fact, it was my own heartbreak, pain, and utter confusion about love that drove me to study it in the first place. I am a woman who has climbed her way out of a childhood darkened with alcoholism and abuse, the invisible fifth daughter of a Sicilian father who refused to see me when I was born because I was a girl. A dad who only said "I love you" once, when he happened to be drunk. As you can imagine, dating for me was a disaster filled with heart-crushing disappointments.

My first love was a radio DJ who I will call Uncle Rich. It was crazy infatuation at first sight for both of us. For eight months, we spent every minute together, taking in artsy movies, having long, deep talks, and taking meandering walks in the picturesque hills, all punctuated by private times when we just couldn't keep our hands off each other. The chemistry was beyond electric. One day while I was listening to him, Uncle Rich proposed—on the air. His words went through my body like a seismic wave and I felt my heart stop. I grabbed the phone and called him shrieking, "Yes!" He promptly put me on the air so that the listeners could hear the paroxysm of shy giggles that took hold of me. His fans voiced their approval and all was perfect. I was delirious with love.

Three months later, as we were looking at a lofty Old World cathedral for the wedding, Uncle Rich tearfully told me he had to leave town for a better radio gig. I cried but he said he would send for me as soon as he had money for a bigger place. We talked every day on the phone, and I blissfully blazed forward with wedding plans, surrounded by every bridal mag available, choosing my flowers and setting the dinner menu.

But one day, something seemed different. Very different. I asked Uncle Rich what he had done the day before, but he wouldn't answer. His weird silence filled me with panicky feelings. My mind went crazy thinking he had met someone else. I quickly made plans to visit, but before I even got there, the dreaded—and *dreadful*—phone call came. Uncle Rich told me he had indeed fallen for another woman. Just like that, it was all over between us.

In shock, I questioned and questioned him. I cried, even pleaded for him to reconsider. There was no way back in. I could not believe what he was telling me, but nothing I said made a difference. The One, my true Beloved, my fiancé, had really dumped me via a phone call. I hit rock bottom. I couldn't eat or sleep for days. I didn't leave my bed. Weeping was my middle name. I was obsessed with thinking about him, rehashing our final interactions, and wondering what went wrong.

It was the worst emotional pain I'd ever felt, and right then and there I decided something: I never wanted to feel that bad, that heartsick, or that depressed ever again. I got out of bed, went to the library, and checked out every book I could find about love. No matter what it took, I was going to answer all the questions I had about how to create a great and lasting relationship.

It dawned on me that I'd never had any role models of what committed, true love could be like. My parents stuck together but lived in a war zone of alienation and physical fights. My friends' parents were *all* divorcing. My older relatives who were married were less than happy. I had never seen love firsthand. Actually, I had only read about it in the soaring words of poets like Walt Whitman:

> *O that you and I escape from the rest, and go utterly off,*
> *free and lawless,*
> *Two hawks in the air, two fishes swimming in the sea*
> *Not more lawless than we;*
> *That furious storm through me careering,*
> *I passionately trembling;*
> *The oath of the inseparableness of two together,*
> *of the woman that loves me, and whom I love*
> *more than my life, that oath swearing,*
> *O I willingly stake all for you.*

As I drank in transporting words like these, something in my gut told me that the poets spoke truth: enduring passionate bonds must really exist. So I decided to go on looking for the elusive secrets of lasting love.

Learning the Secrets of Love

My search continued for more than two decades and led me to earn an M.A. and Ph.D. in clinical psychology, and study Eastern and Western thinking about love. I learned and grew enough to marry Sam, my rock, the true love of my life. I am thrilled to tell you we have created an awesomely fulfilling marriage lasting more than twenty-five years! Sam and I ran a postgraduate training center, the Institute for Comprehensive Family Therapy. Along with our colleagues we interviewed healthy couples, studying videotape after videotape of pairs fighting and making up. We researched the ones that made it and the ones that didn't. Finally, after years of studying everything I could get my hands on, I came to understand the mysterious process of love and the even more difficult process of forming a committed, passionate relationship that lasts. As they say, I "got it"!

It has been more than twenty-five years since that moment when I started my own personal journey out of the abyss to solve the complex mystery of finding and keeping true love. The fiancé who dumped me gave me the greatest gift ever: an understanding of how to build self-love and deservedness and a relationship that is beyond what I ever imagined possible between a man and a woman. And I passed that gift on, because it gave me the knowledge and ability to help so many single women in every decade of life find their own lasting love. But most important, the secrets I learned can help *you* discover how to rejuvenate and deepen your relationship so that you can take the next steps into an exciting future.

This book is based on my personal and clinical experience plus the best research on love available to date. Each chapter contains many references that are spelled out in full in the notes section at the end of the book. So when I give you advice, please consider it carefully. Try it on for size before you reject it impulsively. And please feel free to tailor it for your individual circumstances so that you make it even better and more effective.

Why I Wrote This Book

The truth is, I am writing this book because my heart is bursting with gratitude for my life with Sam. I want to pass on that ultimate treasure—the best friendship and sexy love that heals the wounds in your heart and opens all the possibilities in living your life full-out. It is this gift of a passionate lasting love that I want to share. I want you to have the comfort, ease, and joy, the exhilarating moments of rapture, the juicy bliss that come with living in a secure, committed relationship that is just right for you.

This book is a gift from my heart to yours. May all the wishes of your heart take root, blossom, and come to sweet fruition.

PART I

Retrain Your Brain: First Get Out of Your Own Way (Yes...You're In It!)

1

The Lasting Love Program

The fountains mingle with the river,
And the rivers with the ocean;
The winds of heaven mix for ever,
With a sweet emotion;
Nothing in the world is single;
All things by a law divine
In one another's being mingle:
Why not I with thine?
—*Percy Bysshe Shelley*

Have you ever been involved and in love with one man for months, or even years, only to find that he simply cannot or will not take that next step into living together or marriage? Instead he gets irritated, distant, and angry—or simply hits the highway—if there is any talk of sharing a future together? Maybe you tend to be involved with a guy for a few months and then, mysteriously, he falls away, leaving you alone. Maybe you have been with a man for ten years who brings over the chicken soup when you are sick, is there whenever you need him, and yet is completely unwilling to have a committed relationship or family life. Or perhaps you are in a long-term on-again, off-again relationship where one or both of you periodically withdraw or see other people. You may be living together or even married, and yet feel disappointed, anxious, and insecure because you are drifting apart rather than coming together.

And even though you have the love of your friends, there is a *real loneliness* to doing it all by yourself.

I know because, as a clinical psychologist specializing in relationships for more than twenty-five years, I have heard countless stories like these. I've spent thousands of hours sitting with women who are frustrated, hurt, lonely, spilling the tears of a broken heart. Strong women, caring women, successful women. Great women of all ages. Dealing with the very real challenges of finding and keeping lasting love.

But the great news is that I have helped many of these clients forge ahead to create the close companionship, the adventure, the rapture, and the juicy passion they had all but given up hope of finding. How? I have devoted my life to studying dating, passionate love, and creating and rekindling commitment with the One you really want. And over decades, I have refined my approach so that it works more effectively and faster than ever. Plus I have used these principles to train a group of highly experienced Love Mentors™ (dating and relationship coaches) who have helped single women create fulfilling relationships all over the world. These principles form the basis for the Lasting Love Program.

If you have just met someone who makes your heart sing and feel uncertain about how to move things along…if you are or have been involved with a man who tends to simply disappear…if you keep getting stuck and losing out with commitment-phobes…if you feel trapped in a disappointing and heartbreaking relationship, your love life is about to change on this program!

> Somewhere there waiteth in this world of ours
> For one lone soul, another lonely soul—
> Each chasing each through all the weary hours,
> And meeting strangely at one sudden goal;
> Then blend they—like green leaves with golden flowers,
> Into one beautiful and perfect whole—

And life's long night is ended, and the way
Lies open onward to eternal day.
                                        —*Sir Edwin Arnold*

When Sally Met Gary

Sally*, a bright-eyed zaftig charmer, used the Lasting Love principles to transform her life's long night of loneliness into a beautiful relationship that was even better than she'd ever imagined. We'll follow her throughout the book and see how she changed the same-old, same-old relationship problems into committed, lasting love.

A speech pathologist who is everyone's best friend, Sally battled her pear-shaped figure and was always concerned about her ample bottom when it came to dating. Nevertheless, she pushed on and found Gary online. His profile was laugh-out-loud funny, and the teasing e-mails they exchanged put a semi-permanent grin on her face and helped her melt five pounds off her figure. When Sally met Gary for a first coffee date she felt a tingle of excitement—he was even cuter than his photo! A prominent blogger, he could turn a witty phrase in person and had Sally mesmerized. He was a little short, a fact she easily overlooked once they started gabbing.

Soon, Sally and Gary spent dreamy hours together drifting on a private happy cloud, finishing each other's sentences and cracking each other up. Gary was not only sharp but generous as well. When he sent her two dozen roses, Sally forwarded a photo of the bouquet to her whole posse, who all agreed that he was different—and clearly smitten.

Gary said as much as he teased Sally about one day being "two octogenarians having an affair in assisted living." *This one is different,*

*In all examples, identifying information has been changed to protect privacy. Some identities are composites.

Sally thought to herself with great relief. *He's the real deal!* But as it got better and better between them, it also got scarier. Some of Gary's mannerisms reminded her of her ex, the guy she caught sex-texting with the blonde next door. After that fiasco Sally was on the couch hiding out with the TV remote for a whole year—she couldn't seem to shake it off. One thing Sally was sure about: She never wanted to feel that kind of agony again. The next time she saw Gary, that painful memory of her ex in the back of her mind created a vague anxiety. She tried to counter this bad feeling with reassuring thoughts about how connected she felt to Gary, how they were so totally on the same wavelength, how he had integrity and was not a cheater like her ex.

Just for a little insurance, Sally decided to work on things more, to try harder, to move things forward so that it would all turn out right this time. The months passed. When she met Gary's family, she brought her secret-recipe cheesecake and wowed them with her funniest story about a first attempt at waterskiing—she'd held on to the lead after she went down in the water, garbling away at them to stop while doing her best not to drown. Gary's brother took her aside to tell her how happy Gary seemed with her, how he needed to settle down with someone like her. When Sally shared this with her girlfriends back at home, they all agreed that it was a very good sign.

Sally helped Gary research his blog stories and carefully read and edited drafts of a novel he was aching to finish. Hopefully, she thought, Gary would realize what a catch she was, how much value she added to his life. She couldn't imagine that he didn't realize what a great team they made. She started leaving a few things at Gary's apartment. He didn't seem to protest, so she moved even more stuff into his place.

Then one night, Sally met Gary for a date. For no apparent reason, something felt off. Drastically off. Gary was too quiet. Plus he suddenly started ordering mixed drinks, which he had never done before. He seemed to be more into his cocktails than her. Sally got this awful sinking feeling that made it impossible to finish her dinner.

The following week he didn't call or text much, even though she left him messages. When she finally got ahold of him, he mumbled something about a deadline. Even though the words were reassuring on the surface, she couldn't stop feeling like she was about to burst into tears. The next time they got together, Gary seemed even farther away and emotionally unavailable. His eyes were glued to his BlackBerry. And he started drinking again. Worst of all, he had none of his usual quips and just wasn't gabbing it up with her. Feeling nervous, Sally asked what was going on. Was it her? Was he upset with her? Gary seemed tense and irritated, but he said everything was fine. In her gut, Sally felt just the opposite. She pushed the issue. Gary exploded and delivered the line, the knife that cut Sally's heart in two: He was just not ready for a serious relationship. Sally could barely breathe as he went on to talk about how he needed time for his novel. *His f***ing novel!* she thought.

Somehow, even though she was shocked and reeling, Sally had known that this very moment was coming. But why did he come on so strong? How could he say all those crazy-in-love things to her in the beginning? Why didn't he appreciate how utterly perfect she was for him? After all the things she did for him!

In her mind she held on, waiting and hoping for him to come to his senses, to mature, to change and choose her.

In desperation Sally called me for Love Mentoring™. I referred her to one of my expert Mentors, who put her on the Lasting Love Program. As a result, Sally was able to create an extraordinary relationship. I want you to learn from Sally's journey from heartbreak to love, so we will be following her throughout this book.

Perhaps you can relate to some of Sally's story. Perhaps you've met the One and seen him come on like gangbusters. He establishes a beautiful relationship with you, only to pull back for no apparent reason. All of a sudden, everything becomes murky and uncertain in your relationship. Are you a couple or not? Has he met someone else? Why is he running hot and cold? Do you have a future together? Should you have The Talk about where things stand? And you wonder, *Is it me? Is it him? Will I ever have a committed, solid, and lasting relationship?*

Yes, I know, it's a downer, but you might feel better knowing that I've experienced variations on this story—and so has pretty much every woman I know. In fact, in one study of college students, 93 percent of the females reported that they had *already* been rejected by someone they passionately loved. You are not alone.

But what if I told you that there is a definite path that can free you from all these painful patterns and the guys who turn out to be jerks? A path that will help you get or rekindle the commitment and security you want and deserve? This is the Lasting Love Program. No games, no mind tricks. The program is based on solid, dependable methods that grow out of experience and the latest research on dating, relationships, living together, and marriage.

Whether you have been dating for a few months or have been on-again, off-again for several years, you will learn how to lay the groundwork so that you are comfortable moving forward and your partner is more interested in building a committed future together. You will find ways to let go of your own fears, to profoundly connect with your guy so that your relationship becomes more of what you want it to be. I'll also show you how to move things forward so that your Beloved can know with certainty that he wants and chooses to be with you and only you, and that he is there supporting you as you support him. If you want kids, he can step up and be the partner who will have those children, with all the joy and elation they bring. You can create this life. And I'm going to help you get there.

> Learning about how to get out of my own way, how true commitment works and how to create passionate attraction helped me fulfill my dream of love with the greatest guy. We are so connected, at home with each other and

can talk about anything. The sex is an expression of our love for each other. I have never experienced that before! We were married on the beach in Jamaica with the setting sun and a Caribbean blessing for our union. I was dancing on air and still am two months later!

—Robin, who used the Lasting Love Program
to marry her soul mate

Your Lasting Love Basics

This book will show you the step-by-step pathway to committed love. You will learn how to build an emotional connection and commitment with a man that will carry you through the trials, setbacks, and disappointments that come along in life, a connection that will bring the kind of joy and contentment you have always imagined. I've helped thousands of women get the commitment they want by following these straightforward methods, and now I'm sharing these secrets with you. You will learn how to:

- Handle your own fears, doubts, and baggage from the past.
- Tell if your partner really is Mr. Right.
- Use the powerful natural laws of attraction that underlie that I've-Gotta-Have-Her-in-My-Life feeling.
- Set up the conditions that lead to your Beloved wanting to date you exclusively.
- Help your boyfriend overcome his fears of commitment.
- Tell when you should cut your losses and leave a relationship that is a waste of your precious time.
- Have The Talk so that he listens heart-to-heart and bonds more deeply with you.
- Set the stage so that a man will do whatever it takes to build a fulfilling and wonderful life with you.

The book is divided into four sections. Part I, *Retrain Your Brain: First Get Out of Your Own Way (Yes . . . You're In It!)* covers: the six killer beliefs about love that sabotage your relationship; how to overcome fears that destroy any chance of lasting love; and the single most important thing you can do for yourself and your relationship—get a Love Mentor. Part II, *Is He Really the One?*, shows you: exactly how men think about love and commitment; men's eight common fears of commitment and what to do about them; the powerful Seven "Real" Laws of Attraction that can take your relationship to a deeper level; and how to know for sure if your guy is the One. Part III, *Sealing the Deal*, covers: setting the stage for the commitment you want; exactly how to have The Talk so he really will listen; what to do if he won't commit, becomes distant, or cheats; how to decide about living together or getting married; plus the surprising research that reveals the benefits of a good marriage. Part IV, *How to Be Happily in Love Together Forever*, will show you how to make romantic love and passion last no matter how many years you've been together.

How to Work the Lasting Love Program

I recommend that you simply read the whole book first to get an initial sense of the powerful Lasting Love principles and practices. Then go back and *really* do the suggested exercises. Don't just read the exercises. Do them. Play full-out. Make this the million-dollar course for yourself. The jackpot to end all jackpots. If you hit a downturn, keep going and you will win big-time. Even if you feel that a particular section does not apply to your situation right now, please read it and do the exercises anyway. When it comes to love, things can change rapidly and dramatically. I want you to be fully prepared!

As long as you use the principles and strategies, there is no wrong way to work the program. You can also tailor the program to your unique needs by jumping ahead and then circling back to complete all the work.

The Lasting Love work can be done solo, or you can share parts of it with a guy who's a serious contender (for example, the chapter on the benefits of marriage). Completing the processes with a coach—a wise person who is successful in love and devoted to you and your relationship success—is an extremely powerful choice. Another option is to use the book along with one-on-one coaching from one of my expert Love Mentors who has used Lasting Love principles to get or stay happily married.

LASTING LOVE ONLINE

For even more support, visit my Web sites www.lovein90days.com and www.dating-advice.tv. On these sites you can find a professional Love Mentor, daily affirmations, articles, quizzes, funny and educational videos about the dilemmas of modern love, and other helpful resources. Plus you can e-mail me about your concerns, adventures, and successes! (See Appendix A for more details.)

Okay. Now let's dig into the nitty-gritty.

So You Want a Commitment?

Why is it that when a woman meets a great guy, she tends to hear those wedding bells, or in some way, shape, or form jump straight to commitment? For example, Sheryl, a client of mine who was a brilliant professor, burst into my office, flush with excitement. "I've met the One!" she exclaimed.

"Okay! Tell me all about him," I answered.

"Larry's tall, athletic, in his forties, and just about to sell his own company." Her eyes twinkled. "And he is reading Eckhart Tolle!"

"Sounds great."

"He says he wants marriage and kids."

"Yes."

"He's a sports nut, though. I hate sports."

"Uh-huh."

"But I do like tennis. And oh, I forgot, he said he's writing a song for me!"

"How long have you been dating him?" I asked.

"Well, we've been e-mailing back and forth for two weeks," Sheryl said sheepishly.

"You mean you've never even spoken to Larry!"

Sheryl blushed.

You know exactly where this relationship went.

Why do we *do* this kind of thing? We meet someone of interest, who could be the One, and immediately doodle a hyphenated last name, thinking about how great it will be to stay over at his place and never have to leave. Lost in fantasy, we entertain all kinds of ideas about sealing the deal first. But then when it really starts to happen with the guy, we often get cold feet. We find out about his warts and pimples, both physical and metaphorical. Second thoughts erupt about his not being so great and wondering if it's better to just get out.

Women tend to be hung up on commitment for good reasons. For one thing, we are physically wired to find a mate, bond, and reproduce. Oxytocin, the "tend and befriend" hormone that creates a powerful attachment, is primed and ready to be produced in our bodies. Second, from early childhood we are bombarded with fairy tales, romance movies, and advertisements that position happily-ever-after as the high note of life. And of course a committed deep love relationship is a great and wondrous thing.

I define such a relationship as a monogamous, romantic win–win life partnership; a relationship that satisfies both members' deepest needs for fusion and oneness (the "we"), as well as individual needs for personal space, growth, and self-expression (the "I"). An ancient Buddhist myth says that the universe is the love play of a divine being that split itself in two in order to know the ecstasy of love. According to the myth, all men are fragments of this original god, while all women are splinters of the original goddess. When the divine assumes human form, the male and female search for each other to regain and celebrate their original Oneness, the sacred couple. Our love desires are born out of the yearning for the rapture of reunion. Poets, songwriters, shrinks, and gurus all agree with the findings of hard scientific research: Love makes the world into a garden of possibilities. Passionate, committed love makes us healthier and happier. It is worth everything. No wonder, then, that many women desperately want a committed and close relationship.

Yet at the same time, they sabotage themselves in so many ways. I've seen countless women who say they want a long-term boyfriend, partner, or husband but are undermining their chances of creating what they dearly want. So let's get one thing straight up front: Before you can have a committed, fulfilling relationship, you need to have realistic expectations of exactly what such a relationship looks like.

Expectations and Commitment

Let's first dispense with the romantic notions or common fears women have about commitment in love. It's *not* about:

- A perfect, divine-right partner simply appearing to whisk you out of your lonely, hard day-to-day life.
- Getting to a place where your partner is so much on your wavelength that he magically understands you and provides what you need.

- Moving through some rite of passage where you and Mr. Right become happy together forever.
- Getting the relationship to a point where you never have disagreements or fights.
- Hanging in there and somehow outlasting a commitment-phobe who never chooses you.
- Finally throwing in the towel and settling for Mr. Good Enough, whom you really do not feel the slightest bit attracted to.
- Winning a hard-fought battle in which you finally manipulate the guy into loving and choosing you forever.
- Giving up yourself and your own needs so that you can be the right partner for your guy.

Commitment is a continual process in a couple that deepens over time. You open up, spend more time together, and the best-foot-forward infatuation stage ends. As you relax into the relationship, the not-so-wonderful qualities come out. At times you can be inattentive, thoughtless, cross, or even mean. This re-creates some of the disappointments each of you experienced in childhood, because a partner often represents a parent figure. But commitment means that you and your partner pass these tests, these challenges, these curveballs you consciously and unconsciously throw at each other. You may fight, be sorely hurt, be awful to your partner, but together you recover, repair, and restore the loving connection. Because of commitment, you accept each other despite your worst qualities. This creates something stupendous: being loved with all your flaws!

As you weather and surmount your problems, you become ever closer. Each of you becomes more loving toward yourself and your partner as you share more deeply and grow in mutual loyalty. The process of commitment is difficult at times—there is no perfect person, and as two people begin to blend their lives together, there is always something to work on. But while you work through the commitment process with your significant other, you begin to build something new, something stronger. And that's a relationship in which you help each other grow toward what each of you considers a better version of yourself. This powerful process fuels change and novelty in the couple so that dopamine—the infatuation neurotransmitter (brain chemical)—is created again and again. The result: lovers who are graced to re-experience the excitement of falling in love and that wild ecstasy of newlyweds for ten, twenty years—or even more.

But to reach this pinnacle of committed passionate love, you must be prepared to climb a winding uphill road. The Lasting Love Program will show you how to be successful on that climb. You will learn about:

- Being realistic and settling for less than perfection.
- Forgiveness rather than brooding and holding on to painful grudges.
- Coming together and being content with the present.
- Sharing the day-in, day-out irritations and disappointments.
- Celebrating each other's triumphs.
- Being there for each other through the inevitable suffering and setbacks life throws at us.
- Co-creating plans for a shared future.
- Working as a team toward common goals.
- Supporting each other's dreams, goals, and best self-identity.
- Working through heartbreaking fights, restoring and building an even better connection and commitment.
- Kindling and rekindling shared passion, ecstasy, and joy.

Does this journey, with its twists and turns, call to you? Yes? Read on!

THE OPENING EXERCISE: *CHOOSE A GOAL*

Take a few minutes and think about what you want to create in your love life. What prompted you to buy this book? What do you want to change? What is your goal for your relationship? When you sharpen your intention and set a goal, you are much more likely to transform your reality. I say, imagine what you really want, even if at this point it seems impossible to get! Even if you are dealing with the biggest commitment-phobe on the planet or feel lonely, disappointed, uncertain, anxious, and confused right now. Even if true and lasting love seems to be impossible, especially for you.

If you allow yourself to begin thinking of possibilities, little by little, step by step they can begin to manifest. Since thoughts underlie your moods and your actions, even small changes in your thinking or in the way you talk to yourself can slowly transform everything in your life.

In choosing a goal, just let all I have written here be food for thought, ideas for your heart. Check your idea of what is possible for you at the door and see what ideas about love truly excite you. Just hypothetically. At first. Okay?

On the next page I've listed the eight key steps toward deepening commitment in love. Look over the list and pick out a goal (or a few of them) that calls to you right now. You will know a goal calls to you if you feel a little tug or a tingle or maybe even some sadness in your heart when you think about it. We will work toward your goal(s) together as you go through this book, and I will share specific tools to achieve each one. As you reach your goals, you may even want to add more.

Commitment Goals

1. Create an exciting love intention/affirmation about having committed love in your life.

2. Create greater self-esteem, deservedness, and self-love.

3. Break out of self-sabotage and fear of intimacy.

4. Agree that you and your partner will be dating each other exclusively.

5. Declare love for each other.

6. Talk with your Beloved about what you both want in a shared future; lifestyle; finances; religious beliefs; fears, goals, dreams; and whether you want marriage and/or children.

7. Commit to moving in together or getting engaged.

8. Marry or make or renew a lifetime commitment to create a loving win–win partnership that gives each of you roots (stability and dedication) and wings (fulfilling your personal dreams for the future).

Write your goal down as an affirmation in the present tense, as if it is happening right now. For example, if you chose goal 1, write a sentence like, *I have lasting, passionate, fulfilling love in my life.* If your goal is number 2, you might say, *I deserve a full commitment from my*

Beloved. Or for number 7, you could write, *Brad and I commit to moving in together.*

Post your affirmation(s) where you and you alone can see it (them) every day. Make sure to read your note several times a day. Give the affirmation(s) your full attention for just a few seconds as you read over it (them). You do not have to believe an affirmation in order for it to "work" and come true. Simply say it and let yourself have a fantasy as if it were true.

The latest research shows that the process of attention to and repetition of new material (affirmations) can retrain and rewire the neural connections in your brain! As you practice your love affirmation over time, your brain will create more and more connections that help reinforce your new beliefs and love intention. How can this be? A principle in neuroscience called Hebb's law says, *Neurons that fire together, wire together.* Practicing your love intention regularly will "rewire" your neuronal connections so that thoughts having to do with you in a relationship become associated with the intention, and a whole network of positive connections grows and expands. The net result is a more powerful "muscle" around creating love that is right for you. So start giving your neurons their marching orders.

Throughout Part I, I will be showing you different ways to retrain and rewire your brain so that you can get out of your own way and consciously create lasting and passionate love.

Speaking of getting out of your own way, when negative thoughts do occur, train yourself to repeat your love intention in your mind. Do not fight doubts, fears, worries, or painful feelings—just let them come, but then simply and gently repeat your affirmation. If you do this repeatedly, you will find that the problem thoughts and feelings have far less potency. You can then be more grounded emotionally in dealing with your partner when he becomes distant or hurtful, and you can more clearly and easily create the loving interaction you prefer.

Commitment ultimately stems from making a decision about what you are creating in your life, putting your attention on that decision over and over again, and then acting on it, even in the face of disappointments. You decide, commit, and take action toward your own love-filled happy future. When you do this again and again, no matter what, you will eventually succeed in having all the magical alchemy of committed love for yourself and with another.

EXERCISE 2: *THE CONTRACT*

Here's what I tell my mentees, and here's what I say to you:

As you go through the book, push yourself beyond your limits. Face your inner saboteurs and the behavioral patterns that don't serve you. Expect the exhilaration of a roller coaster, then just hang on for the ride of your life. I'll be there with you, on every twist, turn, climb, and drop.

On the next page, you will see a contract. Make a copy, fill it in, and sign it. Amend it if you like, but keep its spirit. *The biggest commitment of all occurs between you and yourself—that is the unbending intent to give yourself the gift of lasting love.* Only you can do it. The contract is designed to help you stay the course. Post it in a private place where you can see it every day.

L A S T I N G   L O V E   C O N T R A C T

I, _____, understand that I am undertaking an intensive program designed to give myself true, lasting love that is just right for me. I commit myself to doing the exercises and following the recommended program to the best of my ability. This work is now Priority One in my life.

I further realize that this program will raise emotional issues, make me aware of my self-sabotaging patterns, and surface my hopelessness, despair, and fears about committed love. I know that at times I will truly want to backtrack or even quit. Nonetheless, I hereby commit to following the program one day at a time.

To this end, I hereby commit to nurturing and strengthening myself so that I can do what I and only I can do: deliver the committed love relationship I long for.

_____   _____
Signature   Date

Love feels no burden, thinks nothing of trouble,
attempts what is above its strength,
pleads no excuse of impossibility.
It is therefore able to undertake all things,

and it completes many things and warrants them to
take effect,
where he who does not love would faint and lie down.
Though weary, it is not tired;
though pressed, it is not straightened;
though alarmed, it is not confounded;
but as a living flame it forces itself upwards and securely
passes through all.

—*Thomas à Kempis*

May this book be a living flame for you, carrying you upward, securely past trials and tribulations…to that place where dreams are realized and the light of love never dies.

2

Killer Beliefs

HOW HIDDEN THOUGHTS ABOUT LOVE

SABOTAGE YOUR RELATIONSHIP

The greatest barrier to success is the fear of failure.
—*Sven-Göran Eriksson*

Have you ever wondered if you were missing something when it comes to having a relationship with a man? After a whirlwind courtship in which a guy is all gaga for you, he insists on having a relationship with you and then suddenly pulls back, acting distracted and lukewarm—do you sometimes get the sense that all men are screwed up? That love is too difficult? That you will never find that terrific guy who can rock your world and not get scared off when it comes to making the big decision? One who can truly hang in there?

Well, you're not alone. Many women have experienced these thoughts and feelings yet haven't been able to move past them. The good news is that your frustration is about to end. In this chapter, you will learn about a powerful force that is at the root of most of your disappointments in love. This force subtly creates an impenetrable barrier between a man and a woman even while sparks are flying between them. It causes emotional distance, even for women who are good communicators, taking over a woman's romantic life and killing off any chance she has at creating lasting love. No matter how hard she tries, she winds up alone as the man she wants withdraws and fades away.

Like a vampire, this force comes in many insidious forms and often strikes when the woman is least aware of its presence. And even if she vigilantly repels it, often it will return time and time again to drain all the romantic love from her life.

This powerful force is composed of simple little things called thoughts: destructive, pessimistic, and negative beliefs about love.

Relationship Roadblocks

Beliefs underlie and shape our experience, our perceptions of reality, our moods and emotions, and everything we say and do. Psychologists point out that we are aware of many of our beliefs, but others lurk just underneath the surface of our minds. It's these hidden beliefs that tend to shape the most important parts of our lives, without us being truly aware that they are doing so. When it comes to relationships, if you have beliefs based on fear, scarcity, abuse, past disappointments, and loss, they make up a force that can put up a complete roadblock on your love journey. These include negative, false, and delimiting beliefs about men, love, or intimate relationships. I call these the silent relationship killers.

The last time you were disappointed or hurt in a relationship—maybe after a breakup, or when your boyfriend flirted with another woman, or after your partner had to stay late at the office once again and miss your dinner date—what did you think? If you're not sure, examine what you said, out loud, to close friends. Do any of the following sound familiar?

You can't trust men—they all cheat.

I'm too much for a man to handle.

All men are jerks.

Guys are a**holes when it comes to relationships.

What if these were not truths but simply beliefs? Conclusions you reached that just don't serve you? Stories you created in your own head? Yes, you are (or were) in love. Yes, he is (or was) acting strange. But does that *really* mean that *all* men are screwed up? That love is too painful? That you have some fundamental flaw that makes you unlovable? Does it mean you will never find lasting love? No! These are nothing more than self-sabotaging beliefs that you have made up based on past experiences. And they're keeping you from the relationship you want. Knowingly or unknowingly, you bring these killer thoughts into every relationship you enter, even though what you really desire is an emotional connection, a strong bond, and a deeper committed relationship.

How Killer Beliefs Work to Kill Off Love

Lasting, passionate love does exist—this has been proven by recent brain research! But it takes work, and a good part of that work is managing killer beliefs. Let's look more closely at what happens when these core destructive beliefs are not managed, but instead are carried from your past into your present (and future) so that they destroy your relationships.

There are no perfect partners, no fairy-tale meant-to-be relationships that just travel on autopilot straight to eternal nirvana. In the natural progression of falling in love and then getting to know each other, both partners discover aspects of the other that are quite disappointing, disagreeable, and even wounding. All love relationships—even great ones—have challenges. And many people experience some form of anxiety around commitment; after all, moving forward with a partner is a move into the unknown. There are always pulls and tugs among career, personal time and hobbies, and spending more time together as a couple. So tensions and problems surface, and these in turn stir up your killer beliefs.

The killer beliefs shape your mind to seize on any bump in the road as proof that your negative ideas about love are all true. When you experience a big setback, a jealous quarrel, or a heartbreak, you may start to think: *Am I losing myself in this relationship? Is this too hard? Am I settling? Is he really the guy for me? If I really open up my heart, is he going to disappear on me? Am I going to be hurt?* Your baggage from the past gets dragged into your present and leaves you worried and ill at ease with your current partner, killing off the vitality and joy of your current relationship. You react, pull back, attack, smother, or simply become hopeless. You are not forthcoming with your thoughts, speaking your truth, or explaining what you really need. This tension leads to a lack of understanding and emotional distance; it makes it hard, if not impossible, for your partner to see you for who you really are, and consequently for you to see him as he really is—not as your ex.

The trickiest aspect of this negativity is that an intimate relationship tends to bring to the surface the disappointments of past relationships and even our childhood wounds, creating tremendous emotional breakdowns. It's like pressing the replay button; once again you're dealing with the same hurtful scenes, the abandoning father, the judgmental mother, or the first love who dumped you. It is from these experiences in love that we came to form killer beliefs.

Traumatic events actually cause our brains—specifically our neural synapses—to rewire their connections so that they are more reactive and stressed by similar situations. So when we break up with a long-term lover or husband or are betrayed by infidelity, our killer beliefs are reinforced, and with that our neural connections between thoughts and emotions about love and disappointment are strengthened. Not only that, but killer beliefs usually form in clusters, too, so that one cascades into another and another in a stranglehold of negativity.

Don't think this happens to you? Let's take a look at Sharon and see if her situation sounds familiar.

It was Sharon's birthday, and when her guy didn't make a fuss over her, it brought up a defining and critical experience from adolescence when her father ignored how good she looked in her prom dress and made a fuss about her sister Helen instead. It was in this pivotal scene from childhood that Sharon first decided that she was unlovable as a woman. Layered upon that are guys she dated who simply disappeared from her life. So in dealing with her current boyfriend who ignored her birthday, she revisited the killer belief, *I can't have love because I'm not lovable.* This cascaded into a second one, *All men let you down in the end.* And finally, *This relationship is not working.* These core beliefs emerged because of a simple breakdown in the here and now that could easily have been fixed.

Instead Sharon reacted with massive disappointment, sadness, hopelessness, withdrawal, and irritability, punctuated by angry jabs... And what effect did this have on her relationship with her boyfriend? It didn't produce fun and games, that's for sure!

Even though it is not apparent, a man has finely tuned radar about one thing: *a woman's unhappiness.* Often he cannot separate himself emotionally from her; his partner's unhappiness becomes his own. Your disappointment, tension, moodiness, distance, and irritability will usually trigger his hot buttons and lead to arguments and a painful wedge in your connection.

The whole relationship-killer process starts with not taking his disappointing behavior at face value, just as it is. Instead of being present and simply looking at what happened, you take the disappointment as proof of your core negativistic beliefs. You assign it meaning way above and beyond what actually occurred. *He forgot my birthday.* This is the fact. All the drama about your unlovability and everything falling apart is just a story you concocted.

Instead of taking the healthy road—saying in a loving way that you are disappointed and showing your boyfriend how to make it up to you—you worry, fret, sulk, whine, criticize him to his face or to your friends, and distance yourself. Instead of showing him how to be your knight, how to come through and to win with you, your attention is stuck on: how impossible relationships are; how depressed you are because there is something wrong with you; what a jerk he is; and/or how this relationship is going nowhere. You subject yourself to a process that is a whirlpool of suffering. Does any of this sound familiar? Painful?

What happens when you don't identify and manage these kinds of killer beliefs? Bottom line: They consciously and unconsciously sabotage any attempt to pull together with your partner when inevitable relationship roadblocks occur. You're no longer in the here and now, experiencing the relationship as it's unfolding—you're actually operating as if this were an extension of previous failed relationships. In other words, you are living in the past, a practice that will get you nowhere. I've seen this scenario over and over again in my practice— even though the woman is the one who, on the surface, has been pressing for the relationship to work and move forward.

Sometimes it's hard to tell the difference between normal anxieties and killer beliefs. With normal fears, it is easier to ask for and receive reassurance from your partner and then soothe yourself about making the right choice and the fulfillment that lies in your future together. This is quite different from the depressive gravity and the often unconscious nature of killer beliefs. So with that in mind, I urge you to read all the following killer beliefs and do the exercises, being honest with yourself so that you become very present to their appearance and impact on you.

> Deal honestly and objectively with yourself; intellectual honesty and personal courage are the hallmarks of great character.—*Brian Tracy*

The Six Killer Beliefs

If you want out of this mind trap, first you need to uncover what killer belief(s) you are holding on to so you can excavate it from your mind. Scary as it may seem, focusing on what bothers you *most* about being in relationships, about men, and about committed love is what can ultimately set you free. Over the years, I have heard the following six core self-sabotaging beliefs countless times. Some of them, like *All men are jerks*, have become über-destructive urban legends that women freely banter about.

First read through each of the following statements, including their variations, with the attitude of an anthropologist studying the beliefs of a newly discovered tribe. Imagine that you've just discovered these beliefs and are examining them for the first time.

Then go through them again and try each one on for size in your mind. Do you agree with it just a little bit? Good. Does it cause a reaction in you? Even better. Do specific people, places, and events come bubbling to mind? Great! The first steps on the Lasting Love Program are noticing your beliefs and then your reactions to them so that later you can dismantle them and free yourself from their stranglehold.

KILLER BELIEF 1: *THERE ARE NO GOOD MEN*

Other variations on this theme:

- All men are jerks.
- All men are babies.
- All men are cheaters.
- All men are liars.
- All men let you down in the end.
- All the good ones are taken.
- All the available men have defects.
- All the available men are losers.

This killer belief is so pervasive in our culture that it deserves a little more time devoted to it than the others. Just think about the character George Clooney plays in the movie *Up in the Air*. This handsome guy flies around firing people on behalf of downsizing corporations; his dearest passion is collecting air mileage points. He's totally unable to bond or connect emotionally with anyone. The ultimate jerk. And this movie was acclaimed! A recent series of FedEx commercials depicted men as inept in doing something as simple as sending a package. And the cultural references to men as jerky characters go on and on. If you simply pay attention to what women say in casual conversation, you will hear a great deal of man-bashing.

This killer belief usually surfaces in two different ways: as a dead-end dating pattern, Not Perfect—I'll Pass, where every single contender is perceived as having a fatal flaw; or as out-of-control fears of rejection and abandonment that nullify feelings of trust and shut down a woman's heart.

The Not Perfect—I'll Pass Problem

This is derived from the notion that all the good guys are taken and only the defective ones are available. Here, the fear is that to actually choose a man would be settling. As Lori Gottlieb describes in her excellent book *Marry Him: The Case for Settling for Mr. Good Enough*, women can be picky, picky, picky when it comes to their suitors. They practice what I call the laws of repulsion, sitting on their high horses and judging the man's physical qualities or behavioral traits. This guy is too paunchy, too bald, too old, too young, or even too good looking; that one has hands that are just too small. Other deal breakers: bad taste in music, a cheesy sense of humor, loves me too much, is too predictable, or uses the wrong table fork. One perfectly intelligent, accomplished, single-for-a-long-time gal recently told me that she could tell just by hearing a guy's name that he was wrong for her—and it was not some bizarre moniker.

The negative judgments spewing from this self-sabotaging belief are based on superficial characteristics or traits. You become an expert in getting rid of all those defective "bad guys" who could never be the One. But guess what? These complaints—including the typical ones that I've listed above—have *nothing* to do with the qualities that make for a partner who can provide lasting love and happiness. Study after study has shown that the most important variables leading to happy relationships and marriages are a guy's (and your) character virtues, especially empathy, concern for others, and willingness to grow. So not only did you ditch the "bad" ones, but you threw out the good ones, the great ones, and all the in-between ones, too!

Research clearly shows it is contempt that kills off love. Instead of being nitpicky and acting out of these laws of repulsion, it is important to change your perception to notice what is really at the guy's core in terms of his values and character. If you don't, your killer belief and the attitudes associated with it set up a whole host of negative and contemptuous vibes, as well as emasculating and cold, bitchy behavior that has men heading for the hills. If you have this form of deadly dating pattern, you could have already thrown away perfectly great guys, any one of whom would have brought you happiness.

The Chase Me Problem

Maybe you're not Miss Picky when it comes to relationships, but the minute your boyfriend wants to move forward to a deeper commitment, you panic. You pull back and become unavailable or quiet or act crazy and dump him. Even if he acts loving, you insist to your friends that he doesn't really care about you. All this happens almost against your own will and for no particular reason having to do with him or the relationship. I call this pattern Chase Me.

The Chase Me deadly dating pattern is all about fear. Deep down, you believe that no matter how good things are right now, it's not going to last: Somewhere down the road there will come rejection and abandonment. The net-net is that *you* are the commitment-phobe. When you start to seriously fall for someone, you ultimately end up breaking up with him before he can hurt you. In this way, you are in control of the heartbreak. What you really want is for the man to smash through the barricades you've thrown up and ride in on his white horse and claim you. But you never give him even the remotest clue, like where the corral is located, and because you've pushed him away again and again, he doesn't magically come after you. Then you say to yourself and your friends, "All men let you down in the end." As the psychoanalysts used to say, the fear is the unconscious wish. Women who operate under the Chase Me pattern usually wind up helping to create the very thing they fear: being abandoned and alone. If you would like to learn more about the Not Perfect—I'll Pass or Chase Me deadly dating patterns, pick up my last book, *Love in 90 Days: The Essential Guide to Finding Your Own True Love.*

Shayna, a thirty-something curly-haired advertising copywriter, was caught in a Chase Me pattern. She grew up with an alcoholic father who, it turned out, had an entirely separate, secret family with kids he had fathered with another woman. He took up residence with the "other" family when Shayna was eleven. She learned her killer belief from the mouth of her bitter mom, who would often say, "All men are pigs. You can never trust them."

While Shayna spent most of her free time working on a romance novel, she had actually seriously dated only one man, a lawyer named Brian. He wanted to marry her, but Shayna felt too anxious at the thought; the bottom line was that she felt she could not trust him. Shayna started throwing tantrums about his working late and his travel schedule. Among other things, she worried that he was cheating on her. Meanwhile, Brian was with her every possible moment he could be while he prepared for a massive trial. They slept together almost every night of the week and on weekends. He introduced her to his family as the One, texted her sexy notes, and was ready to go ring shopping.

Shayna told her friends (all of whom were single) that the thought of ring shopping with Brian made her feel very nervous—as if she was making a life-threatening and dreadful mistake. Her friends (more like frenemies) told her that being with Brian might spell the end of her writing career. Plus, they pointed out, he wasn't creative or into the arts like she was. Their negative talk reinforced Shayna's killer belief, and she began to sour on Brian. As time went by, Shayna became more and more sullen and bitchy during the times she and Brian were together. After many attempts to break through Shayna's walls, Brian finally threw up his hands; instead of getting on one knee, he packed his suitcase and left. A year later, Shayna heard that he was marrying a painter whom he had met at a museum fund-raising event.

Shayna realized that she had made a huge mistake. She decided to work with one of my expert Love Mentors to help overcome her killer beliefs and dead-end relationship patterns. In Chapter 4, we will return to Shayna to find out what happened with her love life.

THERE ARE NO GOOD MEN
KILLER BELIEF WARNING SIGNS

You keep wondering why a woman like you who has so much going for her is single and alone. In addition, you may be lost in a whirl where you love him, you hate him, you just don't give a sh*t—and you can't stop yourself from acting bitchy or distant.

KILLER BELIEF 2: *I WILL NEVER HAVE LASTING LOVE BECAUSE SOMETHING'S WRONG WITH ME*

Other variations on this theme:

- I can't trust my instincts, choices, or judgment.
- I am unlovable.
- I am too old.
- I am too fat.

- I am not attractive to men.
- I am too successful.
- I am not successful enough.
- I have kids that get in the way.
- I have nothing to offer.
- I'm damaged goods.
- I don't know what's wrong with me.

This relationship-killer belief tends to create fears of being rejected, and it can play out in many different ways. You might be self-deprecating, putting yourself down jokingly to guard against the rejection that you know is coming. You might say: "I'm a great person to fall for; I've got six kids and live in a rented shoe. *Not really.* But I do have teenagers that drive me crazy and our place is so tiny…" You may withhold information about your past or lie about your debt. You may push a man away altogether even though the initial courtship has gone well. Or you might tolerate only so much close-ness; if the guy starts showing real interest and commitment, you react by rejecting him for no apparent reason. On the other hand, if you are saddled with this self-sabotaging belief, you may put up with a distant and unsatisfying relationship or even one in which you're physically and/or verbally abused.

Note: If you are facing physical abuse, remember that this is never acceptable. You need to keep yourself and your kids, if you have them, safe. This is the top priority. See the section on Cautions Regarding a Violent Partner on page 229 for my recommendations on how to deal with a potentially dangerous situation. In my opinion, there is no future for a relationship that is marked by domestic violence.

Now, let's look at a happier example where the guy was not abusive and there was a future, in spite of a woman's self-sabotaging belief.

Robin was a funny, warm, emergency room nurse who was thirty pounds overweight. She had a history of finding guys who were less successful, becoming their best friend and buddy. She would fall in love with them, and yet never reveal her true feelings. With deep-seated beliefs that she was too fat and unattractive, she often wisecracked with guys she liked about being "as big as a hospital wing" as a way of fitting in. She never flirted or even tried to make herself more feminine and attractive. Out of her own fears of commitment, Robin even pushed away Hector, the one guy who was smitten with her. She actually suggested that he date her best friend.

Luckily, Hector was one guy who knew what he wanted. He put on the full-court press, telling Robin of his feelings for her and absolutely refusing to go away. Robin used some of the Lasting Love techniques (we will be discussing them in the next chapter) to overcome her killer belief. She was then able to sit still long enough to accept Hector's attention and love without making a joke or sarcastic remark. They are now living together and thoroughly enjoying their plant-filled hideaway.

I WILL NEVER HAVE LASTING LOVE BECAUSE SOMETHING'S WRONG WITH ME
KILLER BELIEF WARNING SIGNS

You have many self-doubts, especially about your deservedness and attractiveness as a woman. It is very hard, if not impossible, to relax, be real, and speak your truth with a man. You may over-give in order to gain the love of a man.

KILLER BELIEF 3: *TRUE LOVE DOES NOT EXIST; IT'S JUST A DEAL*

Other variations on this theme:

- Men just use women.
- Only weak or needy people stay with each other.

- Relationships are merely tit-for-tat trade-offs, like business deals.
- Lasting love is a made-up Hollywood and advertising fantasy.
- There are no really happy couples, only ones who've settled.
- Lasting relationships are not about love, they are about compromising for the sake of the children.
- The best I can hope for is [fill in the blank].

This killer belief creates cynicism and hopelessness about true, caring, passionate, and fulfilling love. No matter how kind or caring the guy is toward her, this woman still wonders, *What is he after? Is it just for the sex? Does he need a trophy woman to look good? Does he need help to get a new job?* Loving acts are seen as barter chips to get something in return. If a man feels only that cynicism, he will walk away.

Jane was head of sales in a large corporation. She was a fifty-something powerhouse who had been dating a clothing mogul on and off for ten years. But she had tired of their routine of going to social events, helping each other do business networking, and then retiring to his penthouse to have booze-fueled sex. She wanted more than this distant arrangement from her boyfriend but she was so afraid; afraid that he might say yes and terrified that he might say no. Jane came from a wealthy, "proper" family where her parents divorced and she was raised by a nanny. She had never been married.

When she met Greg, an HR professional with a soft touch and an open vibe, Jane broke free from her on-again, off-again relationship. Jane and Greg went out to lunch and dinner together and laughed themselves silly. At first it was mainly focused on talking about work. But one day, after sharing a great dinner and bottle of wine, they slept together. The sex was sweet and yet passionate. But when Greg wanted to sleep over, Jane panicked. Because of her belief that relationships were tit-for-tat trade-offs, she found it hard to believe that he just wanted her. Yet Greg was the first person who made her feel like maybe love could be about something more than a transaction in which you helped each other's careers. She decided he was worth confronting her own fears, and e-mailed me for some relationship coaching. Jane overcame her mistrust and fear using some of the techniques that you will learn in Chapter 3. She also learned how to get in touch with her feminine side and flirt. The last time I talked to her, she gave me the news: They were happily engaged.

TRUE LOVE DOES NOT EXIST: IT'S JUST A DEAL
KILLER BELIEF WARNING SIGNS

It is baffling: Even though you are successful and can pretty much navigate getting what you want when it comes to your career, your skill sets don't work when it comes to attracting men and creating a love relationship. And you think they really should work in that arena, too!

KILLER BELIEF 4: *LOVE IS TOO DIFFICULT*

Other variations on this theme:

- The price for love is too high.
- It's too painful.
- It could be angry, explosive, and dangerous.
- I'm too hard for a man to handle.
- I have to tiptoe around in my relationship.
- I'll never get what I really want.
- I've seen what people go through and they end up miserable anyway.
- Love means suffering.
- Breakups damage you.
- You can never recover from a breakup.
- Relationships can cause you physical or emotional harm.
- We bring out the worst in each other.

This killer belief tends to fuel fears of being damaged by or damaging to your partner. It is common when there has been anger and verbal or physical abuse in your upbringing, or if you have an explosive temper yourself. The fear is that it is really not safe to be in an intimate relationship—for you and/or for your partner. Sometimes this fear is unconscious, and you can't really understand why people would make remarks like "I have to walk on eggshells around you." On a conscious level you are painfully aware that somehow or other you manage to break free of any relationship with a future in it.

Lisa came to me for Love Mentoring after a long history of relationships that lasted only three or four months, which puzzled her. She grew up with a verbally abusive single mother who could turn on a dime from being caring and nice to judgmental, harsh, and punitive to the point of slapping her. Yet Lisa defended her mother's love for her and tried to make her proud when she entered graduate school to study philosophy. As we worked together, Lisa realized that she picked very passive, conflict-avoiding guys who were the opposite of her volatile mother. Yet like her mom, Lisa would have drama-filled outbursts in which she would find fault with her boyfriends and "somehow" drive them away. She discovered that her killer belief was that love is too dangerous. She got in touch with her pessimism and talked about how hopeless she felt about "being too hard to handle." Most important, she learned how to take time-outs to soothe herself and control her anger. I asked her to create the love intention, *I am in a loving relationship with a strong, caring man who appreciates and handles me.* Lisa started a Dating Program of Three, an empowering dating strategy in which you see three men casually at the same time. (For a detailed description of this powerful approach, see *Love in 90 Days.*) This program helped her meet more solid guys who were not afraid of her. Now she is having a great romance with one she describes as a "strong man."

LOVE IS TOO DIFFICULT
KILLER BELIEF WARNING SIGNS
If you are honest with yourself, you have to admit that
you need to control your own over-the-top emotionality
and drama. Plus you need a relationship with a steady
and empowered guy who gives you the sense that drama
from either one of you is not going to be allowed to
burst out and ruin things.

KILLER BELIEF 5: *THIS IS NOT IT*

Other variations on this theme:

- It's not perfect.
- This does not match the image I had.
- This is not the way it is supposed to be.
- This is not my happily-ever-after.
- He's not my soul mate prince.
- He doesn't look like my type, which is [fill in the blank].
- He's not good enough.
- There's not enough chemistry.
- We're not a good match.
- We're going in different directions.
- This relationship isn't working.
- I am not willing to settle for less than my perfect relationship.
- This is not what I expected love to be like/look like/feel like.

The killer belief *This is not it* tends to create fears of settling for a relationship that is not like the script in your head. You have a fantasy, Technicolor version of the ideal relationship that is cobbled together based on childhood images—maybe fairy tales, romance movies, and the like. The reality of what's happening now with your boyfriend does not match that picture. You feel a great deal of anxiety about trusting the relationship and/or about whether he's really good enough. Especially when he disappoints you or you are in the middle of a fight. So when he wants to move forward into a deeper commitment, you tend to pull back.

Twenty-nine-year-old LeAnn was a statuesque dancer and former model. She had dated many men before she came for Love Mentoring. Her complaint: Each relationship was disappointing in one way or another. With one guy things were too boring and predictable, while with the next there was too little sex. Her relationship-killer belief was *It is not perfect.* She had an image of the perfect lifestyle with a wealthy businessman who was also very artistic and completely devoted to her. They would live together happily ever after in a Fifth Avenue penthouse with two long-haired Chihuahuas. I pointed out that what LeAnn wanted actually did not exist! As we worked on LeAnn's beliefs and co-created a vision of a happy, fulfilling love relationship, she let go of her fantasy. She was then able to be realistic in her expectations of guys. LeAnn learned to relax and just appreciate her dates and the wonderful qualities they had to offer. She is now in a committed relationship with a guy she really loves (even though they do not live in a Fifth Avenue penthouse).

THIS IS NOT IT
KILLER BELIEF WARNING SIGNS

You have never actually seen a real-life (movies and TV don't count) couple living out the totally fulfilling happily-ever-after relationship that you are going to have with your soul mate. And you haven't met him yet, but you (kind of) believe he's coming and it's all going to happen one day.

KILLER BELIEF 6: *RELATIONSHIPS MEAN THAT ONE PERSON HAS TO GIVE HIM- OR HERSELF UP*

Other variations on this theme:

- I can't be my real self in a relationship.
- I need too much.
- I have to do all the work to make the relationship happen.
- I am losing my identity in this relationship.
- I can't speak my truth.
- I can't get what I need.
- I can't win with this man.
- I don't have any power in this relationship.
- I have to be the way he wants me to be.
- He has to be the way I want him to be.
- I have to avoid conflict.
- I have to teach him what love is.
- I have to forget my needs and concentrate on fulfilling his.

This killer belief tends to create fears of being smothered or smothering your partner. The woman fears that she will create an empty one-way relationship where one of the partners is completely taken over by the needs and wants of the other. Ultimately this belief and the behaviors it fuels can lead to a relationship where true feelings are never spoken and real wants are not expressed. Such a relationship is not only inauthentic, but also boring and unfulfilling. In some cases, the woman ditches her friends and her independence to submerge herself wholly with the One; sometimes it is the guy who is desperate to please and bond with his partner.

KJ was a struggling actress/waiter who was desperately in love with Kyle, a fellow actor who was bisexual. They costarred as each other's love interests in an Off-Off-Broadway play. There was definitely some chemistry, but Kyle was younger and not interested in settling down. He wasn't even sure of his sexual preference. Even so, KJ was determined to make him see that she was the One. She texted, e-mailed, and called him daily with cheery messages of appreciation and love. Her killer belief was, *I have to teach him what love is.* Kyle responded to KJ's smothering moves by refusing to interact with her outside the theater. When the play ended, so did their so-called relationship. Only then was KJ able to recognize how her deeper beliefs were preventing her from being in a real relationship. She began dating guys who were interested in her. At first, their attention made her uncomfortable. But over time, she came to appreciate how many men love to give to women and how important it is for women to receive that caring. We'll cover more on this crucial dynamic in Chapter 6.

RELATIONSHIPS MEAN THAT ONE PERSON HAS TO GIVE HIM- OR HERSELF UP
KILLER BELIEF WARNING SIGNS

You give, give, give to make it work, till you can't anymore and you end up feeling empty, taken advantage of, and pissed off. Or you take up with an accommodating milquetoast and are bored, bored, bored.

As we've discovered, it is your secret and not-so-secret killer beliefs that can destroy your relationships. In the next four exercises, I'm going to help you uncover, face, and counter those beliefs. Be brave and honest—I am with you. By the time you're done, you will have deep insight into how they run your love life; more important, you will have taken a giant step toward getting rid of them once and for all.

✎ Exercises: Facing Your Killer Beliefs_____

EXERCISE 1: *IDENTIFY YOUR KILLER BELIEFS*

Read through the killer beliefs a couple of times. Write down the ones that caused any kind of emotional reaction or imagery in your mind. Add any other self-sabotaging thoughts or troubling memories from the past that cropped up while you were working with the list.

I am very proud of you for working on this! It takes a great deal of courage to dig deep and face painful thoughts, images, memories, and feelings.

EXERCISE 2: *LEARN HOW YOUR KILLER BELIEFS PLAY OUT*

Pick out at least one and as many as three of your killer beliefs. In a journal, write out several real-life examples of how these destructive beliefs played out in a past relationship. Tell each story with: (a) a beginning that describes your partner and how you came together; (b) a middle that describes how the relationship worked when you were together; and (c) how it all ended.

Now describe how these killer beliefs play out in your current relationship.

EXERCISE 3: *FACE THE DEAD-END FUTURE*

Be brave and journal realistically about how things may end with your current partner if you do not identify and deal with your killer beliefs.

EXERCISE 4: *CHOOSE YOUR THOUGHTS ABOUT LOVE*

If you were your own best friend and Love Mentor, what helpful and loving advice would you give yourself that counters your killer beliefs? What thoughts would you like to have about lasting love? Write these out and post the paper in a private place, like your closet, where you will see it every day.

For example, Sally from Chapter 1 had killer beliefs that she would never have lasting love because there was something wrong with her (she believed she was too fat and unattractive). As she did the journaling exercises above, she also remembered the heartbreak that her mother went through when her dad left for another woman. This memory came up as she journaled about the previous boyfriend who had cheated on her. Sally realized that she also had the killer belief that all men cheat. Here is what Sally wrote as her own chosen thoughts about love:

> *You are a brilliant woman and perfect life partner for a brilliant guy. Think about Uncle Harry and how completely devoted he is to (the not-so-slim) Aunt Elle! There are more like him!*

Okay. Great work! In the next chapter you will learn how to rid yourself of these inner obstacles once and for all so that your killer beliefs transform and you are free to go forward into a deeper and richer love.

> If I believe I cannot do something, it makes me incapable
> of doing it. But when I believe I can, then I acquire the
> ability to do it even if I didn't have it in the beginning.
> —*Mahatma Gandhi*

3

Overcoming Fears That Destroy Any Chance of Lasting Love

The experience of overcoming fear is extraordinarily delightful.—*Bertrand Russell*

It's time to dismantle your killer beliefs once and for all. If you don't, they will produce deep, malicious commitment fears that block off love. Instead of choosing a man who would potentially make a great match and building a relationship, you choose only those who cannot really give love. Instead of taking love in, you put up roadblocks to stop it. Instead of coming closer to your partner, you run away. When these deeper fears loom, it can seem extremely difficult, if not impossible, to have The Talk with your boyfriend to clarify whether you have a future together as a seriously committed couple and/or whether there is marriage and maybe children in that future. You may find yourself lingering in an uncertain, anxious state, wondering about what exactly is happening between you and the guy you consider to be your boyfriend. For all you know, he may not even consider you his girlfriend!

As I pointed out previously, deeper fears emanating from killer beliefs may lead you to undermine a perfectly fine relationship, to head for the hills to protect yourself; or to pursue a guy madly, only to turn tail and distance yourself once he decides he wants you. But more commonly, killer beliefs actually *distort* what you think is going on between you and your man. How? If you've trained your brain to focus on how your partner fails you and not notice his positive actions, you tend to react to him accordingly. It's not pretty.

In one study on the power of self-sabotaging beliefs on couples' perceptions of "reality," married couples were videotaped interacting with each other. Trained observers with no ax to grind observed them, scoring each interaction between the spouses as positive, negative, or neutral. Those who reported being unhappy in their relationships underestimated the number of positive actions by their spouses by a whopping 50 percent! Happily married couples, on the other hand, tended to agree with raters' observations of their spouses' behavior.

So what gives here? According to one couples researcher, the study shows that even in unhappy relationships the partners keep "making bids" for each other's interest, attention, and affection with kindness and caring. Unfortunately, these bids for loving connection are misperceived both psychologically and physiologically. Figuratively and literally, the partners don't "see" the good stuff coming their way. Why? Because unhappy spouses believe that their partners don't have good intentions toward them. If that's not a killer belief in action, what is? We can ignore the goodness that's right in front of us when we continuously sabotage ourselves with killer beliefs and set ourselves up for disappointment.

Where does this way of thinking and acting get you? Alone, and on the couch, with the tissue box and your old friends Ben & Jerry. Enough! In this chapter, we will work on freeing you from these self-sabotaging beliefs so that you can create the loving relationship that is just right for you.

✎ Exercises: Freeing Yourself from Killer Beliefs___

The good news is that there are eight easy-to-follow and effective Lasting Love Program exercises to free yourself from these self-sabotaging beliefs and fears. Let's take each one of your relationship-killer beliefs and use journaling to blow it out of your way.

EXERCISE 1: *JOURNAL ABOUT EACH KILLER BELIEF*

For each killer belief you identified in the last chapter, do the following:

Write down the killer belief at the top of a sheet of paper. Draw a line down the center of the page below the belief. At the top of the left side write NOT TRUE BECAUSE, and at the top of the right side write TRUE BECAUSE. Say the belief over and over. After each time that you say it, alternate writing down reasons why the statement is not true in the left column and reasons why it is true on the right side. *Continue this process until you find that your belief is shifting and you can add more positive statements.*

Sally, whom we first met at the beginning of Chapter 1, did this exercise with her Love Mentor, Beth. She wrote, *I will never have love because I'm too fat.* She alternated saying the sentence aloud and then jotting down her NOT TRUE BECAUSE and TRUE BECAUSE reactions.

Here are a few of the responses she wrote down in her left and right columns.

I will never have love because I'm too fat.

Not True Because	True Because
There are plenty of heavy women who get married.	Men like thin women.
There are guys who like a handful to love.	Everyone is obsessed with weight and being thin.
I have had serious relationships before when I was even heavier.	Thin equals beauty in this culture.
My aunt is very overweight and has a great marriage.	I have cellulite, too.
I am sexy and full of love!	
Men feel very at ease and flirt with me.	
I am zaftig and gorgeous.	
I am like Queen Latifah!	

After you do the exercise, read over the responses that you wrote. Interesting, aren't they? Now that you are beginning to shift your belief, finish the exercise by writing out a positive affirmation that speaks to you and post it where you will see it each day. After Sally completed her entries, she felt her belief shifting to the NOT TRUE column. She then wrote down the affirmation, *I am a sexy passionate woman who radiates lots of love!* Sally posted this affirmation in her closet where she could see it and think about it several times each day. When she did, she felt less anxious about her body. Sally reconnected with her boyfriend, Gary. After one passionate encounter, he started talking about having kids together.

If you are working on one of the variations on the belief *This is not it*, you might find that you are confused about whether the relationship should actually continue or not. That's normal, and I'm not advocating that the relationship you're in is the one you should most definitely stay in. We'll get to all this in Part II, but for now continue to do all these exercises to clear your heart and mind to help yourself make the best decision.

EXERCISE 2: *THE HEART CLEARING*

Make two loose fists and with them, gently tap the areas above and below your heart for about a minute. Imagine the pain and fear associated with a killer belief as black shapes in your heart that are falling down and out of you as you tap.

Now put your hand over your heart and repeat this sentence over and over again: *Even though I believe [whatever the killer belief is about], I deeply accept and love myself. I am entitled to miracles.* Continue this until you feel a shift into a more peaceful or positive state. Here's a description of the process by one of my students, Jorga, who freed herself from a history of being with heartbreaker alcoholics so that she could become happily married.

I just did it again now, and it feels great! It makes me feel so free and empowered and it gives me hope, especially when I go to a dark place. The darkness lifts. As I look back on our first month of marriage, I am so thankful that you helped me change my mind, my life, and my future.

EXERCISE 3: *JOURNAL ABOUT BELIEVING IN LOVE*

Divide up a blank piece of paper; on the left side write NO, NOT NOW, and on the right side write YES, NOW. Repeat the sentence *This is the right time to believe in love* over and over. After each time you say it, alternate writing down reasons why the statement is not true in the left column and reasons why it is true in the right.

Read over your responses and reflect on them.

Finish the exercise by writing out *This is the right time to believe in love*—or another positive affirmation that speaks to you. Post this where you will see it each day.

Here is how Sally did this exercise.

No, Not Now	Yes, Now
I don't want to believe in love, because I will just get hurt.	I met Gary and it's the best relationship I've ever had.
Gary could cheat on me, just like Ed.	I have built up the courage to take risks in love.
I am too busy at work.	I want it and I feel ready!!
I feel ugly and fat when I undress.	Gary said I look adorable naked.
I can't think of anything else!	I'm a fantastic woman who deserves a great relationship!

Sally finished the exercise by writing down this affirmation:

This is the right time to believe in love because I am ready, I'm courageous, and I deserve a growing relationship with a great guy!

The great poet Walt Whitman described this freeing-up process as follows:

> *O to speed where there is space enough and air enough at last!*
> *To be absolv'd from previous ties and conventions,*
> *I from mine and you from yours!*
> *To find a new unthought-of nonchalance with the best of Nature!*
> *To have the gag remov'd from one's mouth!*
> *To have the feeling to-day or any day I am sufficient as I am . . .*
> *To drive free! To love free!*
> —Walt Whitman, "One Hour to Madness and Joy"

EXERCISE 4: *BRAINSTORM ABOUT YOUR LOVE INTENTION*

The most powerful way to break free and create that madness and joy along with the security and depth of connection you really want is to use your untapped creativity. Brainstorm about thoughts, images, and feelings that are relationship-building. And then, once you discover them, combine those thoughts and feelings into a single affirmation that is your true love intention. Your love intention will help you imagine and focus on a fulfilling and exciting relationship in your mind, and over time it will shape your reality so that life becomes a beautiful reflection of that core affirmation.

But first you must brainstorm and find those special thoughts about having love that inspire you, that make you feel good when you think about them. Ideas that express exactly the kind of relationship you want. Brainstorming thoughts about your love possibilities opens new doors.

Otherwise, your negative beliefs and fears of rejection, abandonment, smothering, or being deeply wounded will continue to shape your love life. The only way you gain control over them is to retrain your mind. Emotions flow from thoughts. Actions flow from thoughts. Changing your thoughts is akin to changing the channel that you are tuned to—like turning from the scary and violent suspense of *Halloween* to the beautiful and calming nature documentary *Planet Earth*. As I've said before, all the latest research shows that, contrary to earlier views, our brains are incredibly plastic and highly responsive to new thoughts and stimuli. So if you change your thoughts, you change your brain.

We've done some of this rewiring by creating affirmations. But the best way to retrain your brain is through discovering new relationship ideas and possibilities and then using them to create a love intention. This is why I placed creating a love intention in the number one position on the goals list in Chapter 1. If you take just one thing from this whole book, make it this: *You have the power to completely transform your dating and love life through deciding and focusing on what it is that you want at the deepest level.* Goal 1 is:

> *Create an exciting love intention/affirmation about having committed love in your life.*

What is your love intention for yourself? This is your key brainstorming question.

The word *intention* is from the Latin *intendere*: *in-* meaning "toward," and *tendere* meaning "to stretch." This means your love intention is going to help you push yourself, stretch yourself beyond your comfort zone, beyond your killer beliefs—in a good way.

The *Oxford Dictionary of Philosophy* defines *intention* this way:

> *To have an intention is to be in a state of mind that is favourably directed towards bringing about some state of affairs, but which is not a mere desire or wish, since it also sets the subject on a course to bring that state of affairs about.*

So I ask you, what state of committed love do you want to bring about? And before you answer that question, how much time have you devoted to being thoughtful about and crafting a personal and meaningful love intention?

Not much, right? We're too busy. From the moment we get up, we are doing and doing. We have to get the coffee. Shower. Work. E-mail. Cook. Do errands. Handle the kids. Not to mention a little time for ourselves, keeping up with Facebook, Twitter, or our favorite TV shows. Exhausted just thinking about it, right? And here I am asking you to spend valuable time crafting a love intention, which is just a matter of words. How is that going to do anything? Simply this: It will free you from your enslavement to pessimistic thoughts (and your schedule!).

> Wake up,
> Wake up
> And clothe yourself with strength.
> Put on the beautiful clothes.
> Rise from the dust;
> take off the slave bands from your neck.
> —Isaiah 52:1–2

A love intention will wake you up! Here's how: As we discussed in Chapter 1, research has repeatedly shown the power of positive self-talk, which is what most of us call affirmations. Positive affirmations have been used to lower stress and anxiety levels and boost social confidence. Creating a specific love intention is a powerful type of affirmation that sets you in motion toward creating a particular set of circumstances that we call a lasting love relationship. And it does so both consciously and unconsciously, so that we build associations between love and fulfillment. But it does even more. Through our intention alone, we can activate the full power of our frontal lobe, which is the executive center of the brain. In his book *Evolve Your Brain*, clinician Joe Dispenza describes how this powerful process works:

When we firmly resolve to be, do, or even have something—regardless of how long it will take, or what is happening in our environment, or how our body feels at that particular moment—we spark this structure of the brain into action. At such a moment, we no longer care about the external world or how our body might feel; we align with an internal representation or concept of our intention. When we make up our mind, without considerations or concern as to how our choice to do or be something might happen, the frontal lobe is now fully activated.

What is so amazing about our brain and the frontal lobe is that we have the ability to make a thought become the only thing that is real to us. Because of the size of the frontal lobe, human beings have the privilege of making thought more important and more real than anything else. We are all naturally wired to be this way. When we make our thoughts all that is real and we pay attention to them as if they were, we unite the frontal lobe's primary functions into a force as powerful as anything in the universe.

Now let's go back to how you spend your time and energy. Many of us put attention on what we want to create in work: *My goal is to get a promotion. I want to get a pay raise this year. I want to design jewelry full-time and support myself. My goal is to complete grad school and be a therapist.* Or we put attention on our appearance: *I want to lose weight. My goal is to be two sizes smaller by ___. I'm getting a hot new hairstyle.* If we have kids, we certainly put a lot of attention on them. *I want my son/daughter to be healthy, do well in school, have friends...* We even put attention on vacations: *A cruise to Aruba...And I want a top cabin... With a window to see the water.* But most of us don't put attention on the most important part of life: living in a state of love. This is not a judgment—it is simply, as they say in transformation lingo, *what's so.*

So now ask yourself: What is it that you really desire, really long for in your relationship? It doesn't matter if you have been seeing someone for a few months or have been involved in different ways for several years; there is no need to be shy here or embarrassed about what you want or how realistic it may seem to you. Be honest with yourself and let yourself picture your ideal life.

Would you like to create more of a sense of *we-ness*, connection, and deep trust? Would you like to create an intention in which your partner knows without a doubt that he wants a committed relationship with you and only you? Where you have exciting plans for the future? How about being engaged? Living together? Would you like to be married? Have children? Or would you simply like to run off with your guy to Tuscany and paint your heart out, with his full support and admiration?

What is it you want to create?

Do you want to create that, when you come home and greet your husband, he's the hottest thing you ever saw and you feel like you're having an affair with him, and you two are winking at each other and can't keep your hands off each other? Or do you want to create something where the two of you are scheming to help the world? Where you're laughing, giggling, and running down the hallway together at some institution because you've gotten them to donate $100,000 toward ending malaria in Africa? I know couples who do just that and share a fun, generous, and making-a-difference kind of love together.

Or is the love intention about his tenderness, eye contact, and acknowledgment of how special and incredible you are? Is it that you want him to touch you on your arm in a certain way when you've been hurt, because he knows that's what you need? Or to draw a bath for you when you're crying, put you in that bath, and just listen to you?

Everyone has a different love intention. When you find an imagined state of affairs with images, sounds, and feelings that are right for you, it'll call to you. You'll feel it. You may think, *Oh, my goodness, that's exactly what I want*. You may laugh or cry, or both. Build your love intention from this imagined state of affairs—from *pure possibility*, not with any idea of whether you can or cannot do it—even if you feel that it's totally impossible!

How could I ask you to do something that might seem completely unrealistic? Well, remember how we just talked about how the brain's frontal lobe is activated when we strongly believe something? To get yourself into that state, make your love intention a statement about your love life *as if it were happening right now.* This allows the brain to perform a mental rehearsal of what it expects to find out there in the world. It's like a slalom skier who mentally rehearses going downhill around the gates without a fall or miss till she crosses the finish line. World-class athletes do this all the time so that when they're at the starting line in the race, their frontal lobes and muscle memories know exactly what to expect and how to behave. Just as it works for Olympic athletes, it'll work for you—no matter how far-fetched your ideas and dreams seem to you now. Through repeated rehearsals of your love intention, your brain will shape your perceptions of how the world looks, and then your actions will lead you to creating more love in your life.

> Dreams are like the paints of a great artist. Your dreams are your paints, the world is your canvas. Believing is the brush that converts your dreams into a masterpiece of reality.—*Anonymous*

EXERCISE 5: *CRAFTING YOUR LOVE INTENTION*

So now it's time for you to craft your love intention. Remember, a love intention is *not* what you spit out when friends ask you what you want in a relationship; it is an imaginative statement created *as if there were no limits*, a simple global statement that you make *regardless of your present real-life circumstances.*

State it in one sentence, in the present tense.

Let me give you some examples:

- I am engaged to a wonderful man and we live a lifetime of fulfillment together.
- I have a committed, loving, passionate, monogamous relationship.
- I live with a devoted, loving, excited, and exciting life partner.
- I have a great, devoted companion who goes on world adventures with me.
- I marry a fabulous guy who is just right for me.
- My loving partner and I share a passionate happy life together including art, children, and service to the world.

If it feels great to think your love intention, then it is right on target. If a statement feels scary, that's good! You are pushing the edges of your growth—exactly what those Romans meant when they came up with the word *intention*. You can put your partner's name in the love intention if you choose. For example, the one that I really love to make is: *Sam and I continuously deepen our love.* Other variations:

- Ben and I share a marriage that is exciting, nourishing, and sexy.
- Brandon and I get closer every day.
- Jason and I commit to a win–win, growing love relationship.
- José and I get happily engaged.
- Deepak and I commit to living together as loving life partners.

The next thing I invite you to do is to write your love intention down and put it in a private place. Post it where you can see it every day. You can place it in your closet, near your computer if you're in a private space, or in the top drawer of your desk, where you'll pull it out and look at it daily.

If you are with a conscious, growing partner, have him read this book and each of you create a love intention. Then merge them into a single shared love intention: *We happily help each other grow individually and as a couple.* Or, *We have a loving, healthy family with terrific children.*

A love intention is very powerful when it is truly heartfelt. From my experience with many women and men, a deeply felt love intention will more quickly help you fulfill the goals you set in Chapter 1. Next, we will move on to exercises that will activate your love intention.

EXERCISE 6: *LOVE INTENTION PRACTICE*

Shorten your love intention to about ten words. Now think of your love intention as a mantra. In meditation, you are instructed to put your attention on a given sound, word, or series of words that serve as a mantra. When distracting thoughts or feelings come (*Oh, I forgot to do the dishes,* or *I'm so worried about that deadline at work*), you let them come and go without fixating on them, accepting them for what they are: useless noise. Soon they pass through your mind and disappear. Then you go back and put your attention on the mantra.

In the same way, put your attention, your *full* attention, on your love intention, every day, several times a day, just for a few minutes. As you do this, practice the meditation technique for handling distracting thoughts. Suppose, for example, that your intention is, *I have a beautiful, loving relationship that gets better in every way.* As you think this, a thought comes up: *Oh, that's impossible . . . my kids are too much for him.* This is your old killer belief rearing its head. Instead of fixating on how you will never have the lasting love you want because of your children, you will instead let this distracting thought pass like a cloud going by. Then go back to the intention. Discipline your attention so that you work on this crucial practice and stay with it for a few minutes. As you practice, it will get easier.

You can bookend your days by practicing the love intention

meditation first thing when you wake up and just before you fall asleep. Aim to make it a simple habit, like brushing your teeth. Creating and practicing a love intention that sets you in motion toward your love goal doesn't take much effort, but the results can be amazing.

I know that even with all this encouragement and support, at times you will still feel hopeless or down. And that is okay. It is fine to feel whatever you are feeling. Just know that whatever it is, it will pass. And if you continue your love intention practice, just as you would with exercise or a new language, you will get better at changing your thinking patterns and feelings. In time, your new mental abilities will allow you to speak and act differently around your man. You will become clearer, ask for and get what you need and want, and gladly fulfill your partner's wishes. Through your practice, you can completely transform your love life.

EXERCISE 7: *PRACTICE POSITIVE PARANOIA*

Remember the study that showed that unhappy spouses miss half the good stuff their partners are doing? You don't want that in your relationship. So I want you to practice the opposite of that, or what I call Positive Paranoia, which means you put your attention on the deeper love or the beneficial intention that your partner has rather than automatically seeing him as wounding, awful, and unfair, and letting these perceptions "prove" that your killer beliefs are "real." Positive Paranoia means you notice and put your attention on the good aspects of your relationship. This will help to activate your love intention.

Here is a personal story that illustrates this process:

In the beginning I used to be furious with my husband, Sam, for not listening carefully and for avoiding eye contact with me. His actions or nonverbals proved my killer belief, *I am not important or lovable.* There were other times when he would hold my hand and put his arm around me. But I chose not to focus on his loving touch. I would try to talk with him and then when he didn't look into my eyes or seemed distracted, I would get upset and clam up. My husband, in turn, would become emotionally distant and then angry at me for being "cold." Eventually, things would escalate into full-blown and bitter fights. Do you think my focus on what he was doing "wrong" helped me get more eye contact and better listening? Yeah, right! There is no way behavior like that gets you what you really need from a man.

When I created and practiced my love intention, *Sam and I continuously deepen our love*, I began to notice and even write down the nurturing actions he took and how considerate he was. I nurtured this state of Positive Paranoia and actively took note of how he always did the driving, cleared the table, and worked hard for our family as proof of his devotion. Even when he was mean at times, I still knew his devotion was there and revisited the thought that we were deepening our love (my love intention).

I became less emotionally reactive and more validating, which is a natural outgrowth of noticing the positives in a relationship. As I validated him more for his caring actions, I created a safe space for him to make more emotional contact with me. He began listening, making eye contact, and eventually looking into my eyes in a way that no person ever had. By focusing more on what he gave me, I got back love beyond measure.

This is one example of what's possible beyond an ordinary relationship: the kind of love that you could call extraordinary. There is nothing wrong with wanting extraordinary love—as long as you are willing to be the change you want to see in your partner. Expect more from yourself first in terms of your thinking and actions. In practicing Positive Paranoia, you will be able to be like those happy couples who hold themselves to higher standards and therefore have the best marriages! Later I'll go over the other "real" laws of attraction that I finally "got" after many years and many battles. Don't waste precious time with your man like I did.

The Two-Step Positive Paranoia Practice
1. Every day, write out a list of five positive aspects or attributes in your relationship or partner. Include minor things, like the way you feel great when you have coffee together in the morning. And major things, such as how helpful he is in supporting your career. Think about your list several times during the day.
2. Share your list with your partner. For example, say, "I adore the espresso you brew," or "You rock when it comes to helping me with my work presentations!"

Practicing these steps will help you become established in the state of Positive Paranoia, which, in turn, creates a kind of atmosphere of warmth and appreciation that men love to be in. This simple two-part exercise is surprisingly powerful in bringing more love into your relationship.

EXERCISE 8: *WEAR SPECIFIC GEMSTONES AND JEWELRY*

With all that work for the first seven exercises, it's fair for me to give you something fun now. For this one, I want you to go shopping! You're going to look for a gemstone or a piece of jewelry that symbolizes your love intention. Stop rolling your eyes. Not only have I seen the positive impact that "gem therapy" has had on the women I've helped over the last twenty-five years, there's also some serious science behind this!

Gemstones have been studied for thousands of years, in China, India, and more recently Tibet. Their healing properties and their ability to empower the wearer in matters of love appear in the most ancient texts humans have written. They're even part of human-kind's oldest system of medical practice; in ayurveda, specific gems are used to rebalance the body and heal disease. But of course, as a psychologist and scientist, I had to see whether this was all just superstition. I began to study the literature on charms and amulets and came across fascinating research.

In a recent series of six separate experiments, psychologists at the University of Cologne explored superstitious beliefs in a college population. In the first study, of 173 students, only 15 percent reported *not* believing at all in the notion of bad luck or good luck. The majority reported that such beliefs, including the wearing of lucky charms or amulets, gave them feelings of security, confidence, and reassurance, which helped them in important situations, like taking tests. In the second and third studies, students were divided into groups around the task of putting a golf ball into a hole. In one group the experimenter said they were using a "lucky ball," while in the second and third groups she said it was an "unlucky ball" or made no comment. The results were striking. Students with the "lucky ball" were much more successful at putting than those who got the "unlucky" one or no comment about the ball they were using.

Study number four involved fifty-one students who were assigned to three groups and engaged in a timed motor-skill task. The German experimenter wished group one good luck by saying, "I press my thumbs for you." The other two groups were not given the good luck wish. The good-luck group far outperformed both other groups in terms of accuracy and speed.

In the fifth study, twenty-six students were assigned to two groups who were given two different cognitive tasks in the computer game Tetris. After each practice run, the first group was told they had good luck, while the second group was told they were having bad luck. Again, performance in the lucky group was significantly better. Second, the experimenters showed that those in the good-luck group reported significantly higher self-efficacy beliefs than those in group two. *Self-efficacy* is a fancy term for self-confidence in action.

Finally, in study number six, forty-one students were asked to bring their own lucky charm—like a ring, pearl necklace, or jade stone—to a memory experiment. Half of them were allowed to keep their lucky charm, whereas the other half were required to hand their charms to the experimenter. The results were fascinating. Those with their lucky charm had less anxiety, felt more confident, and did significantly better on the memory test.

In reviewing the data from all six studies, the authors concluded that the belief in good luck, being wished good luck, and wearing jewelry or objects that had positive meanings to the wearer all worked to lower anxiety, improve self-confidence, boost empowerment, and, remarkably, greatly improve actual performance on both physical and mental tests.

Although the study of lucky charms or stones is relatively recent in modern psychology, we've already shown that science has validated the power of belief and intention in reorganizing the brain's perceptions. So I say, what do you have to lose by selecting particular stones that are aligned with believing in "the good luck" of your love intention? These lucky charms will remind you of a positive thought about love, and through that association you will be empowered. Putting the gemstone on, touching it during the day, and seeing it in the mirror will remind you of your love intention and thus serve to activate it mentally. Through these simple actions, your gemstone can help you focus on an exciting love future and interrupt the noise about past or current disappointments.

Below are three categories of love intentions and stones to go along with them based on both Eastern and Western lore. Pick a stone or several (most are inexpensive) and wear them next to your skin as necklaces or rings. Each gemstone is like a string you tie around your finger to remember something.

- **Finding the One:** Rose quartz heart, goldstone heart, lapis.
- **Getting a commitment:** Diamonds or diamond chips, jade butterfly (Chinese symbol of successful love), pearls.
- **Increasing passion/intimacy in a relationship:** Moonstone, sunstone, fire quartz heart.

How Love Intentions Unfold

Practicing the eight exercises in this chapter will optimize your chances at developing committed and lasting love with your partner. Simply put, what we put our attention on tends to manifest. Granted, it often occurs more slowly than we'd want, playing out in a zigzag fashion: There is progress, then setbacks and disappointments, followed by spurts of new progress. You will have some great days and others when the killer beliefs and commitment fears emerge and muck things up. But your continued practice of your love intention and, in particular, your Positive Paranoia work, will fuel a positive trend in your relationship. You will have fewer and briefer fights, with increasing closeness, understanding, and love. In short, you will be that much closer to fulfilling your commitment and other relationship goals.

One final thought: Throughout my years of practice, I've noticed that love intentions almost *never* play out the way you expect. Instead, they manifest as delightful surprises. Continue to practice, and there will be magical times ahead when the love you receive is better than you could have ever imagined.

The time will come
when, with elation,
you will greet yourself arriving
at your own door, in your own mirror,
and each will smile at the other's welcome,

and say, sit here. Eat.
You will love again the stranger who was your self.
Give wine. Give bread. Give back your heart
to itself, to the stranger who has loved you

all your life, whom you ignored
for another, who knows you by heart.
Take down the love letters from the bookshelf,

the photographs, the desperate notes,
peel your own image from the mirror.
Sit. Feast on your life.

—*Derek Walcott*

4

The Single Most Important Thing You Can Do for Yourself and Your Relationship

GETTING A LOVE MENTOR

> Suddenly the fairy godmother materialized and waved her magic wand. In a flash, Cinderella appeared in a splendid dress, shining with youth and beauty. Her stepmother and stepsisters gaped at her in amazement, and the ministers said, "Come with us, Cinderella! The Prince is waiting for you." So Cinderella married the Prince and lived happily ever after.—*Anonymous*

The fairy godmother and her magical wand. Nothing like that really exists, right? Only in children's books and movies that are designed for flights of fancy and moments of escape from the harsh day-to-day grind of relationship challenges and disappointments. Or do they occur in real life?

I never believed in fairy godmothers until something happened to me many years ago. My very own fairy godmother began to oversee and open up my love life—only she took the form of a *he*, a fairy godfather who got me to the ball and deep into my forever love story. Of course, mine had a few more bumps than Cinderella's; it is a *real* happily-ever-after, after all. His name was Dr. Arthur Stein, and he was the psychologist who originated many of the Love in 90 Days principles I have written about. He was the original Love Mentor who saw past my many flaws and ugly bits to the perfect soul in little old *moi*.

Arthur stopped me from screwing up with the prince numerous times in my marriage. When my husband, Sam, and I first met, it was compete at first sight! We were psychology grad student rivals for the same stipends and awards. We were young know-it-alls for whom listening was a foreign ritual and arguing was both of our middle names.

I unconsciously followed the laws of repulsion. *Defensiveness* (the fights were *never* my fault); *stonewalling* (I got my Ph.D. in Cold Shoulder before I got it in clinical psychology); *criticism* (he was always doing it all wrong, whatever it was); and the worst trait of all, *contempt. (The stupid bastard! How idiotic could he be about women and me in particular! Men!)* These are the very traits that renowned couples researcher Dr. John Gottman calls the Four Horsemen of the Apocalypse—because they kill off connection, break apart commitments, and doom a relationship. Sadly, even though we were both therapists (and should have known better) we acted no differently than any other couple on the rocks. We were drifting farther and farther apart.

After a few world wars that exploded between us, I felt like I had no other choice but to leave Sam. In so many ways, he was perfect for me—intellectually, physically, and as a teammate—and he really made me laugh. But I couldn't take it anymore. To deal with it, I discussed our problems and my desire to leave with my Love Mentor, Arthur. As memory serves me, the conversations went something like this:

ME: I think I should just end it.

ARTHUR: You're just following your killer belief that men are all bastards! And you will do it with the next guy and the next, unless you examine that belief, own it, and then distance yourself from it.

ME: I can't.

ARTHUR: Darlin', you can do anything. You got into a Ph.D. program that only took eighteen people from around the world. You finished UCLA in three years. You can definitely do this!

ME: (thinking he's crazy and just shining me on, but eating it up because my father never noticed, much less appreciated me!) Well, how?

ARTHUR: Just notice how your mind starts working when he does something to upset you.

ME: Come on! Like that is so easy to do...

ARTHUR: (ignoring me) You give his action or inaction so much weight and negative meaning, as if he were deliberately trying to hurt you. You c'mon! Most of the time he's just making stupid mistakes because he's young and immature.

ME: He just shouldn't be saying these dumb things to me!

ARTHUR: Try to look past his mistakes and see his intention. His love for you. Even if it comes out upside down. You are the most incredible woman he has ever been with.

ME: (feeling touched by the Love Mentoring validation and rising to be my best self) Well, I think it does cut him to the core when I pull away and refuse to speak to him.

ARTHUR: To Sam, the silent treatment is like a knife in the heart. He can't handle it. Yet.

ME: But it's not all my fault!

ARTHUR: Do you want to be right and alone? Or do you want to be an empowered woman who is disciplined and goes for the love? Would you rather be right? Or happy in Sam's arms?

ME: When we fight, I feel beyond miserable.

ARTHUR: But at the same time you're enjoying feeling self-righteous and like any judge or jury would agree with you. So is it worth it?

ME: (defiantly and somewhat sheepishly) Yes!

ARTHUR: Please! Cut the crap.

ME: Well...*no!* Happy now? (I almost stuck my tongue out at him, but I had some self-control.)

ARTHUR: So are you ready to work or do you still want to pout some more?

ME: I'm ready.

ARTHUR: What kind of future do you want to create right now?

ME: Being in love with Sam.

ARTHUR: Okay. Hold that thought!

As I write this, I have to say that I'm embarrassed by my immature reactions to someone who clearly was trying to save me from my own self-sabotaging beliefs and behaviors. Yet that's how many of us act if we don't have someone in our lives to help save us from ourselves. We can make all kinds of mistakes—mistakes that have long-term negative consequences.

Luckily, Arthur got through to me enough that I could admit I needed serious help in the intimate relationship department. My Love Mentor was filling some of my needs for something I call TTLC: Tough and Tender Loving Care. Like a good and loving parental figure, Arthur was providing the validation, confrontation, and limit-setting that I lacked and sorely needed. He was helping me to see and overcome my killer beliefs so I could evolve into my best identity, what I call the Diamond Self. He helped to hold the vision of me as a deserving, gracious, kind, assertive, and empowered Diamond Self. And he held to that vision even when I felt and acted like a disappointing self, an inconsequential self, or a worthless self, as I often did during times of conflict with Sam.

Arthur also taught me about the other species, men, and how to have a loving relationship with one of them. He taught me about how men have real problems dealing with their own negative feelings, like anger. Later, research confirmed this idea that men more than women experience a physiological process called flooding when they are upset: Their blood pressure and heart rate soar, and it is very difficult for them to calm down. In other words, they go into flight-or-fight mode. I began to see that their biological engines are simply different from ours. During conflict, they get revved way up and have a hard time self-soothing and slowing that engine down. So while you feel like your argument about never going out to see your folks together really helped clear the air, your significant other may feel upset and annoyed with you for the next hour. Imagine that! And we are the excitable, hysterical ones?

Well, once I "got" this difference between us, I slowly stopped escalating spats into world wars. More often than not, when Sam *started* fuming and getting mean, I could just put my arms around him before things exploded. My act of unconditional love took us almost immediately out of the right–wrong game and into the close sweetness of win–win happiness. You see, Sam loves to be touched. So the more I did that, the more he paid me back by being under-standing and holding me when I became the b*tch from PMS land.

I would have left my husband (or he would have left me) a few times if it weren't for the teachings of my Love Mentor. I am forever grateful to him because I was so close to losing my soul mate forever. Instead we've been able to weather one of our families disowning us and refusing to even meet our baby girl because one of us is Jewish while the other is Italian; the devastating death of a baby; a life-threatening illness; and the usual deadly boring stretches when we seemed to be going in "different" directions.

While my personal experiences with Arthur have fostered a deep belief in the value of Love Mentoring when it comes to creating lasting relationships, it's much more than just my own experiences on both sides of the couch that support this idea. Research on the impact of mentoring on adults has shown how effective it is in many walks of life. For example, numerous studies have shown that those who are mentored are more successful in their careers and in school.

Women, in particular, have benefited enormously from mentoring, with reports of greater self-esteem and a heightened ability to break through the "glass ceiling." They also do better having multiple mentors. Besides being a Love Mentor to many women, I've also played the role of business mentor to women in large companies here and in Europe. I can vouch firsthand for the life-changing difference it makes both at work and in creating great love relationships.

One of the most important things you can do to create the commitment you want in your relationship as you're following the Lasting Love Program is to work with a straightforward, knowledgeable, and devoted Love Mentor. This is the secret, the strategy that has totally transformed my life and the lives of thousands of others: Love Mentoring involves reeducating yourself and developing critical skills to build your most important and intimate relationship.

In *Love in 90 Days*, I described the importance of having a mentor when you are dating, but as I've shown in my story about Sam, most women also need one when they are in the throes of working out a fledgling or struggling relationship. Maintaining and building higher and higher levels of committed love is the hardest task we face in life. As the great poet Rainer Maria Rilke wrote:

> *For one human being to love another is perhaps the most difficult of all our tasks, the ultimate, the last test and proof, the work for which all other work is but preparation.*

Part of the reason it is so hard is that our killer beliefs lead us to reenact the most powerful love traumas from our past. According to Imago relationship therapists, we tend to revisit these negative scenarios in three different ways: We *pick* men who are similar to our problematic fathers or exes; *project* those hot-button traits onto boyfriends; or *provoke* our partners into acting like our problem parents or exes behaved. So our tendency is to keep picking commitment-phobes, or alcoholics, or [insert your type of heartbreaker]. Even if he doesn't seem that way at first. Then, if the person does not act in the same old hurtful ways, we tend to project—that is, perceive—him as doing it anyway. And finally, we can be so scared, so expectant of the same traumatic and disappointing behavior that we actually may provoke our partners into doing it.

Because of this pick, project, or provoke pattern, we wind up with the same disappointments, the same rejections, the same abandonment, the same abuse we suffered growing up. Not to mention other conflicts, pains, and misfortune that life hurls into the midst of a couple's work and family life. It is certainly easy to get lost in a murky whirlpool of pain and confusion, and this is why a wise and loving mentor whom we respect can make all the difference in whether things move forward with your happy ending, or whether they simply fall apart.

Here is an e-mail that is similar to ones I get all the time. It is from a woman named Sheila, who tends to pick commitment-phobes:

Why does this always happen to me?? I just broke up with my boyfriend, Gene, after eight months. The exact same thing happened with my last boyfriend, but we only made it together for about four months. In both cases, it was just not clear where it was going and it was driving me crazy. Gene said he wasn't sure that he wanted the whole white picket fence thing. I don't really want all that but I am 39 and really want a child. When I first brought it up, he just changed the subject. When I brought it up again, I couldn't stop myself from getting angry and we wound up having a huge fight where he stormed out of the restaurant. After that Gene stopped calling me every day and we didn't see each other for a whole weekend. I was beside myself and went over to his place, where we had a screaming match. I was the one who told him it was over, but I think it's what he really wanted. It has been two months now and I am devastated. I want him back more than I can say, but I don't know what to do.

If Sheila had a Love Mentor, she would have had someone to advise her about how to steady herself and envision the future she wanted to create with Gene. A mentor would have helped her to be patient for a while to see if Gene could work through his ambivalence about the future. That way Sheila would be more conscious about her tendency to project the worst onto Gene and to provoke fights with him. A mentor would have been able to help Sheila feel more self-confident and shape the shared-future Talk with Gene so that it unfolded *without drama*, thus maximizing the possibility that he would share Sheila's vision and commit to her.

A wise mentor would have counseled Sheila to busy herself with other passions and hobbies instead of obsessing about Gene and his commitment, ensuring that she continued having fun with Gene instead of being so tense and anxious with him. He or she would have warned her that drama and joylessness would play big roles in driving him away. A knowledgeable Love Mentor would even know exactly how to counsel Sheila so that she could make the right moves that could possibly reengage Gene, even if there was a cutoff.

We'll get to all those relationship skills later, in Parts II and III, but for right now it is important for you to understand that having a coach who knows the winding switchbacks on the road of love and who totally appreciates your Diamond Self can help improve your relationship and speed you along the way to the commitment you want. We all have blind spots. We all need coaching. Especially in love.

Here is an e-mail from a fifty-something woman who used Love Mentoring to get happily married for the first time:

> *Having a Love Mentor was what allowed me to get married. That guidance helped me get over my tendency to blame the other person and want to be right. Nurturing loving guidance combined with a firm hand in letting me know when I was being a spoiled brat allowed me to look at my own patterns from a neutral perspective. I learned that I deserve to be supported on all levels,*

including financially—that I could have a true reciprocal loving partnership.

Many of you saw me do Love Mentoring on the 90 Day Love Challenge on Fox's *Morning Show with Mike and Juliet*. If you didn't, here's a nutshell recap. The *Morning Show* issued an official challenge to me: Could I really help someone to find love in just ninety days? Over thirteen consecutive weeks, Fox viewers watched—and ratings hit an all-time high—as I used Love Mentoring to help thirty-seven-year-old Amelia go from zero dates to having twelve great prospects, including two guys who she was really interested in.

When I first met Amelia, she believed she had to work hard to make people love her, to be accommodating and approval seeking, especially with men. What I saw in her was how fantastic, how enormously gifted, how adorable she really was. To help Amelia access, value, and nurture her Diamond Self, I gave her an exercise to do in which she shyly nicknamed herself the Wonder Diva of Love, something that flew in the face of her lack of deservedness. Over time, she came to identify with her new name in a playful, happy way. In the process of Love Mentoring, I taught her to do her own thing, not be too available, and not be over-giving in the dead-end pattern I'll-Make-You-Love-Me kind of way. Amelia even snagged her dream job as a by-product of her growing self-esteem.

Leaving Behind the Loneliness of Doing It All by Yourself

Think about the people who have left a positive lasting impression on you. It's amazing how a teacher, a boss, a minister, a therapist, or a family member can help you change your life. Other self-help books talk endlessly about how you can't rely on other people to give you what you need. Yes, on one level that's true—you ultimately have to do it for yourself. But it's an awfully long and *lonely* road, pulling yourself up by your own bootstraps; and in the end, you won't succeed anyway, trying to be Ms. Independent.

Nowhere is that more true than in going from casual to committed or rekindling a close passionate connection and finally finding the lasting love you want. It's almost impossible to do it by yourself, and yet many of you keep doing it just that way. Because you think you're supposed to. The result: You're not successful in deepening intimacy and love with someone *you really want.*

The Four Steps of Love Mentoring

I know that Love Mentoring sounds like pie in the sky for some of you or some hokey theory that can't really work in your life. But you owe it to yourself to work through these four simple steps of Love Mentoring and try it—just to see where the process takes you.

STEP 1: *FIGURE OUT YOUR TTLC NEEDS*

Here is a list of tough and tender loving care (TTLC) needs you may have that is divided into three categories: Nurturance; Guidance and Envisioning; and Limit-Setting. Women tend to disregard their own needs and therefore make it even harder for their partners to fulfill them. So even if it is hard, read through and note which ones tug at your heart.

You must be very clear about exactly what you need because you will work on fulfilling these needs not only with your Love Mentor, but with your partner as well. Creating a healing partnership with your Beloved, where you help each other feel more grounded, safe, special, and empowered to live your dreams, is the ultimate path to a committed happy future together. As you choose items from this list, you are defining what true love means to you.

Take a notepad and look carefully over the following list. Jot down what you really needed growing up but didn't get or anything that you intuitively feel would be helpful to you right now. While it is easiest to identify needs for nurturance, also look for items in all three categories, because usually, much as we might hate to admit it, we need some combination of nurturance, guidance, and confrontation.

Nurturance

- Being accepted.
- Being chosen and wanted as the special one.
- Being helped to feel safe.
- Being loved unconditionally.
- Getting hugs and physical affection.
- Being understood.
- Being prized.
- Being told I'm attractive.
- Being treated as if I'm desirable.
- Being told I'm lovable.
- Being told I'm unique and special.
- Being supported when I'm failing or feeling vulnerable.
- Receiving acts of caretaking and service.
- Being treated with respect.
- Being forgiven.
- Being treated fairly.
- Being given to.
- Companionship—shared time together.
- Being protected from frenemies or bullies.
- Getting time and attention.
- Getting what I really need, even if it is a lot.
- Being listened to.
- Being treated as if my wants and needs are very important.

Guidance and Envisioning

- Getting a commitment for a shared future.
- Being encouraged to live my dreams.
- Being helped to explore the world and my place in it.
- Getting recognition for my accomplishments.
- Belief in my unique potential and talent.
- Being praised and rewarded for accomplishments.
- Being encouraged to be real.
- Being encouraged to play, to find my bliss.
- Being taught, guided, or advised.
- Getting symbolic and thoughtful gifts.
- Belief in and validation of my Diamond Self identity (ideal self identity).

Limit-Setting

- Getting constructive and helpful critiques.
- Being told to "suck it up" when I have to do something difficult or scary.
- A "swift kick in the butt" to help me get motivated.
- Being confronted when I'm out of line.
- Getting constructive limits on my behavior.
- Receiving reasonable consequences for abusive or destructive behavior.
- Being helped to make reparations for destructive acts.

Every person deserves to experience nurturance, guidance, and limit-setting. They are the cornerstones to building a solid and loving human being. Yet sadly, most of us have missed out on one or more of these basic inputs, either as children or as adults. And not having them has left lasting impressions on our inner template, the model of love that is made up of a set of beliefs that ultimately guide our love relationships. The faultier your model, the more impossible love seems to be for you and the more killer beliefs you have. These unfulfilled needs are the ones that you need to work on with a Love Mentor and eventually with your partner.

STEP 2: *FIND A LOVE MENTOR*

When I'm on radio or TV, women are always calling in with this type of question:

> *"Dr. Diana, you say that a Love Mentor is so important in helping me find love. Where in the world do I find such a person? On Craigslist?"*

Not exactly! Here's how:

Make a list of all the kind and wise people in your social network. Love Mentors can be male or female and may include good aunts, stepparents, therapists, coaches, ministers, rabbis, and 12-step sponsors, among others. Then pick out three people who might be able to meet your TTLC needs. Choose ones who you look up to and admire. Important: *These need to be people who have or have had great love relationships themselves*—not *your single friends.* They know the road you want to be on, while your single friends do not. And often your single girlfriends will simply tell you a guy's great while you're dating him and then how awful he really was after you break up—because they're afraid to hurt your feelings. This is not useful!

In addition to being in a wonderful relationship, another plus is if your prospective Love Mentor is an informal matchmaker who has helped a few people get married. She or he also needs to think highly enough of you to want to spend the time to help you. If you are choosing to work with a therapist, make sure that he or she is accomplished in working both individually and with the couple as needed. Obviously if some of the folks on your list are paid professionals, you have to be prepared to invest in your love life.

Cultivate a closer relationship with your potential Love Mentor. Reach out and spend an hour or so with them face-to-face and/or via phone and e-mail each week. I don't care if you're nervous or anxious or feeling not good enough around the person; do it anyway. These feelings actually mean that they are in the position to be able to help you even more with your self-esteem! If you are working with a nonprofessional Love Mentor, give back to the person in any way you can: Take them to lunch, give them thoughtful gifts, make introductions to people who can help them. But be sure to ask them to spend more time with you, talking about your relationship with your Beloved.

If you are unable to find a good Love Mentor on your own, you can also consider hiring a professional Love Mentor. I now have handpicked, expert Love Mentors who have used my principles to get or stay happily married themselves. They have long backgrounds in transformational work and are closely supervised by me. For more info on how these mentors can coach you by phone or Skype, contact me at www.lovein90days.com/coaching.

STEP 3: *ASK FOR TTLC*

In your meeting with your Love Mentor, use straight talk about yourself, your boyfriend or partner, and the trouble spots in your relationship. Share your dating history and what self-sabotaging patterns you think you've been playing out. If possible, and your Love Mentor thinks it is appropriate, introduce your Love Mentor to your guy. Ask your mentor a lot of questions and get guidance and advice. Remember, there are no stupid questions.

Come right out and discuss the TTLC needs you wrote up from step 1. Most people automatically react well to nurturing input like listening, acceptance, or validation, yet in fact they may be lacking in guidance or limit-setting. Unfortunately, tender love from a mentor is *not enough* by itself to help us become actualized as our

Diamond Selves. If you don't believe me, reread the transcript of the session with my Love Mentor. We need coaching, guidance, and sometimes confrontation. Some women need help in setting limits on their own emotional drama, taking the victim role, or acting like bitchy out-of-control divas. Trust me, you don't get help or gain self-control over those behaviors from someone who just pats you on the back.

Ask your Love Mentor to give you the healing input you need to become your Diamond Self. A validating yet honest relationship will help you be centered and clear on the commitment you need and want. You will have a safe haven, a loving anchor to buffer you when you are confused, angry, or upset. Your mentor will serve as a guide to help you when you are uncertain about how to proceed toward the relationship you want. Also, should you find that you have to back away from your Beloved in order to help him respect, appreciate, or choose you, your mentor will be there as a strong supportive ally.

STEP 4: *TAKE IN THE HEALING INPUT*

The last step in the process is for you to take in and internalize the loving guidance that you receive. You can have the most perfect, most adoring, toughest Love Mentor in the world, but if you argue with her, fight her advice, and generally block the love by defining it as not real or useless, it will do you no good at all. Often it takes internal discipline to correct yourself and accept the caring that is coming your way. Do not discount and throw away the love that is being given to you.

> When we talk about understanding, surely it takes place only when the mind listens completely—the mind being your heart, your nerves, your ears—when you give your whole attention to it.—*J. Krishnamurti*

Pay attention, listen carefully, and repeat in your mind the loving statements your mentor offers you. Focus on your mentor's intentions by actively imagining yourself the way she or he sees you, in all your glory. Mentally rehearse what it might look, sound, and feel like to bring that best self-identity to life. Remember the power of mental rehearsal and how it helps rewire the brain? The process of visualizing and rehearsing will increase your self-esteem and bring out your charismatic Diamond Self. Everybody has one; yes, even you. Even if right now you are feeling just the opposite.

As you take in the validation and guidance from your mentor, your self-esteem and self-love grow. This process in turn will allow you to be more intimate on every level with your boyfriend as you are more and more able to take in and give love.

One powerful way to help you take in your Love Mentor's healing input is a technique that has helped many women called the Mirror Exercise. We all know what it is like getting ready for a date or a big event, peering into the mirror and not liking what we see. The extra pound, a bulge here, a wrinkle there, a zit we can't get rid of, not to mention hair that absolutely will not cooperate with the brush. Yes, the mirror often shows us all the things we do not like about our bodies. It generates lots of negative self-talk and doubts about our attractiveness, especially when we are about to meet our guy's family or go to a friend's wedding with him.

Well, new studies have shown something remarkable, something that flies in the face of all that! Researchers found that a mirror can actually work its magic in a positive direction if you know how to use it. In these studies, obese adults and adolescents were told to look in a mirror and discuss their bodies in a positive way. After six mirror sessions, the subjects started to naturally shift their focus from what they thought was wrong to what was right with their bodies. In other words, their self-talk changed. As a result, these obese people had an increase in their body satisfaction and experienced less disgust and anxiety about their appearance. This was true even for those who were depressed! Remember also that many clinical studies have shown that shifting to more positive self-talk reduces anxiety and stress, especially in social situations.

Let's put this powerful research to good use.

EXERCISE 1: *THE MIRROR EXERCISE*

1. Every day, look in the mirror and practice repeating the positive things your Love Mentor says about you.
2. Find five things that are right with your body. Notice the way your eyes twinkle, the definition in your arms, your beautifully shaped hands. Appreciate each part of your body that you really like.

Doing the Mirror Exercise regularly will bolster your self-confidence and help you on your journey to committed love. Your journey to a great and lasting relationship starts with your inner self love.

Love Mentoring and Shayna's Forever Love

Remember Shayna, the thirty-something curly-headed writer who lost her Brian in Chapter 2 because she couldn't take in his devotion? She found and hired a Love Mentor, Sherri, who worked on helping her learn to take in nurturance. At first, Shayna phoned in late for her appointments or missed them altogether. She tended to ignore the kind and validating things that Sherri said or did. Although she was asked to do the Mirror Exercise, Shayna did it only once in a halfhearted way. She also managed to not go out on any dates. Sherri took a firm stance with Shayna and confronted her in a strong way. For the first time, Shayna experienced a strong maternal figure that cared about her, who was entirely different from her victimized mother. Sherri said, "You will never have love in your life. Ever."

Shayna was taken aback. "What?"

Sherri said, "You heard me." This confrontation pierced through and got Shayna's attention. She started to weep. Sherri explained that Shayna was holding tightly to her killer belief that *All men are pigs and can't be trusted*. Sheri further confronted her, saying, "You're pushing me away the same way you pushed Brian and loving men away. If you continue, no one in the world will be able to end your loneliness. You are wasting both of our time in these Love Mentoring sessions." There was a long silence as Shayna cried.

Finally, a more open Shayna sincerely asked for help. Sherri responded that she needed to see Shayna cooperate in order to proceed with the mentoring. Shayna agreed. Over the next week, she actively did the Mirror Exercise and experienced a breakthrough in self-confidence about her body. She even sent thank-you flowers to Sherri.

This loving confrontation was the beginning of a turnaround for Shayna. She started a Dating Program of Three (for more information, read *Love in 90 Days*) where she saw three guys at the same time casually. In her Love Mentoring sessions, she was asked to practice Positive Paranoia so that she listed the positive things about each guy. Over the course of six months, Shayna dated more fulfilling guys and finally found the One. With Sherri's support, she did not distance from him, but instead told him when she felt insecure or like running away. When he proposed, she accepted. Shayna became much calmer and more peaceful. She wrote that her Love Mentor taught her how to be a strong woman who could ask for what she wanted. Most important, Sherri taught Shayna how to overcome her anxiety so she could sit still and take in the experience of being loved and prized.

> The good life is inspired by love and guided by knowledge.
> —*Bertrand Russell*

Give yourself the gift of a caring, validating, and devoted Love Mentor. Create a close relationship with a wise, affirming person who is in a successful, committed relationship. If you can't find one in your own network, I can steer you in the direction of expert professional Love Mentors. So feel free to contact me at www.lovein90days.com/contact. Through mentoring, you can learn important skills and internalize hopeful beliefs toward intimate relationships and thereby become a better mentor to yourself. You can then create a whole new inner love template that makes the "impossible" possible in your most precious relationship.

> Sometimes people come into your life and you know right away that they were meant to be there, to serve some sort of purpose, teach you a lesson, or help you figure out who you are or who you want to become. You never know who these people may be (possibly your neighbor, professor, long lost friend, lover, or even a complete stranger), but when you lock eyes with them, you know at the very moment that they will affect your life in a profound way.
>
> —*Anonymous*

You have come to the end of Part I on your journey to lasting love. This has been deep work, and I am so proud of you for whatever piece of it you did—even if it was just reading the material! I celebrate you for having the courage to examine your own beliefs, tackle your fears, and consider the guidance and inspiration of a Love Mentor.

I know you can succeed in creating the love you want if you simply press on with your love intention leading the way.

PART II

Is He Really the One?

5

Inside His Head

MEN AND COMMITMENT

> Don't disturb the exotic bird!
> —*Jerry Seinfeld, on how to talk to your wife*
> *on HBO's* Curb Your Enthusiasm

Have you ever wondered about what goes on in the minds of men when it comes to relationships? Do you wish that you could quickly move past the dating games guys play and finally get to a connection that is the real deal: comfortable, exciting, and *lasting*? After all, you have spent so much time thinking about the relationship, figuring it out, trying hard, and being committed to it. Still, despite all your efforts, he is confused, ambivalent, and even anxious about committing to you, leaving you with all sorts of questions, like:

> *How could he stop texting or calling for a whole week after he was so totally into me for months? Why does he pull away every time we open up and get real and close? How could he not appreciate all the great things I do for him and how great his life is with me in it? Doesn't he understand that we were meant to be together? Why isn't he interested in moving in with me? Will he ever commit? Am I wasting my time with this guy? Will he ever propose? After all the time I have clocked with him, will I ever have a chance to be a mother?*

What is going on with these guys? Men seem to want you and then, when they can have you, they forget about it. Their confusing, conflicting, mysterious behavior can just about drive you nuts. And *we're* supposed to be mysterious! Truth is, men are at least as hard to figure out as women. They tease us with clever e-mails, thoughtful gifts, daily texts and calls, only to turn around in the blink of an eye and disappoint us. Who hasn't fallen for that grand opening game in which they lure us with intimate talks, funny dates, soft kisses, maybe a perfect little heart bracelet, and more? A man can be attracted to you, have mind-blowing sex with you, see you regularly, and be caretaking to a fault, and yet deny the fact that you are a couple! Or at the same time be secretly seeing another woman. He may fantasize about a future together with you and speak about those fantasies, but hasn't the slightest inclination to make it all come true. So what exactly is going on here?

Through my work as a therapist and clinical supervisor of other individual, couple, and family therapists, I've heard just about every issue that single, married, and divorced guys have. I've logged thousands of hours in the trenches listening to men as they've completely opened up and explored their deepest issues, problems, needs, and fears. Those private moments have given me a unique window into understanding guys' fears about maturity, commitment, forming a couple, and creating a family. I understand how their minds work— how men tend to view love relationships and the different resistances they have toward choosing a woman for the long haul. I also have guided many men (including hard-core commitment-phobes!) through the process of making a true lasting commitment to a woman, and in a few cases run up against guys who have an impenetrable wall when it comes to moving forward into an exclusive future with one woman. In this process, I learned that it is absolutely critical to know and understand your significant other's deeper commitment fears in order to assess whether he really can step up and be the One. And as this is a key part of the Lasting Love Program, I'm now going to share men's secret fears with you.

Men and Their Mothers

Have you ever felt that men sometimes give off vibes of discomfort, uneasiness, or anxiety about relating to us women? Like they feel they can never understand or please us—but it also seems that it's critically important that they make us happy? Well, you are picking up on real gender-based differences that are not just due to biology, but also based on the structure of men's early childhood experiences. Most men had a woman as their first and primary caretaker in infancy. Their comfort, their happiness, their very survival depended on this all-powerful figure. Yet, of course, there are no perfect mothers. Which means that there was anxiety in that early relationship. And depending on how good or bad it was, real fears developed.

A man's mothering one was his original source of happiness, comfort, and sustenance, and when he is an adult that is the role his partner takes on automatically. The security, the warmth, the caretaking, the validation, the discipline, the boundaries, the amount of space, the problems, the tensions, and the general ins and outs of the mother–son relationship created a template for how to interact with a woman. This means that to some degree, depending on the progress he has made in becoming psychologically independent, a guy will transfer his baggage from his upbringing to your relationship.

As anthropologist Henrietta Moore put it: "All relations are with M(others)."

Nowhere is this more true than with a man's intimate partner. Typically it is very difficult for a man to remain separate emotionally from his girlfriend—her happiness is his happiness. Just as he felt a need to please his mother, he has a strong need to satisfy his partner. This is one of the most critical aspects of the relationship for men: *Can I please this woman?* The need-to-please issues start a self-imposed pressure to perform that he feels whenever he's with her, especially if she is upset or seems to have a problem that needs to be fixed. On the other hand, the more his girlfriend is in a happy or satisfied frame of mind, the less he will feel this burden. Now, I'm not saying that your man is conscious of this pressure. All I'm telling you is that he *feels* it, and that this changes how he reacts to you.

Believing they can't please a woman is one of the biggest reasons men won't commit.

In *Seasons of a Man's Life*, Daniel Levinson describes how a man may have various unconscious fantasies about women and relationships based on his memories and experiences of mothering. If that was a somewhat negative experience, depending on what his mother was like, he may experience a woman as an erratic abandoner, a devouring witch (we all have seen that kind of mother, at least in movies!), a feeding smotherer, a humiliating rejecter, an all-giving servant, or a demanding master. When these images are transferred to a girlfriend, they can create all kinds of commitment fears.

Pick, Project, Provoke

Just like women, men tend to reenact these negative scenarios in three different ways: They *pick* women who are similar to their mothers; *project* mother-like traits onto girlfriends; or *provoke* their partners into acting like their mothers. As adults, they tend to do at least two out of these three behaviors.

Take my client Grant, who was an engineer. He was raised by a critical woman who served in the armed forces. Grant could never do the right thing by her. His first serious relationship was with Roz, a big-time TV producer who was like a barking general with her troops both at work and at home. He basically *picked* a woman like his mother. She criticized and he withdrew, retreating into the world of computer games. When Roz would call him, Grant saw her as intruding on his free time and being critical of his game playing, no matter what she said (*projecting*). He would talk to her in a distracted way, which she took as a sign of disrespect. And voilà, Grant *provoked* Roz into angry outbursts that reenacted his mother's worst traits.

When Grant broke up with Roz (he texted her with the "it's over" message), he tried his hand with a woman who was very different from Mom. It was almost love at first sight with Ally, a shy yet nurturing type. In the beginning, Ally hung on Grant's every word and catered to his every desire. But after six months of dating exclusively, Grant "discovered" Ally's heretofore hidden traits. She became stubbornly controlling at times, much like his mother. For example, Ally began deciding how and where they would spend weekends together. One Sunday, when Grant complained about yet another brunch with Ally's girlfriends, she gave him the hurt silent treatment. Grant reacted by *projecting* onto Ally's negative vibe that she was angry and about to explode. Then he *provoked* her by several cutting, out-of-line remarks that escalated things to the point that Ally defended herself in a harsh, shrill voice. After the last of these fights, Grant decided that Ally was not the One and ended it with a long e-mail.

This pick, project, or provoke pattern really takes effect when things start to get serious and there is talk of a future together. That's when points of difference and conflict surface. She wants kids, he does not. He's into hanging out with the guys on the weekend and she wants more date time or time with her couple friends. These types of disagreements make it easy for projections and provocations to surface so that the woman seems to be and often acts out the role of a killjoy, a controller, a witch, or an abandoner.

In light of this, do you see how the exercises in Part I not only benefit you, but also benefit your partner and the whole relationship?

It's critical for you to work on being able to make yourself happy and to work with your belief systems and moods so that negativity and drama do not take you over! The more successful you are at the self-work, the less likely you will be to react to your partner's pick-project-provoking behavior. And you will be able to help remove self-imposed anxieties and pressures to perform from your boyfriend's shoulders, which means he will be able to be much closer and more loving toward you.

Men and Their Fathers

Negative or problematic experiences with a father also play a significant role in a man's commitment fears. If Dad mistreated, invalidated, criticized, controlled, or abandoned him, he will grow up with negative expectations in forming a love relationship. A father is usually the second most devoted and bonded parental figure, and to a certain extent a man's partner is also symbolic of the father. Dad's role as an early source of care and sustenance is close to the role played by the man's significant other in adulthood. Experiences with a rejecting or abusive father can be projected onto a girlfriend, so that she is seen as cold or cruel.

There is little doubt that commitment fears are also aroused by the role model that Father presented as a man in a love relationship or marriage. Did he suffer through massive henpecking? Did he sacrifice himself and work two jobs to eke out a living? Was he shackled to a job he hated for twenty-five years because the family's livelihood depended on it? Was he the total financial and emotional support for his wife and children, who sucked him dry? Did he die at an early age from a stress-induced heart attack? Did he stop having sex or start sleeping in a separate room? Did he ever have time or opportunity to pursue his own hobbies or dreams? Or even downtime with peace and quiet?

When a son grows up observing his father's overwork and suffering for the sake of marriage and family, he is often not eager to commit to some woman and follow suit. It is not appealing to go down the same awful road that leads to a boring sexless picket-fenced cage in the suburbs. Pop culture only reinforces the stressed-out heart-attack-prone dad role models in movies, TV, and even on YouTube.com. In response to a Web video in which a married machinery worker supposedly died, a male viewer posted the following:

> *Bob won't be in to work tomorrow, due to an incredibly boring death today.*

Maybe a man grew up not with a miserable father as a role model, but in an entirely different set of circumstances that negatively impacted his ability to commit—the all-too-common history in which the guy's parents divorced. Did his father leave the family, meet someone else, and shower his love on a new set of children? Did his father lose contact with him altogether?

As a child, did he have sporadic or unpredictable contact with his dad, where he would wait for him, only to be disappointed? Did his mother hate his father and forbid or interfere with their having contact? No matter which scenario describes your significant other, one thing remains the same: When a son grows up without a steady or validating paternal figure, or a steady, supportive, affirming, and happy maternal figure, he is quite vulnerable to having serious commitment fears.

Men's Eight Common Fears of Commitment

As I've worked with men over the years, I've discovered eight specific types of commitment fears, all of which have their roots in childhood and adolescence. Through the process of picking, projecting, and provoking, these fears lead men to re-create their negative relationship scenarios and sabotage themselves when it comes to romance and love. Some men have more than one fear. Unfortunately, if a man is not growing and working on his issues, he will often follow these same patterns over and over again with woman after woman—sinking his possibilities of committed love into the netherworld.

You might be thinking, *Dr. D, I already know plenty about men's commitment fears; what's the point of rehashing them here?* What I'm offering is a much deeper understanding of the minds of men, a way for you to be able to determine if your man is mired in his issues—in which case you need to get out quickly and cut your losses—or if he is growing and working on developing himself. Understanding these self-sabotaging patterns will show you how to key in to his psychology and understand whether it is worth your time and effort to stay involved in the relationship.

1. *SHE WON'T WANT ME:* THE FEAR OF REJECTION

This is a man who is afraid a woman will suddenly lose interest and abandon him. Because of this, he has a hard time having honest straight talk and is very afraid of conflict. When the inevitable disagreements and differences come up in a relationship, he stuffs his feelings and drifts away. He prefers e-mail or texts when dealing with uncomfortable issues. He doesn't have the courage to stand up to his partner, so problems fester and blow up. When tension reaches the boiling point, he doesn't have the cojones to break up. Instead he becomes passive-aggressive, gently slipping away as his texts and calls fade out—or he quickly dumps his partner before she can dump him. Above all he fears rejection, a feeling so painful for him that it is almost like annihilation, like being completely destroyed. Instead, he slithers around any direct conflict.

Many men suffer from some degree of this conflict-avoidant

pattern because, as we learned previously, guys tend to have much more difficulty dealing with stress, experiencing soaring heart rates and blood pressure that are hard to bring back to normal levels. As a result, they may pull away and distance themselves emotionally in order to calm down.

Fear of Rejection: The Story of Emmett

Emmett, one of my therapy clients, was a computer security expert who had a history of falling for gorgeous Asian women whom he believed were "out of his league." Emmett met Riko, a much younger Japanese woman, online. He was awestruck by her delicate beauty. Riko looked up to Emmett and his great intelligence. Nonetheless, he told me in numerous sessions how he was sure she would get disenchanted and leave him. Emmett's fear wasn't based on reality; Riko's e-mails to him were filled with thank-yous, smiley faces, and flirty jokes. Nonetheless, Emmett let himself get "tied up with work" so that he did not promptly respond to Riko at times. And feeling abandoned, she pulled away from him. After several months, Emmett was very unhappy with Riko's passivity during sex. He complained to me about his unhappiness and how this made him feel rejected, like she didn't really want him. But even after my prodding, he refused to tell his lover what he would like her to do to spice up their sex life.

Eventually, Emmett agreed to a joint session with Riko. He was very nervous that when he was straight with Riko, she would storm out (like his mother, who had a difficult personality), but with support he was able to speak his truth. This was just the first step in Emmett overcoming his fear of rejection. Riko reacted calmly and was open to talking about it. When Riko started to discuss her own issues about Emmett's lack of support for her work as a graphic designer, he tended to clam up and withdraw emotionally. When I confronted him about his silence, he admitted that he was afraid that he would say something "fatally stupid" that would make Riko leave him. But both were committed to therapy, and over time the couple worked together and, to Emmett's great relief, became engaged.

FEAR OF REJECTION WARNING SIGNS

He avoids angry exchanges like the plague. If there is a disagreement, he tends to pull away and use texts or e-mail or simply does not respond to your messages.

2. *SHE'S GONNA TAKE AWAY MY FREEDOM:* THE FEAR OF BEING CONTROLLED AND SMOTHERED

Because of the strong need-to-please pressure that most men experience, they often develop the fear of being controlled. As a clinician, I've observed that men value their independence and freedom even more greatly than women. In order to define their own separate identities, they really had to pull away from Mother early on in their lives. Both boys and girls have to individuate from Mother in order to form a separate identity. But a boy faces a twofold task—he must learn to perceive himself not only as an individual distinct from her, but also as being male as opposed to female. Failures in achieving a separate identity can then lead to failures in developing a male identity. This battle for a separate identity is, according to some scholars on gender differences, harder for men than for women.

As a result, many men grow up with a view of women as weights that hold them down or as controlling objects that won't let them go. You can hear these fears echoed in the phrases men use, like *the old ball-and-chain* and *she had me by the balls*. It's easy to see then how marriage becomes the definite marker of a change in power, where the woman-as-wife simply takes over the man's life.

When the fear of smothering is very strong, it leads to classic commitment phobia. Talk of a future makes this guy quiet, nervous, upset, or angry. He may be reluctant to act like he's in a couple when you are with friends or out in public. He may only speak in the first person, saying "I" instead of "we" or "me" instead of "us." He may keep you away from his friends and family. A man who is afraid of smothering may be in an on-again, off-again relationship for years—where he always seems to want you when you break up because he then feels free and unencumbered—yet he just cannot pull the trigger and commit when you are together because it feels like he is losing his independence, the lifeblood of his very existence as a man.

If the relationship has progressed to having regular sex, he may need to make an escape by asking you to leave or going home instead of spending the night. He may feel distant and emotionally unavailable to you. He may say he is not sure what love really is or that he is incapable of experiencing love. This is the guy who comes right out and says that he does not believe in love and marriage or getting serious and settling down with one person.

No matter what he feels for you, this is a man who is terrified of jumping fully into a long-term relationship. Bottom line: He believes he can't be himself and fully be with a woman. In his view, he has to give up the lead role in his own life if he is stuck in a supporting role with you and/or the children. It seems like his golf, buddies, bar days, sports, even the Super Bowl, are going to be ripped away by the all-powerful, all-controlling vortex of the couple. For this man, commitment, love, and marriage mean being trapped in a cage from which there is no escape.

Fear of Being Controlled: The Story of Jon

Jon, a forty-year-old businessman, had a series of relationships, each lasting around six months to a year. He fell madly in love with brunette after brunette and pursued each of them vigorously until the moment things became serious and "her thoughts of marriage" were in the air. At that moment everything would reverse and he would feel like the prey instead of the hunter. Jon would become anxious, agitated, and feel like he had to get away from each woman at all costs, as if his very life depended on it. In his last relationship, Jon claimed that he was forced into an actual engagement, but he was saved by an unlikely ally. He told me that right after he gave her the ring, he started having full-blown panic attacks. Jon described them as attacks in which he couldn't breathe and his chest became so tight and painful that he was sure he was having a heart attack. With these frightening symptoms, Jon felt like he had the excuse he needed. He told his girlfriend that something was really wrong with him and broke up with her. Jon walked away from her and never had another panic attack.

During therapy, Jon came to realize that his fear of being smothered had destroyed his last relationship and would prevent him from any chance at real love. Only then did he begin working seriously on facing and overcoming his severe commitment fears.

FEAR OF BEING CONTROLLED WARNING SIGNS

He may totally act like you are the One and be very accommodating and nurturing—until he has to say the three magic words or you want a definite wedding date or commitment. Then he says to you that settling down doesn't work for him because he is incapable of living that way. You begin to see a pattern in which he says no to any requests you make of him.

3. *THERE'S SOMETHING WRONG WITH ME:* THE FEAR OF NOT BEING LOVABLE

Because of not being prized and validated growing up, a man may have a core unconscious fear that he is simply not lovable. He feels insecure and not-good-enough. This type of guy is looking to you for approval, asking what you think, before he makes decisions. In the beginning, he tries hard and works overtime to make you happy. His feelings depend on what you think and feel. If you are sad, disappointed, or afraid, he is really upset and takes it as a measure of his fundamental lack of worth.

The net effect is that he feels emotionally uncomfortable in the relationship, like it is not a good fit for him. He may feel like the woman is out of his league. So when it comes time to take that next step to commitment, to say the L-word or talk about a future, he is passive, quiet, and tends to pull away from you.

Another sign of this particular type is the man who cannot tolerate your innocent flirting with guys or talking about your ex. He gets depressed, moody, and withdrawn. If you cheat, forget about it: This man will not fight to win you back. Instead he will collapse internally under a mountain of insecurity and self-hate.

Fear of Not Being Lovable: The Story of Jason
Thirty-one-year-old Jason, an Internet marketer, suffered from a fear of not being lovable or worthy. At a local bar, he met Felicia, a sloe-eyed and beautiful Pilates trainer. Jason was tipsy and confident as he swept Felicia away with his quick wit. They wound up sharing that first night together. Felicia then pursued Jason, asking him to join her at various parties and events. Jason came along, but usually had a few drinks to loosen up. A few "good" months went by. One night, Felicia met her ex at a party and flirted with him. Seeing this, Jason sulked and withdrew from her. He was not responsive to any of her attempts to reconnect, even refusing to come over for "make-up" sex. A few weeks later, he called the whole thing off, rejecting Felicia before she could reject him.

FEAR OF NOT BEING LOVABLE WARNING SIGNS

He may be very quiet or shy, or he seeks approval by doing things that are helpful or giving. He finds it hard to talk about his own wants and needs. He may be more passive and tends to enjoy solitary activities including sports or computer games. He cannot handle any competition from other guys—it usually spells the end of the relationship.

4. *I'LL NEVER MAKE IT:* THE FEAR OF NOT MEASURING UP

While the fear of not measuring up is closely related to the fear of not being lovable, it has its roots in men's biology and in our culture. Men are biologically wired to perform and produce. Plus they have been taught by this materialistic culture that the measure of a man's worth is how successful he is in terms of power and money. Men often feel they must succeed at everything they do: in school, sports, video games, relationships, as lovers, as parents, and as breadwinners. Some men feel that if they fail in any of these arenas, they are losers.

The fear of not measuring up also has its origins in families where boys are driven to be perfect, to get all A's, to excel on the football field, or by their mothers (often single or divorced) to be the "men of the house." It's very difficult if not impossible for a boy or even an eighteen- or twenty-one-year-old to feel like a man, so you can understand how that kind of pressure at a young age might make him still feel like he isn't man enough or that he doesn't measure up as a grown adult.

Sally's significant other, Gary, who started to pull away from her in our story from Chapter 1, struggled with the fear of not measuring up. His mother, a super-successful doctor, divorced when he was ten. His rather distant father pretty much disappeared from his life at that point—he did not have much in the way of a role model for how to be a loving male partner. Gary's mom drove herself and him to excel. Yet Gary's dream was to be a respected author—which is a tough and slow career path. So he worked as a real estate agent part-time to supplement his meager blogging income. His mother was not impressed, and Gary internalized that negative assessment. Down deep he felt like he could never really please his mother—or Sally. The critical incident that caused him to pull away from Sally was that he brought the manuscript of his novel to a harsh but prominent writing teacher who actually told him he did "not have the writing gene"! He was completely crushed, believing even more strongly that he couldn't measure up to Sally's expectations and would disappoint her. Gary's only solution was to withdraw from her before she saw through his witty facade and realized what a loser he was. More on Sally and Gary later.

The fear of not measuring up can make it very difficult to move forward into a committed relationship with a partner, no matter how terrific she is. At his core, this type of man is terrified that he can't give a woman what she deserves or needs. His anxiety can be magnified if he is really smitten with her; the more he is into her, the faster he thinks he will fail in some irretrievable way.

Often this type of guy needs a "trophy" girlfriend who is sexy and over-the-top beautiful to "prove" that he is measuring up as a successful man. He may or may not have real feelings for her, even if they are together for years. This in fact is Wayne's story—and like Gary, he felt he couldn't measure up.

Fear of Not Measuring Up: The Story of Wayne

Wayne, a twenty-nine-year-old event promoter, had a strong fear of not measuring up. He grew up with a "Great Santini" father, a career military man who constantly pushed Wayne but rarely praised him. However, Wayne turned out to be very successful at a relatively young age, winning over club owners with his brash can-do attitude. On top of that, Wayne had managed to win the heart of the stunning Li, a thirty-year-old Broadway dancer who had her choice of suitors. They had been together for two years, but as she pressed to move into his place, he nervously told her he was not sure and that he did not know what love really was. When Wayne's business slowed down, he began withdrawing from Li so that they were down to seeing each other about once a week. Then, at one of his events, Wayne met a young model and took her right to bed. He began courting the new girlfriend while still maintaining some contact with Li. Finally, Li confronted Wayne, and he confessed. Wayne tried to make it up to her, but he refused to make any real commitment for the future. After a few torturous months, Li told him that she was done. Li packed up the things she had left at Wayne's apartment and slammed the door while he watched helplessly. That's when Wayne came to see me.

After a few months of therapy, Wayne realized how he had self-destructed when his business started to fail. His fears of not measuring up had grabbed him by the throat, and to make himself feel like a man again he went after the model. That only worked for a short period of time. Wayne told me that he was ashamed that his fears had driven away the only woman he had ever really loved.

With my encouragement, Wayne asked Li to come back. Actually, he begged her. Wayne also invited her to join him in a few therapy sessions. When Li saw that Wayne had true remorse and after he asked her to marry him (with a ring), she did forgive him. They continued in couples therapy until after they were married.

FEAR OF NOT MEASURING UP WARNING SIGNS

He brags and may exaggerate his accomplishments to the point of lying about them. Winning at work or with women is critical to his feeling okay. If this type of guy experiences a setback at work, he may slink away in shame or, like Wayne, find another woman to boost his ego.

5. *I'VE GOT A SECRET*: THE FEAR OF BEING FOUND OUT

As a man gets closer to a woman, he may fear that he will become exposed, because he has to reveal fears or feelings that are "unmanly" or a shameful family secret. This is especially true if he had difficult, demanding parents who shamed him when he cried or acted like a "wuss." A similar fear of commitment can also develop when a man is ashamed about his history or family. He may harbor secrets about relatives who are in mental hospitals, in jail, or just poor.

You may have seen this type of guy depicted on film or TV as the man who can only get married if he completely hides his past. On the award-winning series *Mad Men*, the super-successful hunky lead, ad executive Don Draper, has completely hidden his background and even changed his identity, including his name. For a long time on the show, no one, including his beleaguered upper-middle-class wife, knows his true history. Draper's whole life is about keeping secrets, all driven by the fear of being found out. For this type of guy, opening up and expressing his deeper feelings is impossible because he will have to come clean. And in his world, confession is definitely *not* good for the soul.

Another variation of this fear has to do with an inner sense of having some horrible and uncorrectable flaw. It might be a perceived physical defect like his height or the size of his "package." Or it might be a feeling of intellectual inferiority, a sense of being a B player who's not good enough to be an A. This type of man works harder, tries harder, and puts down competitors with sarcasm or contempt.

In relationships, he will often project onto his partner by being super-critical and judgmental and looking for her fatal flaw. Unconsciously, he doesn't want to be with anyone who would be in a club that would have him. In therapy, he says that there are no great women out there and that he is super-picky because he deserves "the perfect woman." As he makes progress in therapy or some other growth process, he will admit that the truth is that he is afraid to commit because he's afraid he will be found out as the imperfect man.

Fear of Being Found Out: The Story of Guy, the Little Napoleon
Guy was a lawyer who was somewhat short in stature, something that had bothered him since he stopped growing at fourteen. His brutal father, a big and burly Italian pizza restaurant owner, frequently beat him when he was a child. But Guy was tenacious, studied hard, and made it into one of the top law schools. Years went by, and with his hard work ethic and pit-bull attitude he became one of the top litigators in Philadelphia.

When I first met him, he was dressed impeccably in head-to-toe Armani. He had dated Keisha, a quiet social worker, for three years. She looked up to Guy and was very shy socially. Guy complained that even though Keisha was kind and beautiful, she was boring, especially in bed. According to Guy, his friends really liked her because Keisha had humanized him and made him "tolerable to be with." Guy told me all this with a smirk as if he "gave a crap" about "being more human." I wanted to meet Keisha but Guy refused because then "we would gang up on him." Guy really was afraid for Keisha to find out the truth about him: that he came from a brutal and humble family of modest means.

Finally, as Guy continued to waffle, Keisha got the courage to have The Talk. Faced with what he saw as an ultimatum, Guy broke up with her. It was only then that Guy's progress in therapy really began. He lost a great gal, but the next woman he really liked learned about his sad but true history.

FEAR OF BEING FOUND OUT WARNING SIGNS

He denies having any needy-type feelings, like being anxious, insecure, or lonely. He may not be able to use the L-word. He can be extremely judgmental about others, especially if they make demands of him.

6. *SHE'LL USE OR SCREW ME OVER:* THE FEAR OF TRUSTING A WOMAN

If a man had an erratic or manipulative mother and a history of being cheated on, used, or disappointed by women, he may have major trust issues when it comes to making a commitment. Mistrusting all women, he vows never to be vulnerable again—because if he is, he will just be hurt. If he took a hit financially in a divorce and/or is wealthy, he may be afraid that women just want him for his money. He may fear that all women are mean, manipulative, and exploitative.

Sometimes this fear can develop when a guy is stuck struggling to extricate himself from an ugly divorce or an angry battle with his ex over their children. He may come right out and say that he will never marry again.

Fear of Trusting a Woman: The Story of Kai

Kai was a flight attendant who navigated a difficult divorce from a very nasty alcoholic woman, who was very much like his raging mother. To get out, he basically caved in and gave his wife the house that he loved and "most" of his money. When he met Saidah, an earthy warm woman on one of his flights, he was entranced. They had a delightful six months together. But when she started asking about a future, he started to experience her as pushy, just like his ex. He said he didn't think he would ever be able to live with a woman again—and definitely would never marry.

Saidah was patient and kind. She felt Kai would come around, especially if she nurtured him. But after two years went by with very little movement on Kai's part, she gave him an ultimatum: Move in together or break up. Kai felt put upon and abused. He went MIA, finally writing her a long good-bye letter. Saidah, on the other hand, learned her lesson and went to one of my expert Love Mentors. She quickly started dating guys who were more open to creating a committed love relationship.

FEAR OF TRUSTING A WOMAN WARNING SIGNS

He talks negatively about his mother and/or exes. He feels like he has been victimized by women. He may come right out and say he doesn't believe in love or will never marry.

7. *I'M TOO YOUNG:* THE FEAR OF GROWING UP

A man may not feel like he is an adult who is ready to take on the responsibilities of a relationship, children, and family life. This Peter

Pan syndrome may have its roots in various types of family dysfunction. He may have been coddled by parents who protected him from the real world, from the possibility of failure. Any difficulty or trouble at school might have been dismissed as someone else's problem and never his responsibility. Or he may have never been encouraged to try something really hard like a competitive sport or an accelerated course at school—a situation where not succeeding is a real possibility. He may have been sickly and had overprotective parents who wouldn't allow him to play with other kids and compete in sports. Other Peter Pans were just ignored by a divorced or missing father and an overworked mom.

As a result of any of these dynamics, the young man often fails to build up his identity as a competent and solid adult male. Internally, he feels like a child, a kid who wants to play, get high, sleep late, and work menial jobs with little to no responsibility. No wonder, then, that our Peter Pan is boyish in his leisure activities. He may be a video game addict glued to his game console at all times; spend many hours watching or playing sports; or worry about his health while smoking pot every day. He may be still living at home into his thirties. This is a guy who wants to date and have fun, but balks when it comes to having a committed, ongoing, and serious relationship.

Fear of Growing Up: The Story of Jermaine

Jermaine was an eternal student, with two master's degrees and not a pot to pee in. He worked at Starbucks and lived with his single mom, who was a teacher. His main passion was writing, and although he had never published anything, he was always starting a new novel—"his big breakthrough." When Shelly, a frustrated nurse whose dream was also to be a wife and mom, first met Jermaine in a graduate course, she was drawn to his creativity and over-the-top ability to spin yarns. He had a childish air about him that Shelly found endearing. Thus began an on-again, off-again relationship that lasted ten years. During that time, Shelly would leave Jermaine because the relationship and his career were "going nowhere." He would then pull his act together and get a full-time job. They would reunite, but never in a serious, fulfilling way. Eventually Shelly met with me and decided to end the relationship for good. Once she was finally free, she began dating men who actually had their own homes and real careers, who were also looking to be in permanent relationships. Eventually, through an online service, she met the "nerdy guy" of her dreams, a man who was successful and crazy about her. They are married and have adorable twin rascals.

FEAR OF GROWING UP WARNING SIGNS

He acts juvenile, makes ridiculous jokes, or even burps or farts like a little boy. In a conflict, he tends to either quickly back down or have a tantrum to get his way. He may be very concerned with his bodily functions or getting ill.

8. *I CAN'T DECIDE*: THE FEAR THAT HE CAN'T MAKE THE "RIGHT" DECISION

This type of man has a very hard time making up his mind or trusting his own judgment. When he picks one movie to see, he immediately regrets not choosing another. He is not sure that the company he works at is really the best one for him. This guy is afraid of making a decision that forecloses on all his other options—including choosing you. Every time he does so, he has a burst of anxiety and thoughts about other, "better" women.

This guy may struggle with attention deficit disorder, in which he finds it very hard to focus on anything. More typically, he's a real commitment-phobe who is just not sure about committing to whichever woman he is with at the moment. And the fear of making the wrong decision has him ready to stop seeing her at a moment's notice whenever a new "better" chickie appears at a party or on his computer screen.

Fear He Can't Make the "Right" Decision: The Story of George

Leeza, a forty-something cosmetics manager at a department store, was a zaftig blonde who met George online. George was a community college professor who was close to fifty and yet had never been married. Leeza was drawn to George's constantly active mind and loved the fact that he didn't have an ex or kids. George introduced her to sushi, opera, and comedy clubs. At first Leeza was blown away. But as the months wore on, she noticed that George was really very depressed and never seemed to enjoy the fantastic activities they shared. He had a hard time being present with her and instead was always worrying about work, reading his "Crackberry," or quipping that the service or the meal wasn't good enough.

After about nine months, Leeza wanted to know where things were heading in the relationship. George said that he just didn't know for sure if marriage was for him although he thought it was time and Leeza was really terrific. Leeza asked him to figure out where she stood, but all he could say was that he was afraid of making a mistake. With the encouragement of her Love Mentor, Leeza finally left him and started dating other guys. George begged her to come back. After he went into therapy and attended some growth courses with her, Leeza did take him back, under the condition that they get engaged. George says it was the best decision he ever made.

FEAR HE CAN'T MAKE THE "RIGHT" DECISION WARNING SIGNS

He is very intellectual. He tends to overly think things through and obsess. He is always second-guessing himself with his grass-is-greener mentality. Often this type of guy needs to be dumped to realize what he's lost.

The Fear-O-Meter

You can think of the Fear-O-Meter as a continuum of intensity of the eight fears. They can occur at a normal level, where they are being faced and overcome, or they can be exaggerated to the point that the man is so completely neurotic as to be unable to move into a committed love relationship.

SIGNS OF EXTREME COMMITMENT FEARS

When men's fears of commitment are extreme, they can play out in many different ways. Some men become addicts: compulsive video game players, eaters, drinkers, or workaholics. Others become argumentative, contemptuous, critical, or domineering. Still others may act extremely passive or shy or withdraw from any meaningful conversations about the future. Some act more like hypochondriacs or children. Others disappear on you. Still others cheat. *When fears are extreme and the guy is acting out in response to those fears, there is often nothing that can be done.* It's not about you; you can't fix it by being the perfect person or staying with him to "prove" your love. When your partner's fear is out of control, it is operating at an unconscious level and therefore determines the outcome of any love relationship. In other words, no matter how much love you pour into him, it goes nowhere.

Once the deeper fear is triggered, whether it is by the prospect of seeing each other more regularly, discussing a future together, moving in, or getting engaged, a man with extreme fear will at a fundamental level do all he can to pull back. He is not willing to examine himself, his motives, or his fears. Here's what you need to understand: *This type of guy is fundamentally happy with the status quo of his love life and does not want to change.* It's best to get out quickly and cut your losses, no matter how hard or unfair it seems. You're better off leaving because if you stay, all you will end up with is a lot of wasted years you can never get back, not to mention bitter disappointment and heartache.

NORMAL FEARS

All of us are faced with two conflicting urges: *to merge and become one* versus *being independent and free.* When a man and woman fall in love and come together, it is normal and common to have fears come up about losing one's separate sense of self, one's space, one's own identity and unique pursuits and interests. Both men and women experience these fears. This is reasonable—compromises have to be made in order to have a relationship. Time needs to be set aside. After all, how many times has it happened that you got involved with some guy and wound up having little or no time for your girlfriends?

So it is normal in the development of a new relationship for your boyfriend to have doubts, to have some measure of virtually all the fears we have been talking about. The key variable here is this:

If a man's fears are at the normal level, they do not stop him from moving forward over time into increasing intimacy and commitment.

Sometimes it is hard to tell if your boyfriend has an unworkable commitment phobia or more normal fears that he is willing to work on. Here is a ten-part checklist to help you tell the difference between normal fears and commitment phobia. In the last several months or year is he:

1. Trying to be self-reflective by talking about his issues and fears with you in an effort to deal with them and move forward?
2. Responsive to you when you soothe his fears?
3. Showing willingness to work on himself by taking growth or spiritual courses?
4. Actively in therapy or coaching?
5. Opening his world of friends and family to you?

6. Introducing you to people as his girlfriend or significant other?
7. Sharing his physical space?
8. Growing in his ability to discuss what he wants for his future?
9. Becoming more open to discussing the next steps in your relationship?
10. Saying "I love you" more easily or at times entertaining thoughts or joking about getting engaged or living together?

If he is moving forward in five or more of these ways, chances are his fears are more manageable and in the normal range, and he is interested in becoming serious with you.

Helping Him Overcome His Commitment Fears

If a guy is truly into you and willing to grow, he will face down his fears and make it work with you, especially if you accept his need for space and independence, validate his worth, and continue to nurture yourself. Remember, he will tend to project his fears and negative expectations onto you and even unconsciously provoke you into being angry, critical, or distant. If you understand this, you can practice loving-kindness and not engage in that negative pattern from his past. A key part of your Lasting Love Program is to show him that love is possible. You can gently let him know that, as James Baldwin says,

> To defend oneself against a fear is simply to insure that one will, one day, be conquered by it; fears must be faced.

Here is a list of the eight common male commitment fears once again, and how you can help soothe each one. If your boyfriend takes in your input, you will see that he becomes calmer, happier, and closer to you. This indicates that you are on target in your approach.

And he will then be much more able to provide exactly what it is you need from him.

1. *SHE WON'T WANT ME:* THE FEAR OF REJECTION

- If you would like to help your Beloved soothe this demon, it is important to let him know you are not leaving him.
- Honestly validate him and let him know that you are truly enjoying being with him. That he is, in fact, in your league.
- When he withdraws in the face of possible conflict, show steadiness by sending a nonchalant text, e-mail, or voice mail that suggests you are still connected the way you usually are and it is "business as usual." Later you can deal with the issues.
- Share your steady belief in the strength of your ongoing connection, and as time passes your Beloved will lose his fear of losing you.
- If you feel it is appropriate, have sex with your Beloved. He will not feel rejected, and both of you will benefit from the bonding biochemicals it releases.

2. *SHE'S GONNA TAKE AWAY MY FREEDOM:* THE FEAR OF BEING CONTROLLED AND SMOTHERED

- This is such a common fear! Luckily it has a clear antidote: Encourage your man to do his thing separate and apart from you. Send him off to watch the World Cup with his buddies.
- Make sure there are times when he misses you and actually wants more contact with you!
- When you are together, ask him to make decisions and lead the way.
- Flirt and then withdraw so he has to pursue you.
- Point out good role models—real couples you meet where the fellow is happy and relishes his sports, or other hobbies, but

the two are truly in love. Try to cultivate a relationship between the two of you and this kind of couple.

3. *THERE'S SOMETHING WRONG WITH ME*: THE FEAR OF NOT BEING LOVABLE

- When this is a core fear, your Beloved needs a great deal of TLC. If you want to be helpful, be positive and nurturing in a steady way.
- Show by your words and actions that you enjoy being close with him.
- Tell him if he smells good to you.
- Tell him his touch is good for you.
- Let him know that his words connect with you.
- Tell him how just being with him makes you happy.
- Give him a validating nickname, using baby talk if he likes it.
- If you feel it is appropriate, have sex with your Beloved. Both of you will feel more lovable and loved.

4. *I'LL NEVER MAKE IT*: THE FEAR OF NOT MEASURING UP

- With this fear, it can be very helpful to assist your Beloved in owning his competence, abilities, and success.
- Pay real attention to his work product at times (read his court brief, look at his Web site design, and so on). Tell him honestly what is very right or great about them.
- Detail his career accomplishments and appreciate each one so that he can take it all in.
- Celebrate each of his triumphs with him.
- Tell him how proud you are of him.
- Tell others how proud you are of him—in front of him.
- Get him symbols of his success—a fancy briefcase or pen, or the like.

- Realistically envision how great his accomplishments will be in the future and tell him about your vision.

5. *I'VE GOT A SECRET*: THE FEAR OF BEING FOUND OUT

- The bottom line in helping your Beloved conquer this fear is that he has to share his secret with you. So set conditions where he can share in a safe way.
- Sitting or walking side by side while talking can help your man open up, as men feel less threatened in that position.
- Share some of your secrets with him when the time is right, to be a role model, create more trust, and establish a safe space.
- If you guess what his secret is, mention it casually as if it were no big deal.
- Once the shameful secret is out, be accepting and validating of your partner for sharing. Show him that it is still "business as usual."
- This whole process can be enormously healing for your Beloved and open new depth in your relationship.

6. *SHE'LL USE OR SCREW ME OVER*: THE FEAR OF TRUSTING A WOMAN

- If you are interested in helping your significant other overcome this fear, the key is showing him your own steady, giving, and good nature.
- Be reliable and true to your word with him.
- Be nurturing and devoted.
- Give to your Beloved and over time share in the financial and day-to-day responsibilities.
- Be there when your Beloved has a crisis and needs you.
- If you feel it is appropriate, have sex with your Beloved. It will help him to relax and feel more connected and trusting with you.

7. *I'M TOO YOUNG:* THE FEAR OF GROWING UP

- If you would like to help your man overcome this fear, the key is to set constructive limits on his childish behavior so that he sees that he can step up and mature.
- Simply and quietly say "No" to immature behavior like burping at the dinner table.
- Encourage your Beloved to take on more responsibilities at work.
- Be firm in showing your unwillingness to put up with his fearful or self-indulgent behavior.
- Show your Beloved what life is like without you (spend some time apart doing your own thing).
- Be willing to leave if your man will not move forward to the level of commitment you need to see. This firm boundary will help maximize his own growth pressure to step into being a man in a real love relationship.

8. *I CAN'T DECIDE:* THE FEAR THAT HE CAN'T MAKE THE "RIGHT" DECISION

- If you want to help your Beloved overcome this fear, support his belief in his own ability to make good decisions in his love life.
- Suggest that, when making decisions, he listen to his gut or intuition instead of being too lost in flights of thoughts.
- Most important, show your Beloved what life is like without you (spend some time apart doing your own thing). This will help him get in touch with missing you and see that choosing to be with you is the right decision.
- Be willing to leave if your man will not move forward to the level of commitment you need to see. This firm boundary will help maximize his own growth pressure to step into being a man in a real love relationship.

Helping a guy face his demons isn't easy, especially when you have your own issues about love and commitment, along with your own needs, as we all do. But by overcoming your killer beliefs in Part I, you have given yourself the freedom not to drag old wounds or bitterness into your future and to be able to love from your best and highest perspective of self. In so doing, you can inspire your Beloved to find his strength and courage. And you will gain all the more for it.

Perfect love casteth out fear.—*1 John 4:18*

6

The Seven "Real" Laws of Attraction

THE LITMUS TEST FOR YOUR RELATIONSHIP

> I love thee—I love thee!
> 'Tis all that I can say;
> It is my vision in the night,
> My dreaming in the day.
>
> —*Thomas Hood*

Our intrepid heroine Sally started off with the fine madness and joy of new love with Gary. As we saw early on, those I've-Gotta-Have-Her-in-My-Life fireworks died off for Gary after a few months. Unbeknownst to Sally, Gary hit a setback in his career and was struggling with issues and fears about measuring up. And there went his focus and feelings of attraction for Sally. When Sally hit that dark and anxious downtick in her relationship, she started wondering whether Gary was Mr. Right or not. She became anxious, tense, and picked fights with him. At times she ached for him, while at others she angrily rehashed different ways he had let her down in the past. Then Sally learned about what I call the Seven "Real" Laws of Attraction. As she applied them to her relationship with Gary, they started laughing it up together and sharing sexy fireworks again. His quick rebound into being present and connected showed Sally that he was indeed the One.

Understanding and using these laws of attraction are key elements of the Lasting Love Program. They will help you determine if your boyfriend or partner is truly Mr. Right or not. As you apply these laws over time, they will also help your Beloved overcome many of the common male fears of commitment we just discussed. They set the stage for a high-intensity, passionate connection where, if he truly wants to, your Beloved will naturally take the next step forward to being committed and having lasting love with you. On the other hand, if you use these "real" laws of attraction and your man does not respond, you have a strong indication that he may not be the One.

Let's start with a look at how attraction first unfolds and then naturally wanes at the beginning stages of a relationship.

Falling In and Out of Love

When we fall in love, our brains make large quantities of dopamine and norepinephrine, which also happens when you take speed. These brain chemicals create the excited, exhilarated, and focused state that allows us to have five-hour dates and remember every detail about what our new hottie did and said. The speedy chemicals also can drive up our levels of testosterone, which increases sexual desire. On top of that, when we fall in love, serotonin levels fall until they resemble what's found in people with obsessive-compulsive disorders. So we tend to ruminate, fantasize, and obsess about our new (drug-like) boyfriend.

But this hot and bubbly love cauldron and the irresistible feelings of attraction it brings are biologically timed to fade out after somewhere between six months and two years. Sometimes even sooner. Then you can easily find yourself with a man who is emotionally distant, pulling away from you, and staunchly avoiding any whiff of commitment. Sound familiar? No amount of convincing your man about how perfect you are together, no amount of showing him how upset you are because you need him, no amount of giving to him outside or inside the bedroom can get him back. It just doesn't make sense, does it?

Yet some women are able to find a man who does not back away over time, a guy who maintains such a deep emotional connection and attraction to her that nothing else seems to get in the way. These gals don't always have the best looks and aren't the youngest, hottest, thinnest, or curviest. They are not always the most helpful types. Yet the guy is smitten and nothing can stand in the way of his interest and commitment—not cultural or religious differences, family pressures, issues of "not being ready," or work or career demands. He doesn't give any of the usual excuses. Because with this woman, the man is experiencing something at the gut level—a continuation of that infatuated feeling, an attraction that blows everything else out of the way.

So what then are the secrets that ensure that your Beloved has the I've-Gotta-Have-Her-in-My-Life feeling that is absolute and ultimately unshakable? What are the secrets that keep the yummy and immensely powerful attraction between you and your love alive and growing? The secrets that unleash that natural gut level of attraction and a forever love that cannot be stopped by time or circumstance?

You've probably seen or read a number of authors who say it's really easy. All you have to do is call in the One by making an affirmation about having committed love with a great partner. The universe does the rest. It simply brings in the divine right partner, and you stay in love forever.

Of course, I agree with them to some degree. In Chapter 3, I showed you how to create a love intention, which is critical to attracting the kind of love you really want. And that can rewire your neural networks such that the world occurs differently for you. It becomes a world full of rich possibilities; a world in which love with a great man awaits.

But in my experience, it's not enough. To create lasting love also requires learning about men and then discovering what actions truly make them attracted to women. And that's what my program is designed to accomplish. It shows you how to develop those relationship skills in a way that fits with you and your personality, so that you can come together with your Beloved in a beautiful win–win dance. In other words, contrary to what *The Secret* and other law of attraction writers believe, *thinking about what you want is just not enough if you want lasting passion to evolve!* Initial attraction, whether it's based on dopamine or New Age thinking, doesn't last. It's a step, yes. But only one.

So then what are the mysterious secrets that keep love growing and him wanting more of you? In this chapter you will learn them: the Seven "Real" Laws of Attraction. You can use these powerful secrets whether you have been together two months or ten years.

This is not about compromising yourself or giving yourself away. It's about growing as a woman and becoming the change you want to see in your love life. When you are that change agent, you will find a great deal of happiness and joy for yourself. You will naturally act in ways that are powerfully attractive to your partner, that draw him closer, so that he feels at home around you and wants to be with you more and more. When you understand how attraction works and go with it, if your guy is Mr. Right he will be able to see that his life is much fuller with you in it, that being with you feels great, *and that life would be empty and much worse without you.*

These laws of attraction are not the immutable laws of physics or of Newton. But they're also not just New Age ideas that have very little foundation. They are actually based on clinical experience and observation, along with a lot of data from psychological research. They are also the fundamental relationship skills that have been studied, that have stood the test of time, and that some women know naturally. In fact, I believe most of us know these basic love skills and have practiced them at least to some degree. By acting in accord with these principles, you will help your Beloved deal with his issues and fears. Then he will be able to take the initiative and move forward toward commitment and a deeper love relationship with you.

The Litmus Test for Him

Acting in this loving and magnetic way is a great litmus test: Fear-bound or uninterested guys will pull away—and that's a good thing! On the other hand, a reliable and true life partner will find you irresistible. He will give you more of the kind of intimacy, affection, caring, praise, and passion you need—so that both your cups are full.

The core principle underlying these laws is this: *Treat your Beloved as a best friend—with whom you happen to be having an affair!*

The Seven Laws of Attraction

> I learned from my Love Mentor to comfort, appreciate and nurture instead of blame. So many times I held my tongue and thought how would she (my Mentor) handle this? Without learning how attraction works, I would not have been able to have gotten happily married! I am so happy and forever grateful.
>
> —*Anna, forty-something Love Mentee*

There are seven keys that underlie attraction in couples: having fun together; being receptive; appreciation and validation; making yourself beautiful in your own eyes (and his); having an ongoing affair with your partner; giving him space; and keeping drama to a minimum. *Just practicing these behaviors for a few minutes each day can make a vast difference in your personal happiness and in your relationship.*

LAW 1: *HAVE FUN TOGETHER*

> Laughter is the closest distance between two people.
>
> —*Victor Borge*

Remember how you first fell in love with each other: going out on dates that were fun? Your first question is "What can we do to keep having fun together?" Four kinds of fun are important: *quiet enjoyment, humor, excitement, and novel activities.*

Quiet Enjoyment
First, create situations and interactions where you are happy, content, enjoying yourself, and having fun, and he is, too. Share activities like museum exhibits, plays, movies, parks, picnics, day trips, long walks, cooking a new dish, preparing a feast for friends or family, playing card games, hanging out at a community pool, or lounging in front of the TV and watching an entire season of that sci-fi or comedy series you both love. These activities lead to holding hands, touching, looking at and appreciating each other, which in turn produce the hormone oxytocin—the bonding and attachment hormone.

Quieter activities for your downtime together are perfect for couples who lead stressed lives because of either work or family responsibilities such as children or sick parents. If you want to really connect with a highly stressed guy, try not to run him around too much, and make gentle physical contact with him that tends to slow his motor down—rub his back, lie with your feet touching, or whatever works for him. When I interview these guys about their mates and why they chose them, they nearly always point to how they felt at peace around them. I'm not saying you should never go to a club and stay out all night or go bungee jumping. There's a place for that as well. But for bonding, there's nothing like being alone and hanging out doing something you both really enjoy.

Humor

The second type of fun is easy to incorporate into your routine. You could watch funny movies or more sophisticated cartoons together; go to comedy shows, joke around, or share funny moments of teasing or clowning. Shared laughter is a great stress reliever and bonding agent. Humor can be used to validate the other person or for you to lightly make fun of your drama; these are different ways of connecting. It can also break through and defuse your arguments and soothe upset or bitter feelings. For all of these reasons, shared humor has been shown by research to be a key component of happy marriages.

Excitement

I didn't forget you thrill seekers. This type of fun gets your adrenaline pumping and simulates the speedy brain chemistry of falling in love. You could hit the amusement park, go bungee jumping, take a helicopter ride, hike a high mountainous trail, scream yourselves silly at a basketball game, have a footrace at the beach, or even compete in a high-voltage video game. Studies show that people who are emotionally aroused by any feeling, including joy or fear, fall in love more easily. As two love researchers once wrote, "Adrenaline makes the heart grow fonder."

Novel Activities

Novelty has been shown to be a key factor in developing personal and relationship satisfaction. It helps to produce dopamine, the neurotransmitter of pleasure. Change things up—where you eat dinner, where you make out, or where you go on vacation. Do something out of the ordinary, like taking a cross-country road trip or going camping at the beach instead of staying at a hotel.

Case Example: Sonal and Jeff

Sonal and Jeff met through shared fun and games—literally. They loved cracking each other up as they played the Guitar Hero video game, enjoyed long hikes in the pristine woods near their city, and poked around historical museum exhibits. Then after a year, they hit a downturn in their relationship when Sonal began working at a job that seemed to be 24/7. Jeff became withdrawn and hypercritical. When she realized they were drifting apart, Sonal decided to recapture the magic to see if Jeff could step up. She bought a new music video game for them and arranged to see a new antique armor exhibit. Playing together brought back the sparks and the old connection, letting Sonal know that Jeff was still the right partner. They have since married and still play video games for fun. They also work together increasing sales for their online business (excitement); and plan for and go on cruises to different islands (novelty).

Action Plan

Share quiet enjoyment, as well as humorous, exciting, and novel activities. That way you will satisfy the inner couch potato and the adventurer side—of both of you. If you have been dating a guy for a while, you may feel like he needs to put in the effort because you plan all the time. It could be invigorating to suggest that since having fun is such an important part of shared love, you both come up with date or activity suggestions. Or you might suggest that each of you rotate a weekend of planning, or each week one of you picks a new movie or TV show to watch while snuggling, a video game to play, a new hiking trail or ethnic food restaurant to try out, or a challenging new recipe where you cook together. No matter who plans it, make sure it happens.

LAW 2: *BE RECEPTIVE*

> Love is a gift. You can't buy it, you can't find it, someone
> has to give it to you. Learn to be receptive of that gift.
>
> —*Kurt Langner*

Women tend to do the caretaking and the giving. When it comes to relationships, we feel like we understand, we are in charge, we usually have to manage things and make it all happen. The right way. Our way. Which makes for not being such a great partner. Because (surprise!) many men need and want to give to women.

But what happens when men do give to us? If too much intimacy comes our way, or they shower us with unexpected compliments, expensive gifts, and trips, some women instinctively tend to push it all away; to say no thank you or, worse, start a fight for no reason. If we are lucky and our Beloved sees our cellulite bumps as Botticelli-esque, we might shrink away, squirm, and feel uncomfortable. If he just wants to give to us in bed, we feel vulnerable and tense. If he comes up with an exotic, pricey vacation, we worry about the tab. If he wants to drive an hour out of his way to come pick us up, we worry it is not the best way to work the travel arrangements.

Sound familiar? You'd be surprised to learn that many women fear being freely given to. They fear being out of the manager's seat. They fear receiving all the abundance of love that could flow to them. *Why on earth?* you wonder. Simply, most women (not all) are used to giving and not to receiving. So often we find that when women are on the receiving end of caring, their issues of self-worth and deservedness surface. They become anxious and afraid and feel the need to turn the tables and give back three times over. Women don't know how to simply say, "Thank you!" and think, *I'm worth it. I deserve it!*

Instead we have conscious and unconscious protective barriers in place in order to not be disappointed. We feel we have to cook, clean, decorate, give great sex, and do whatever it takes to make a man love us. We have fixed ideas about how we should be given to and are therefore not open to new possibilities, new surprises: a heart-shaped stone instead of a flower; a nuzzle to the neck instead of a kiss on the lips; the appreciative once-over he gives us when we emerge dripping naked from the shower despite the extra poundage flopping around that we try to hide. We slough it off, turn away, or destroy it with a self-deprecating joke.

In short, we are often not able to be receptive, to be in that great archetypal feminine mode of the earth goddess who by her very being, her consciousness, brings an all-is-okay peace to her Beloved. The emotionally available one who bestows upon him the gifts of present-time living, richness, and joy. The archetypal goddess in every woman who deserves jewels, pearls, and gifts to be strewn at her feet just because being with her is so settling and wonderful.

In this archetypal male–female dance, the man can play out the more active principle and you can leave your managerial take-charge hat at the door. You can let him plan and do. Of course, in a great relationship, nothing is rigid and the lovers can fluidly reverse roles, but make sure you have made the receptive aspects of the dance available to your man.

Before you shut down and wonder if I've gone back in time and forgotten all our strivings for equality, let me assure you: I have not. What I am doing is reminding you of the receptive goddess part of you that you may have forgotten, suppressed, or never fully honored. Being receptive means being attentive to your partner's loving words and actions, the affection, compliments, gifts, and pampering that he gives to you. It is about leaning back and enjoying what unfolds as your man is the active one who *does* for you. And not simply on special occasions like your birthday!

Being receptive means letting your Beloved think about and solve your problems—even though you are perfectly capable of solving them yourself. Clever women know they are giving their partner a gift, one that allows a man to feel powerful and generative in the relationship. In my experience, most men have a very strong drive to take care of their partners. When we receive their nurturance, love, and help, we are sending them a message that says, *You are clever, smart, and competent. I accept, trust, and respect you.*

Case Example: Anna and Don

Although he was mega-successful in business, Don was also under a lot of pressure. A friend recommended meditation to help reduce his stress levels, and Don took to the practice in the same disciplined way he ran everything in his life. One morning during meditation, he had an unusual, clear, and startling vision of a ruby necklace. What was even stranger was that Don wanted to run out the door and find the nearest high-quality jeweler so that he could buy the necklace for his girlfriend, Anna. But Don knew that Anna was a no-nonsense nurse who loved a bare, no-frills look and lifestyle. And they'd already had a number of fights when Don suggested pricey dinners or theater tickets. So he proceeded with caution. Later that day, Don told Anna about the vision and how he was driven to buy her the gem. Anna felt like rolling her eyes but kept herself in check. *What a frivolous expense, what a stupid idea. I don't even know if we can make it, if he is the one for me*, she thought to herself. These thoughts saddened Anna greatly because she was witness to her killer beliefs emerging in the face of real caring by a man. So she simply said, "Don, you're so crazy generous," and hugged him.

Anna immediately called her Love Mentor and asked for help. The mentor explained the second law and the importance of being receptive. With her support, Anna decided to go against her killer belief and stretch herself in the direction of being open and allowing a man to give to her. Anna went with Don to a jewelry store, and there he saw just the ruby necklace he had envisioned. Laughing with joy, he bought it and put it around Anna's neck. Just seeing his face light up when she wore the necklace touched Anna's heart. Don said, "I love you for taking this gift. It will bring me tremendous luck! You are the light of my life!" Right at that moment, Anna saw that she had been caught in the scarcity consciousness of her austere, naysaying, fear-bound mother. She understood that Don's generosity could be extremely healing for her and that he was indeed the One for her.

Action Plan

Accept, be grateful for, and enjoy the gifts, the care, the pleasure, he would like to give to you.

Speak clearly about what it is that would truly please you and make you happy, even if sharing it seems weird or like you're asking for too much from him. Let your man know anyway so that he can figure out how to make it all happen. Men love to stretch themselves and flex their creative muscles, to feel like exceptional providers for their partners. Remember, as we discussed in Chapter 5, to men psychologically all others are M(others), and most especially you. So their desire to please is very high. Receive what he has to give and enjoy it, *even if it doesn't quite hit the mark.* Do not criticize his efforts! Because he will merely shut down. If you are receptive, he will hang in there, keep trying, and get to where you want him to be. Just take it all in and let yourself feel good, savor, and enjoy.

LAW 3: *APPRECIATE AND VALIDATE HIM*

> There is more hunger for love and appreciation in this world than for bread.—*Mother Teresa*

Because psychologically you are the symbol of the all-important mother to your Beloved, your opinion of him over time will become more important to him than that of any employer, colleague, sibling, or friend. You have that special place in his heart and his mind. Therefore, it's important that you make time when you give him your full and complete attention, noticing all the wonderful qualities he has. During these moments, you want to look upon him with unconditional positive regard. Let the literal and figurative warts, flab, pimples, and flaws fade away in your perception as you see him in all his glory, his shining spirit and good soul and handsome bits, too.

Be thankful as you count your blessings that occur through him.

Research clearly shows that appreciation and gratitude lead to happiness. Daily counting of blessings leads to less depression and a more elevated mood. So being in this state of appreciation and gratitude increases your own happiness, which, in turn, increases his. Even when he screws up, look for his good intentions, or his sincere apology.

On the other hand, be especially careful with your criticism. As I showed earlier, contempt—when you are on your high horse, looking down on your partner, judging him critically and harshly—is one of the most damaging emotions in a relationship. Simply, it kills off love. Men are very sensitive to being judged by their partners, and it drives them away. Appreciation, validation, and gratitude are just the opposite of contempt. They function like magnets.

Case Example: Radha and Bob
Radha's first husband died of a brain tumor. She experiences each day with her second husband, Bob, as a gift, noticing and appreciating the many wonderful things about his rotund, mirthful, and giving nature. Bob, in turn, feels like his life began when he met Radha. His gratefulness toward her shows Radha that she is with her soul mate. Radha and Bob have been married for ten years. But they are often mistaken for newlyweds—because they exude that certain glow, innocence, and delight in each other. This is the power of appreciation in action.

Action Plan
Research shows that healthy happy couples have a five-to-one ratio of positive to negative interactions: five expressions of interest, affection, humor, or nurturance to one expression of disagreement, anger, hurt, or upset. So make it a point to notice all the wonderful qualities, large and small, that your Beloved has. Practice telling him about it. Be sure to thank him for affectionate gestures, outings, gifts, or helpfulness. Bookend your morning and evening encounters

with a few minutes of the loving-kindness that comes from true appreciation. Notice how he responds.

Get him thoughtful gifts that speak of your appreciation. Make him a playlist of his favorite music sprinkled with a love song or two. Leave him loving notes or cards around the house. Surprise him with a fancy dinner to celebrate his latest win at work. Fly his beloved sister in for his birthday.

Appreciate your man and act on that appreciation. You can tip the scales to the plus side and reap more positives by changing the focus of your own outlook. Appreciation is like magic dust that will allow your Beloved to open himself up emotionally, to trust and connect at a deeper level with you.

LAW 4: *MAKE AND KEEP YOURSELF BEAUTIFUL IN YOUR OWN EYES (AND HIS)*

> Beauty is truth's smile when she beholds her own face in a perfect mirror.—*Tagore*

Every single one of us is beautiful. This means you. It just needs to be brought out. Assets highlighted. Flaws minimized. Personal style and pizzazz developed. So I want you to construct yourself as the emerging star of your life. I know. You can't afford the people who work in Hollywood. But you can find exercise classes and gym trainers, clothing saleswomen, free department store makeup makeovers, hairstylists, and yentas who can become your beauty mentors. Ask them for help. They will show you how to eat, exercise, dress, style your hair, and put on makeup in a way that may be strange or hard at first, but then turns out to be fun and, amazingly, just right for you. These mentors will help turn you into the woman with charisma that your guy can't keep his hands off.

They will also teach you about the power of push-up bras, décolletage, the right heels and skirts, feminine touchable hair, and subtle, fresh, natural makeup. They will help your most beautiful self emerge. Sorry if this offends you, but there is no getting around male biology. Research shows that men are visual creatures that are turned on by: an hourglass figure—which can always be created with a great belt and the right outfit, no matter how many extra pounds you have; full lips; sparkling eyes; some décolletage; and red clothes. Dress in novel and different ways that are attractive and sensual—and during alone times are provocative and sexual. Find out which looks turn your Beloved on and use them. Walt Whitman speaks to this power of the Feminine:

> *This is the female form,*
> *A divine nimbus exhales from it from head to foot,*
> *It attracts with fierce undeniable attraction,*
> *I am drawn by its breath as if I were no more than a helpless vapor,*
> *All falls aside but myself and it,*
> *Books, art, religion, time, the visible and solid earth.*

In addition, science has been uncovering other physical traits that underlie attraction. For example, we now know that women rank the body odor of men whose immune system genes are different from their own as highly sexually attractive. Both sexes are attracted to certain voice qualities, a fit body, clear skin, and a symmetrical face. I'm sure that some of these characteristics led to the dopamine-fueled falling-in-love infatuation stage that started it all with your Beloved in the first place.

Of course, some of you may believe that focusing on your physical appearance is superficial. That a guy should love you for who you are on the inside. There is nothing wrong with that belief. It's just not enough. Like so many things in life, one approach is not sufficient for the long haul. So consider this: If he sees you in the same sweat-pants for five years, do you really believe that outfit will turn him on? More important, are you turned on?

Making and keeping yourself beautiful is really an act of self-love, a way to honor yourself. Jewelry, clothes, and a crowning hairstyle are ways to respect the body that houses you. These things do not foreclose on spiritual and psychological development, but can actually augment them. So adorn the temple of your body and you will be pleasing yourself and attracting him as well.

Case Example: Chloe and Ron
When Ron took his girlfriend, Chloe, shopping for clothes, she found a line of short dresses that showcased her amazingly long and gorgeous gams. Chloe was shy in coming out of the dressing room with the dresses on, but Ron's appreciative grins and comments made her feel like Heidi Klum. She bought two dresses and wore one of them for their next date. Even though they had been together for two years, Ron was so enamored and in love that it poured out of his eyes at their ultra-romantic Italian dinner. Chloe was confident, radiantly happy. It felt like they had just met. After dessert Ron shyly presented a ring to her. As she looked at him in the candlelight, Chloe just knew that he was the One for her.

Action Plan
The next time you are about to see your Beloved, take a real look at yourself in the mirror. What does your appearance say? Do you want to be broadcasting that? What look would he enjoy seeing you in? Do what you need to in order to change your look so that you feel like your Diamond Self and you are attracting compliments and flirty romance from him.

LAW 5: *HAVE AN ONGOING AFFAIR WITH HIM*

> Sexual love is the most stupendous fact of the universe,
> And the most magical mystery our poor blind senses know.
> —*Amy Lowell*

Having sex with your partner is a decision you need to make only after careful consideration. I believe there should be at least two months of consistently improving contact, where you are sharing more and more of yourselves, before you make that plunge. See *Love in 90 Days* for my thoughts on the matter. But once you enter the realm of a sexual connection, it is critical to deliberately keep that spark fanned and hot. How?

Decide that you are having an ongoing affair with your Beloved.

You're wondering, what am I talking about? First of all, I am not advocating having an affair with a married man. I am referring to *acting* like you are having an affair with your partner who is in a monogamous love relationship with you. If you want to set the stage for a win–win sexual relationship that is relatively cheating-proof, you must be creative and in a sense "the other woman." You know, the one he's having the affair with. Think it sounds crazy? Based on many years of experience with clients, students, and mentees, I know that practicing having an affair with him can lead to years of passion if he truly is the One. In order to conduct an ongoing affair with your man, practice physical touch, flirting, and sex play.

Acting like you are having an affair is a powerful relationship enhancer no matter how long you have been together. Here is the key principle:

> *Ask yourself,* What would I be doing or saying right now if we were having an affair? *Then go for it!*

What's interesting about having an affair is that the partners are not automatically available to do the deed. The lingering touch, the sweet nibble on the ear, the deep French kiss may or may not go any farther. There is a playful novelty and uncertainty that drive up dopamine, the falling-in-love brain chemical that is synonymous with anticipation, excitement, and focus on the Beloved. Infatuation sizzles.

Make Physical Contact

Sex begins with physical contact. In fact, couples with great sex lives often are the ones you see holding hands and touching in public. As we've discussed, physical nonsexual contact creates oxytocin, the cuddle, bonding, and trust hormone. In order to amplify this even more, if he is receptive, hold hands, kiss, or stroke his face. His hands, lips, and face are all highly touch-sensitive areas! Gazing into his eyes also releases oxytocin and is an extremely powerful bonding move. In one study, strangers shared intimate details about themselves and then stared into each other's eye for four minutes. Many reported being extremely attracted to each other. One couple in the study actually got married!

Trace the outline of his bicep with your finger or give him a mini massage on his neck and shoulders. Find out what kind of touch he enjoys: stronger, softer, or in between. You both will feel great as the oxytocin works its magic.

On the other hand, many men don't like to be touched unless it's on the playing field (why do they slap each other's butts?) or in the sack. Yet they crave contact with us. And it's often communicated in a strange way. Here's a brief excerpt from an actual therapy session with a couple where the touching-versus-not-touching issue was threatening to destroy the relationship.

SHE: Greg never touches me unless it's sexual.

HE: I'm not a touchy-feely guy, but I love to be with you.

SHE: You sure have a funny way of showing it.

HE: Doc, we were watching a TV show last night and were sitting together on the couch.

SHE: Tell her how you started a fight.

HE: Well, it was nice and cozy and then Ellen left the room and just disappeared.

SHE: It didn't seem to matter whether I was there or not. You weren't paying me any attention.

HE: What, are you kidding? I was really upset that you left.

Okay. What is this man saying that she missed? Translation: *I want to be in your space, your presence, because it feels like home.* Now, obviously he needed to demonstrate more physical affection, but that was easy to achieve once Ellen got how much Greg loved being around her. She learned to be specific about the kind of touch she needed from Greg. The key is to ask for it in a positive and validating way, as in "I really love it when you [put your arm around me, play with my hair while I lie in your lap, rub my back—fill in the blank]." So from that day on when they watched their favorite shows or movies, she would curl up on him and he would touch her till she was purring. They even had more fun in bed.

Flirt

Flirting is defined by a kind of teasing quality, where you offer, then take the offer off the table, and then offer again. Flirting keeps you in the great feminine–masculine dance. It shows your partner that you still find him attractive. To amp up your flirting, do a Queen Latifah (aka Dana Owens) move—give yourself a sexy, sensual nickname. Have fun. For example, you could call yourself *Venus Rising*, *Aphrodite Anna*, *Vivacious Vixen*, or *Saucy Minx*. Dress yourself in line with your Diamond Self name and use an affirmation like, *I am sexy, beautiful, and irresistibly attractive.* Here are fifteen flirting moves that will amp up the sizzle:

1. Make eye contact, smile, and lick your lips.
2. Wink.
3. Look him up and down, look away, look back.
4. Give him a lingering French kiss.
5. Touch your lips, neck, or chest.
6. Suggestively play with your hair, clothing, or an object.
7. Whisper a line into his ear about meeting him later.
8. Stroke his thighs.
9. Give him a massage and slowly move toward his erogenous zones.

10. Compliment his performance in bed (the part you really liked).
11. Give him a "stud" or fun nickname.
12. Send him suggestive texts, notes, or phone messages about what you want to do to or with him.
13. Do a little striptease.
14. Suddenly appear in new sexy lingerie.
15. Pull out a surprise sex toy or feather for future use.

There are many other flirting moves you can make. You can have fun reading erotic stories, magazines, and comics, or watching erotic movies together. Share fantasies. Don't worry, only about 95 percent of people report having sexual fantasies. Start off slowly and just describe a fantasy about the two of you. Begin the story and ask your Beloved to end it. And if a "quickie" happens, be sure to enjoy it!

Go for Win–Win Sexual Fulfillment

Sex releases endorphins, which elevate mood and lower stress and pain levels. After having sex, each partner associates feeling good with the other. Testosterone, the sexual hormone engine for both men and women, also generates feelings of connection. And finally, having sex drives up levels of oxytocin, which explains why for many men (and women), having sex is usually synonymous with feeling intimate and close.

Earlier in the chapter, I talked about how dopamine is produced when we first fall in love, and in law 1 I described how novel activities keep dopamine infatuation going. Well, nothing keeps the dopamine going more than novelty in bed. So vary the places you make love, vary the way you set the stage through candlelight, a bubble bath, feathers, sex toys, whipped cream, or new kinds of lingerie and sexy outfits. Vary your foreplay and try different sexual positions. You might end up laughing yourselves silly as you experiment. Neither my husband nor I is a gymnast, so some of the Kama Sutra is a laugh riot for us. Take it all as fun and games. In the end, make sure that both of you are fully satisfied no matter whether that's achieved orally, manually, or through intercourse.

Sex is a wonderful gift to be enjoyed and shared by both of you. Good, frequent sex promotes your own physical and mental health, that of your man, and the vitality of the relationship. Among other things, it is associated with a reduced incidence of breast cancer in women who have never had a child, more restful sleep, greater pain relief, elevation of mood, looking younger, overall fitness, longevity, and happiness! Researchers have found that there are three primary ways in which couples interact with each other sexually: sexual trance, partner engagement, and role play.

Sexual Trance

- Sexual trance involves an inward focus where each partner focuses on his or her own pleasure and sensations and creates a fulfilling sexual release. In win–win sex, each of you is pleasured and finds a strong release in orgasm. Learn by experimenting so that you know what works for him and what works for you.

- In order to learn what works for him, try touching, massaging, licking, or stimulating all the different parts of his body. Observe and ask him questions about what feels good. Try different sexual acts, variations of intercourse positions, and, most important, oral sex. Virtually all men adore oral sex. If you have a problem with this, consider the fact that if your man showers, chances are his mouth has more germs than his penis does!

- Ultimately you are responsible for knowing your body and creating the conditions for your own sexual pleasure. You can work on sexual trance by using what sex therapists call sensate focus. This simple but effective technique requires only that you be in an undisturbed place where you playfully touch and stimulate different parts of your body and learn about what sensations feel good to you.

- The more you know about your own body, the better your lover will be able to please you. Guide him by saying positive things like, "I love it when you stroke my breast gently." Or "I would love you to use your magic mouth on my tummy and work your way down."

Partner Engagement

- Partner engagement is interactive sex and sex play. The Beloved is seen as a separate person whose happiness and satisfaction are as important as your own. At the highest level of partner engagement there is rapture, bliss, plus a feeling of oneness with each other.
- In partner engagement, you each are dedicated to the fullest sexual expression and fulfillment of the other. This is the arena where you stretch to accommodate what he wants to do. Note: Never go to the point of unwanted pain or trauma.
- When you're having an affair with your man, be adventurous and take the initiative at times with pleasing him. A spontaneous ambush for a quickie is a great idea. There's nothing like "surprise sex" to cement your relationship with him.

Role Play

- The last type of sexual intimacy comes from role play. The couple creates a kind of magic theater where sex is a stage for each partner to share and enact fantasies with the other. This helps the partners explore all the different aspects of self. Plus it helps a man not feel the urge to cheat with other women, because he is already having the novelty of a "different" partner.
- Role plays often emerge from fantasies. The most common fantasies for women involve an imaginary romantic lover, being overpowered or forced to surrender, reliving a sexual experience, or pretending they are doing something wicked or forbidden. Men tend to have more images of domination or force, or doing

something sexual to their partner. Males also tend to have more visual and explicit imagery and fantasies of multiple partners or fantasies of being with two women lovers. Most common roles include: seductive doctor (nurse) and/or seductive patient, bad cop and lawbreaker, master and slave, and the romantic bodice ripper.

Sexual Issues

If you or your partner has problems in this area, first try creatively breaking through your barriers on your own. If he has erectile dysfunction, there are medications available that have been very effective. Don't let a physical problem prevent either of you from having sex. Check with your physicians. If your issues are not simply physical, then by all means seek out a sex therapist or a couples therapist who specializes in sexual dysfunction. Treat this problem as you would diabetes or any other serious illness. It will be well worth it.

Case Example: Isabella and Hector

When Isabella first slept with Hector, she had problems getting turned on. After a series of failures, Hector felt so bad about himself that he stopped contacting her even though he had strong feelings for her. Isabella told Hector that it wasn't his fault and that she had a history of sexual problems. In fact, she had never experienced orgasm. Isabella entered sex therapy, learned to pleasure herself, and reached orgasm for the first time. She invited Hector back into her life, and they started dating without having sex at first. Meanwhile, Isabella told Hector what he could do to turn her on and asked him what he liked. The fireworks began and they became devoted lovers. After a few years, Hector proposed; they had a gorgeous sunset wedding at the beach. Isabella has been married for almost two decades to Hector, but she has kept an affair going in their relationship. Sometimes she surprises Hector, as they are driving to a party, by suddenly announcing she has no panties on under her skirt. They role play meeting each other as strangers at a bar; then they go home to have wild sex in the living room. In later life, Isabella has discovered that she is multi-orgasmic. (It happens to a number of lucky women!)

Action Plan

Try on the concept that you are having an affair with your guy. Dress, act, and speak accordingly. Give yourself permission to have fun with this! Read some erotic literature or a *Cosmopolitan* mag, or watch a sexy movie together and begin to share some fantasies that come up. Talk about what you love having done to you. Ask your Beloved what he likes to experience sexually. Suggest a brief role play that could be fun. It can just start with a sentence or two. Don't worry about pulling off the role—you can do it poorly and it still will work. Just experiment.

LAW 6: *GIVE HIM SPACE*

> Once the realization is accepted that even between the closest human beings infinite distances continue, a wonderful living side by side can grow, if they succeed in loving the distance between them which makes it possible for each to see the other whole against the sky.
>
> —*Rainer Maria Rilke*

One of the most common of men's commitment fears is that if they become serious with a woman, they will lose their buddies, their free time, their sports, their downtime, their whole non-work-related world. One key law of attraction is paradoxical: Men love women who have their own independence, who give them man-cave time to veg out and hang out with the guys. They are attracted to clever and confident women who know that a man needs his space *and who don't hold it against him.*

The more a woman has self-confidence and her own world of friends and hobbies and interests, the more attractive she becomes. It's simply because her partner does not feel smothered in the relationship. He does not have to be her constant savior, caretaker, provider—her whole world. She is not whiny, needy, being overly dramatic, or constantly needing his care and attention. She is not jealous and possessive and having to monitor everything he does. In short, she is not smothering him and driving him away.

Remember that men are wired to feel like they have to perform and produce. It is refreshing when a partner is simply able to take care of herself. To enjoy time away from him, to be able to soothe herself or turn to friends when she is upset is a great thing. When his Beloved is independent and spending time away, he gets to experience missing her and being the one who longs to be together. Many women are so ever-present, clingy, and demanding that their partner never gets a chance to feel what it is like when his woman is not there. So he feels like he has no choice in the matter of being partnered with her. Clinging behaviors almost guarantee that he will feel smothered and then become emotionally distant and pull away.

Another benefit to being independent is that your Beloved recognizes that you could leave him. This is one of the most powerful attractors of all. You are not in the bag, taking any and all acts of abandonment, mistreatment, or abuse because you feel you have to. The notion that you could leave fosters his appreciation that it's a gift being in a relationship with you. It is when something is lost that we truly experience the miracle of having it.

Case Example: Bea and Kumar

Bea was in a relationship with Kumar for only two months, but he was already showing that he was the One by texting and talking to her several times a day, seeing her as often as possible, and taking her out on great dates to hear the jazz they both so enjoyed. Bea's lease was up, and on the spur of the moment they decided to move in together. After that, Bea became more demanding and expectant of Kumar. She felt they should spend the whole of every weekend together, that he was watching too much baseball and "abandoning" her. Kumar announced that it was over and that he was planning to move out. Stunned, Bea broke down emotionally, lost her appetite, and couldn't get herself to work. She called one of my Love Mentors for help, who advised her to give Kumar space by moving into the spare bedroom. After Bea followed through, Kumar stepped up and they had great coming-together sex and a new connection. In her mentoring sessions, Bea learned the importance of practicing law 6, giving space. Since that time, Bea has handled Kumar's need for alone time with great respect and appreciation. For example, she has encouraged him to see his baseball games on TV and at the stadium. Kumar, in turn, has introduced Bea to his whole family, and engagement plans are in the works.

Action Plan

Tell him to go have a night out with his buddies (or in, with his hobby) and that you're going out to see a movie with a girlfriend (and make sure you follow through with your fun activity!). Encourage the natural ebb and flow of spending time together and time apart in a way that makes both of you happy. It is critical to enjoy and savor your own passions, friends, and hobbies. Become the woman who feels like she could leave and do perfectly well by herself or with another guy if things did not work out with this one.

LAW 7: *KEEP THE DRAMA TO A MINIMUM*

> Wise [wo]men, when in doubt whether to speak or to keep quiet, give themselves the benefit of the doubt, and remain silent.—*Napoleon Hill*

In my experience, one of the biggest attractors to a man is when a woman is easy to be with, laid-back, and not overly emotional or dramatic, content with what is so and the present moment as it unfolds. Not in some convoluted and upsetting mind game with herself or her frenemies that consumes her attention and puts her in a foul, depressed, bitchy, or withdrawn mood. Why? Once again, the reason behind this is that it is very difficult for a man to separate his own mental state from his Beloved's. If she is upset, he is upset. He feels the need to fix things, but often he is ill equipped to be truly helpful in the face of drama that is out of control and over the top. So he feels not only upset, but incompetent to boot. When that happens, he will find it very difficult to be around his partner because the environment feels frustrating, draining, and depressing.

When there is drama, the relationship feels bogged down in seriousness and emotional negativity. Usually men use logic as their means of being helpful, which often fails because the upset party is not being particularly logical. If his Beloved then becomes bitchy and takes her anger out on him, you can be sure that he will be repelled. She may become critical and judgmental of him, or she may feel the need to win and be right about the feelings that have caused her suffering. She may withhold sex to punish him. The quickest solution for him is to become emotionally distant and back away from her ASAP. This pattern is very toxic for your relationship.

Drama generally has its roots in your killer beliefs. It might be: "All men are jerks"; "This is not perfect"; "Love doesn't exist"; or "I'm too damaged." If not handled, any of these beliefs can trigger dripping negativity, clingy fearfulness, or prickly anger that can contaminate other people's space. For your own sake and for that of your partner, keep your whining, pestering, neediness, complaining, criticizing, or withdrawing to a minimum. When you are overly depressed, worried, or busy counting your misfortunes, try to remember that these thoughts are not only harmful to you, they can also kill off your love relationship. Avoid being a drama queen or a constant damsel in distress where nothing is right or okay as it is.

Case Example: Leela and Steve

Leela was a curvy redhead who was used to getting her way. When she met Steve, she fell headlong into madness and joy with him. Even though he was a bit paunchy, Steve was a powerhouse attorney who, in the beginning, loved to show Leela a great time. Unfortunately, Leela found it hard to have a great time. Something was always off and making her cranky and irritable—a blowout with her best friend, her hairstylist chopped her hair too short, what have you—and she just couldn't deal. Leela blamed it all on her menstrual cycle—her PMS, heavy periods, cramping, bloating. Well, you get the idea. Steve loved Leela, but after a while he did not feel good being around her. She always seemed to be upset about something. And when he communicated this, Leela was horrified. They had a huge blowout. Steve later called to suggest that she take a growth course called the Landmark Forum. At the course, Leela learned to look at the beliefs that were underlying her drama. She learned to have shorter emotional outbursts and would apologize for being bitchy. Leela felt closer to Steve than ever before and he, in turn, appreciated her for being courageous and working to overcome her killer beliefs and self-sabotaging behaviors.

Action Plan

Here are two techniques to help you with this task. First, challenge the notion that each thought you have is so important. Most of the thoughts people have when they're upset are garbage ideas that just float through. In the Buddhist tradition, they are called the thoughts of the "monkey mind." The monkey mind is unsettled, confused, and uncontrollable. In other words, they are not that profound. Let them pass before inflicting them on others.

Second, don't think that you can just blurt out anything because you're with this person. Before you open your mouth, ask yourself,

Where is this going to get me? Often the answer is in a fight, lonely, and hurt.

If you find that monkey mind chatter often gets the best of you and puts you into a foul emotional whirlpool, I highly recommend that you take personal growth courses that help you deal with your negativistic thoughts and feelings. Some of the approaches that have helped my students gain the ability to distance from and eliminate unwanted self-sabotaging thoughts include the The Work by Byron Katie and the Landmark Forum. You can also use therapy, see a psychiatrist for medication if needed, and/or use a spiritual practice like meditation to help yourself become more peaceful and detached from troublesome thoughts and circumstances. If you are a drama-prone diva, definitely take one or more of these actions before you drive your Beloved and all other men away.

As you learn to discipline and control your emotional reactivity, you will feel a sense of presence and connection to the present moment that is grounding and healing. And if you are with the right partner, he will move much closer to you. Both of you will feel more whole and happy together.

So these are the Seven "Real" Laws of Attraction. Here is a little cheat sheet to remind you:

1. Have fun.
2. Receive.
3. Appreciate.
4. Make yourself beautiful.
5. Have an affair.
6. Give space.
7. No drama.

Once again, it is difficult to practice these behaviors all the time. But begin with a few minutes a day working on the ones that are most important for your situation (you know well which ones those are!) and following the suggested action plans to put them in motion. In this way you can avoid being like many women, who, without knowing it, are driving the men they love right out of their lives, men who could have been the One—like Sally almost did with her worrying and tenseness around Gary.

Instead Sally practiced several laws of attraction with the encouragement, support, and direction of her Love Mentor. In particular, she rekindled the fun and laughter that had first brought them together by inviting Gary to a comedy club, where they laughed themselves silly (law 1). Right away, Gary's mood picked up, and he wanted to see her more often. She e-mailed his latest blog to an editor friend of hers, who wrote Gary a glowing comment. Because Gary respected the editor, the review soothed his fears of not measuring up and he had a creative spurt of writing. Sally read some of his new work aloud to him, marveling at how great it was (law 3). He was beaming when she was done and he threw her on the sofa, where they had truly memorable sex (law 5). All of this coming together led Sally to the conclusion that Gary was the One. But of course, the story doesn't end here.

As a staunch feminist, I learned all these laws the hard way! During blowouts with my husband I would become all serious, acting cold or like a drama queen over some monkey mind chatter that was ridiculous. He would try to fix things and I would attack him. He wanted things sexually that I didn't want. And we were on the verge of calling it quits. Luckily, we had our Love Mentor, took personal growth courses (and still do), learned to control our mental BS, and expanded our whole sexual repertoire. And I am a zillion times happier for it. And so is Sam. Before I practiced the Seven "Real" Laws of Attraction, I used to wonder if he really was Mr. Right. After I did, things between us soared and I had no doubt that he was.

When you practice these laws of attraction, you, too, will be able to tell if your guy truly is Mr. Right-For-You. A man who truly wants a great and lasting relationship with you; a man who is committed to the feast of forever love.

> Sooner or later we begin to understand that love is more than verses on valentines and romance in the movies. We begin to know that love is here and now, real and true, the most important thing in our lives. For love is the creator of our favourite memories and the foundation of our fondest dreams. Love is a promise that is always kept, a fortune that can never be spent, a seed that can flourish in even the most unlikely of places. And this radiance that never fades, this mysterious and magical joy, is the greatest treasure of all.—*Anonymous*

7

Is He *Really* the One?

HOW TO KNOW FOR SURE

> Find a guy who calls you beautiful, who calls you back
> when you hang up on him, who will lie under the stars and
> listen to your heartbeat, or will stay awake just to watch
> you sleep...wait for the boy who kisses your forehead,
> who wants to show you off to the world when you are in
> sweats, who holds your hand in front of his friends, who
> thinks you're just as pretty without makeup on.
>
> —*Anonymous*

You may be in a relationship that is good, perhaps the best
you've ever had, yet you aren't sure if it's the right one. Well,
you are not alone. I get e-mails every day from women say-
ing, *My boyfriend is nurturing and sweet, but he's boring, boring, boring.*
Or, *All my BFFs are crazy for him; he's so hot but he's broke and lives with
his mom.* There's this kind of situation: *I'm seeing a guy who owns four
car washes who's crazy about me but he's fat and has two wild teenage
boys from his first marriage.* And, finally, this classic: *I'm going crazy,
Dr. Diana. I've been living with my boyfriend for two years and lately I've
just started to get the feeling that he may not be able to commit.*

These e-mails and the hundreds I get each week show that the road
to love is rarely a streamlined superhighway. It has many twists and
turns, bumps, detours, and potholes. The journey to lasting love may

be scrumptious and live-wire hot, while at other times it's as dead as the bodies on *Six Feet Under*. After a nasty fight when he completely withdraws into his man cave, you might think that the H-word (as in *hate*) is not too strong to apply to him and the whole relationship. Maybe you are madly in love some of the time and couldn't care less at others. Perhaps you thought you were crazy about him, but then things cooled off into routine autopilot texts, e-mails, and dates, and now it is only when you are *not* together and he doesn't call you that you really want him. Bottom line: You may feel confused, and wonder if you can really trust your own instincts and judgment. To complicate matters, you may be dealing with your own unconscious or conscious commitment fears. That's why I have devoted three chapters to assessing whether your significant other is really the One. I've asked you to look at his psychology, help him with his fears of commitment, and see what manifests when you implement the seven laws of attraction in your relationship. Now we will add specific questions to help you ferret out the bottom line about whether or not he is truly into you; to help you know whether to fish or cut bait. The Lasting Love Program gives you three reality checks, so you will know whether you are dealing with a STUD (Seriously Terrific, Utterly Devoted Dude) or wasting time on a DUD (Definitely Unworkable Dude).

The Three Reality Checks

The key questions to ask about your boyfriend are: *Is he crazy about me? Is he willing to grow? Is he meeting the basics?*

REALITY CHECK 1: *IS HE CRAZY ABOUT ME?*

Is he crazy about me? This is a critical question to ask yourself because you cannot *make* someone love you. At the end of the day, he is either into you or not. You can fool yourself. You can have a fantasy that the whole enchilada of committed lasting love is going to be there with him. Or that you can be giving enough, devoted enough, or sexy enough to make him want you as the One. But it will not work if he is just not feeling it.

To help you answer this key question, here is a simple quiz based on my clinical and Love Mentoring experience that examines whether this guy is into you or not. You need to have been together at least three months in order to use the quiz. Give your boyfriend 1 point for each of these twenty characteristics:

1. Eager to see you.
2. Reluctant to leave you.
3. Wants regular consistent contact; asks for dates.
4. Interested in you and your life.
5. Wants to be helpful in ways that meet your needs.
6. Is verbally and physically affectionate.
7. Wants to be romantic and sexual with you.
8. Texts, e-mails, or calls regularly.
9. Acts like you are very special; doesn't want to date others.
10. Respects you and your opinions.
11. Becoming more attentive and loving over time.
12. Becoming more open to sharing his feelings and thoughts.
13. Becoming more open to sharing his living space.
14. Becoming more open to introducing you to and spending time together with his friends and family members.
15. Acting like a couple in front of his family and friends—using "we" instead of "I," being physically affectionate.
16. Calling you his girlfriend when talking to you, friends, or family.
17. **Saying he loves you.**
18. **Saying he wants a future with you.**
19. **Actively planning a future with you (talking about living together or getting engaged).**
20. **Proposing that you live together or get married.**

You *must* be 100 percent honest with yourself as you rate your guy. When in doubt, *ask your closest friends to help you.*

Score Results
If you have been dating him for at least three months but less than a year:

- 9 or more points = He might develop into a contender.

If you have been together more than a year:

- 8 or less = He is most likely a DUD (Definitely Unworkable Dude). Move on and date others.
- 9–13 = He's still in the running.
- 14 or more, including *at least one if not two of the last four questions (in bold)* = He's a contender and just may be the One. Look for more of these qualities to appear over time.

Bottom line: If you want to find the One, look for a man who provides regular and consistent contact that gets better over time. You should find yourself continually surprised at how he fills your needs to be chosen, appreciated, romanced, and celebrated for who you are. Envision this kind of love and choose guys who *are* that into you. They exist, and that's what I wish for you. There is definitely a lid for every pot, no matter how gigantic, dented, or burned it is.

REALITY CHECK 2: *IS HE WILLING TO GROW?*

There are no perfect guys! So the question is: Is he willing to grow? That is, is he working on himself as a person? If he is crazy about you and if he respects you and your own growth process, he will want to evolve along a similar path as yours. So to help you assess whether your boyfriend is on a positive growth trajectory, I've designed a quiz based on my many years of clinical experience with men. Give your partner 1 point for each of these eleven characteristics:

1. Takes suggestions/advice.
2. Is self-reflective.
3. Can tell you what he (not his partner) did wrong in his last relationship.
4. Is willing to go to therapy or life coaching.
5. Has a mentor at work.
6. Takes growth courses.
7. Meditates/prays.
8. Was or is in a 12-step program or men's group.
9. Has made positive changes in his behavior or his ability to speak his truth.
10. Is growing in self-esteem and self-confidence.
11. Has grown or reinvented himself in his career.

A score of 6 or more indicates that he is an open and evolving person. He has the potential to become a wonderful life partner who continuously reinvents himself. In the last chapter, we talked about how dopamine is stimulated by novelty, and a man who reinvents himself is a guy who understands that new vistas in work, career, or helping others will also fill your lives with passion.

On a personal note, this growth quality in my husband, Sam, is what keeps me crazy about him after decades of marriage. He has reinvented himself several times over, and I never know quite what to expect. He has worked as a clinical psychologist, run a postgraduate training institute for marriage and family therapists, served as a management consultant to large family-owned businesses, co-authored books for therapists and investors, and in his spare time acted as my business manager. Actually I feel like I am having an affair with an old and new lover a lot of the time!

Bottom line: There are no perfect princes. But a frog-prince who is evolving could make a great and wonderful partner.

REALITY CHECK 3: *IS HE MEETING THE BASICS?*

In order to create lasting love, it is of critical importance that your partner is a good person, a mensch with integrity, who does not lie. He needs to have his own work ethic so that he has strong self-esteem and is not overly dependent on you. He has to be able to be a solid, dependable teammate in the game of life. This quiz will help you assess whether your partner meets the basics. Give him 1 point for each of these fifteen characteristics:

1. A good guy who shares similar values and cares about others.
2. Reliable, a man of his word who tells the truth.
3. Willing to admit he makes mistakes.
4. Willing to compromise.
5. Able to forgive.
6. Wants a real, committed relationship.
7. Is willing to sacrifice and invest time and energy for the sake of the relationship.
8. Has the same end goal as you (living together or marriage).
9. Willing to have children if possible.
10. Successful/good income.
11. Is a member of your religious faith.
12. Comes from a stable family of origin.
13. Willing to pull his weight financially, physically, and planning-wise as a team partner.
14. Attractive and sexy to you.
15. Able and willing to have fun with you.

Your partner should score a 10 or higher to be a contender as the One. Meeting the basics is a very core question. Research shows that

lasting romantic love is built on compromise, integrity, and dedication to a shared partnership. You do not want to be wasting your precious time with a guy who does not stand for these values. *Even* if he
has great chemistry with you. *Even* if he makes you come alive. *Even*
if the sex is unbelievable. Chances are, that's simply infatuation that
will end soon enough.

Bottom line: Your partner's character and integrity are critical to
your long-term future happiness with him; no exceptions.

When Sally did the three reality checks on Gary after they had been
together about a year, she found good news. Even though he wasn't
talking about having a future with her, Gary was into her in eleven
ways, including often being reluctant to leave her, interested in her
life, thinking she was very special, calling her his girlfriend, acting like
a couple, becoming more open to sharing his feelings and thoughts,
and saying that he loved her. In terms of the willingness-to-grow
reality check, Gary showed six signs, including taking advice, being
self-reflective, having a work mentor, making positive changes in
his openness about his fear of not measuring up, and growing in his
career. When Sally did a reality check on Gary meeting the basics, he
showed ten great signs, including being a good, reliable person, willing to compromise, able to forgive, willing to sacrifice time for the
relationship, being sexy, and having fun with her. Sally was thrilled to
find that Gary was a serious contender for being the One. But things
still had to develop to the point where he wanted to move forward into
a committed future with her. More on this crucial step coming up!

How Can I Tell If It's Just Infatuation?

Infatuation is more sensually and sexually based than love. It carries
more adrenaline and excitement and is often based purely on physical attractiveness and magnetic energy or charisma. A connection
with the One has these sensual qualities and more: a fitting together

of intellects, personalities, styles of being and relating, values, and vision for the future.

This is the most telling difference between infatuation and a real connection: Infatuation often fades as you get to know each other, and sometimes disappears in a heartbeat (along with the guy). In Chapter 6, I shared research that the biological part of infatuation can fade in as little as six months. But a connection based on the three areas we've just explored improves as you become closer. Couples who have lasting love find that their relationships get deeper and better over time.

Go back and review the list of the fifteen meeting-the-basics characteristics your partner may have. Only one of these has to do with attractiveness and sexiness. Women who make their decisions based mainly on that one trait are sadly missing the boat. You may be wondering, *How the heck can she say that?* Well, it's easy. Lasting love means that you have to rekindle passion that has faded over and over again. It's a pathetically small percentage of long-term couples who have sexual chemistry over twenty or thirty years that never have to work at it. That's why in the chapter on the "real" laws of attraction, I emphasized doing exciting and new activities together, having an affair with each other, and using three different types of sexual play in your relationship. So even if it's just a spark initially, real chemistry can be there if you know how to turn on your own juices and passions when you're with him. And in the long haul, you will need to know how to do just that.

Bottom line: For most happy couples, it's all about generating and regenerating novel ways of being infatuated with each other. So when I say "work on your chemistry," I really mean learn fun new ways to open up sensually and sexually!

Am I Settling?

On the other hand, maybe your partner meets many of the above criteria with flying colors, or at least comes close. But there is still a question in the back of your mind about the possibility that in choosing this man, you may be settling.

It is often difficult to accept someone who actually wants to be in a club in which we are the only other member. If a guy is into us, we tend to get up on our high horses, put on the spectacles of judgment, and peer down at him very critically. So you may be wondering, is this man good enough? Or am I settling? Remember, just like you, each guy has his ugly bits, literally and figuratively. When you are fighting with him and feel disappointed in him, you are going to feel ambivalent. Even in great love relationships, there are times where one partner views the other as not good enough.

It is also very important to be honest with yourself about whether the Not Perfect—I'll Pass deadly dating pattern fits you. In this pattern, you magnify any negative traits the guy has and minimize the positives. Quite often this is a projection of your own unconscious negative beliefs about you not being good enough. If this is your relationship tendency, you have to work extra-hard on appreciating each guy you date and learn to bring out his Diamond Self by being your Diamond Self. That supercritical b*tch is, in most cases, not going to appeal to a really loving guy. Make sure you are ridding yourself of your perfectionism and arrogance. I have seen too many stubborn women hold on to this pattern as if it were a life preserver, only to end up alone in a bitter sea of loneliness and regret.

Ultimately, however, you don't want to choose a guy and a relationship where you have "settling" worries more often than not. To help you decide, I've put together the list below of twelve questions I want you to ask yourself about your man:

1. Am I superior to this man?
2. Do I feel smarter or cleverer than him?
3. Am I really more talented?
4. Is there a complete lack of chemistry with him?
5. Does he fit in with my social network?

6. Am I more educated?
7. Is he too unsuccessful?
8. Is he too old for me?
9. Is he too young for me?
10. Is he too unattractive?
11. Is he too short?
12. Is he too boring?

Now that you've answered the questions, ask yourself this: Are *many* of the questions *frequently* a part of the background conversation you have with yourself or actual conversations you have with your closest friends? If many of them are not frequently dished and hashed over, you're not settling.

But if you do have a few persistent nagging questions in any of these areas, take time to journal about your thoughts and feelings in that area. List all the negatives. Then list any rebuttal positive ideas that come up. End with a list of good qualities that your boyfriend has. Then I want you to review the three reality checks to see if despite his flaws, he is crazy about you, willing to grow, and meeting the basics. Finally (and this part is very important!), envision him five years from now as he might be if he continues to develop and be loved by you. What do you see?

Yeah, I know, *he's too short and can't grow anymore.* Seriously, don't let a dumb thing like that, and I mean *dumb,* stop you from being with a great guy.

THE STORY OF RACHEL

Rachel, a thirty-nine-year-old social worker, wrote to me after reading *Love in 90 Days.* She was involved with Mario, a fifty-year-old who owned a small construction company. Mario was smitten with Rachel and after eight months wanted to fulfill her dreams of getting married and having children. But Rachel was ambivalent. So

I suggested she journal about her negative and positive feelings around the relationship and whether he was willing to grow. Here's what Rachel wrote:

Negatives

I feel superior to Mario because he doesn't have an advanced degree. Heck, he doesn't even have a college degree. Sometimes I am embarrassed to introduce him as my boyfriend because he looks like a construction worker, and, much as I hate to admit it, I look down on those guys. He is just not what I thought I would end up with. A doctor, a lawyer, my mother always said. I am actually afraid to introduce him to her! But that pisses me off!

Positives

But I feel great when I am with Mario. I don't even know why. He makes me laugh, I guess. And he is so affectionate. Something I never got from Dad. The sex is the best I have ever had. And Mario makes good money. More than me.

Willing to Grow

He says he wants to fit in with my family. He even said he would convert to Judaism. I took him shopping and he let me give him a makeover. Mario looks great in tight jeans and a jacket! He also wants to build his business by buying properties at auction, fixing them up and selling them at a profit. Looking into the future, Mario could be quite the success. Even if he is not a doctor. Of course, neither am I.

The journaling process opened Rachel's eyes to her own superficiality, superiority complex, and fear of her mother's disapproval. In fact, Mario was crazy about her, willing to grow, and met the basics. He was humble, generous, willing to compromise, and sincerely wanted the best for Rachel. Although she didn't recognize it at first, he was way ahead of Rachel in some fundamental ways including his ability to compromise and his ease with gratitude, two traits that form the basis of lasting love. When Rachel finally "got it," she knew that Mario was the One.

Bottom line: Feeling like you are settling may have more to do with your own insecurities than what you're thinking about the guy. Take a good close look. He may be a prince-in-the-making!

But Is He My *Soul Mate?*

> A soulmate is someone who has locks that fit our keys, and keys to fit our locks. When we feel safe enough to open the locks, our truest selves step out and we can be completely and honestly who we are; we can be loved for who we are and not for who we're pretending to be. Each unveils the best part of the other. No matter what else goes wrong around us, with that one person we're safe in our own paradise. Our soulmate is someone who shares our deepest longings, our sense of direction. When we're two balloons, and together our direction is up, chances are we've found the right person.—*Richard Bach*

Another interesting question that I've been asked a lot is: "How can I tell if he's my soul mate?" Maybe you also believe that there is a soul mate out there for you. If you said yes, you're not alone. Studies have shown that more than 90 percent of young adults believe in the concept, and 88 percent believe that destiny has determined that there is one and only one person who is your soul mate.

Amazing, considering that the idea is thousands of years old. In *The Symposium*, Plato described the soul mate as the person's "other half" that has been split from him. The quest of life is to find that missing half, that twin flame. The theme has been exploited in movies like *The Butcher's Wife*, *The Time Traveler's Wife*, and *City of Angels*. Other views of soul mates include reincarnation and that the person is someone with whom we have shared other lives. The movie *What Dreams May Come* beautifully explored the profound connection that may continue after the death of one's Beloved.

But the soul mate idea also carries with it the belief that a perfect person exists for us; if only we could find him or her, then love and life would be easy. This last belief has gotten people into a lot of trouble, especially in the area of commitment. By insisting on finding a *perfect* partner, many women have walked away from really great potential partners. Why? Because something was missing. Maybe it was chemistry, or maybe he didn't match her ideal of the One, and so on. So they've ended up alone, still looking for that perfect soul mate. No wonder, then, that the renowned family psychiatrist Frank Pittman once said, "Nothing has produced more unhappiness than the concept of the soul mate."

So what does science have to say about all this? Psychologists have found that people fall into two groups on the question of what makes for a successful relationship: Group one believes it's based primarily on finding the "right person" (soul mate); while group two believes in the "work at it consistently" approach to lasting love. The soul mate group believes that choosing the right person helps overcome most of the problems that love throws our way. And if it doesn't go so easy, we must have picked the wrong person. Therefore, on to the next partner. The "work at it" group believes that there are no perfect princes or princesses and that we are all works in progress. Therefore, a lasting love relationship is never an easy process, and we shouldn't ever expect that.

Having been a psychologist for more than twenty-five years, and married to one man for the same long stretch, I can tell you that there are no perfect partners out there. Not me. Not my husband. Not any of my many clients, mentees, friends, or family members.

Lasting love is a hard-won battle of personal discipline, compromise, dedication, and commitment.

But neither is everyone a good match for us. For example, in the last chapter we discussed research about scent and other physical traits playing roles in sexual attraction or desire. Other research shows that those who are of similar educational levels are more compatible. Therefore, while the one-perfect-person idea can lead to a long road of disappointment, there are certainly better and worse matches for us. If we are with a more compatible person, we are more likely *to have the experience* of being with the One who is a soul mate.

Chances are very good that there is more than one person—in fact several "Ones"—who could fit the bill for you. *And all of them are less than perfect.* But if there are no perfect partners, how can you know whether your current partner can fit the bill as a soul mate? Here are eleven relationship markers to help you know to what degree he is one of the *Ones*:

1. When you're with him you feel like you've come home.
2. You feel like your partnership was meant to be; as if kissed by destiny.
3. In your communication with each other, there is a rapid "knowing" of what each of you means.
4. You have a shared mission in life, perhaps a cause, a career, or the creation of a family.
5. When you're together, the world seems like a better place.
6. Your mood is elevated when you're together. It's not necessarily passion or excitement, although that's there, too, at times.
7. When you look at him, you see a part of yourself that's been missing. Perhaps it's his assertiveness or joy of adventure. But it's something that, when added to your life, makes you feel more complete.
8. Being together makes you more hopeful about the future you are creating.

9. You can be more authentic and fully yourself around your partner.
10. Being together makes each of you work harder on overcoming bad habits and becoming more loving people.
11. These special qualities of connection are growing over time, not disappearing completely or diminishing.

Don't worry if you don't feel all eleven of these things happening when you're with your partner. That's where the imperfection comes in—either in you or in your partner. If you are experiencing six or more of these markers, chances are you are matched well. Over time you can work toward having all eleven of these soul mate qualities.

Bottom line: There are probably a number of guys who could click with you in a magical way as your soul mate. But if you are experiencing some magical moments of communion with your boyfriend, he could be the One of Ones. The connection usually happens in a variety of different ways. So stay open!

Understanding If He Really Is the One

Let all of the mini journeys you have just taken about your partner percolate for a while. Just let your intuitive mind integrate all the different factors. Ultimately your intuition—that is, the gut feeling you get about a man and your relationship—will tell you which way to go. Always remember that it is the overall trend of things in the couple that determines whether it's a good match. There are always ups and downs. The question is: Are things getting better over many months or years? Are you, in fact, moving together toward the goal or goals you chose in Chapter 1?

Many couples break up for no reason at all: Things are tough and they don't get better immediately. It's splitsville because both partners lack the perspective of the overall trend. Do you really believe that your sex life will be great when you have an infant? That you'll be closer when you are sleep-deprived? That it will be all fun and games when you're working on a project, traveling on business for extended stretches, or he's sleeping at the office on a cot? Maintain the perspective of time. Notice if your communication and connection are deepening; if the commitment is improving; if the warmth and passion are more quickly rekindled in the face of fights or loss of intimacy; if he still thinks you're the best. If the answer is yes, keep working at it.

On the other hand, if it's no, you may want to exit gracefully. There are other partners who could be soul mates to you (albeit imperfectly!). Or, if things are strained and painful and they are not improving, you could be much happier living alone. If you feel strongly that this is the case, see the section *Ending Things Gracefully* in Chapter 10.

No matter what, as we end Part II of the Lasting Love Program, I want you to know that I have the highest respect for you for taking charge of your love life by examining what matters to you and whether or not your partner fits the bill. So many women do not take the time to do this and instead just follow the sirens of chemistry, opening their hearts and minds to men who fail them in the end. It is critical to take an inventory of your partner's pluses and minuses and of what you want and don't want in your relationship. From this knowledge base, you will build lasting, passionate love with a soul mate who adds immeasurably to your life. In Part III, we will look at how, if he *is* the One, to seal the deal and launch that glorious process.

> The most wonderful of all things in life is the discovery of another human being with whom one's relationship has a growing depth, beauty and joy as the years increase.
> —*Sir Hugh Walpole*

PART III

Sealing the Deal

8

Setting the Stage for the Commitment You Want

Yes, your desperation has its place, but it must not be in the driver's seat. It belongs in the back of the car and secured in the baby seat and facing behind while you drive.—Michele Ritterman, Ph.D.

After Sally had been with Gary for about a year and a half, things were great between them, except that there was still no talk of a shared future. Even though Gary said his *I love yous*, he would shy away when Sally made any living-together allusions, like, "It would be so much fun to renovate a loft together." He would either change the subject or get annoyed with her. Living together was Sally's goal—and she saw marriage and kids as the next steps after that. But Gary had commitment fears about not measuring up and issues about being able to provide. And he had no role models of guy friends who were happily living together with their significant others. One day, Sally just couldn't stand it anymore. Feeling certain that Gary would never come through for her (based on her killer belief of not deserving love), she was extremely tense and moody when he came over to her place for dinner. She greeted him with a cool peck on the lips and he reacted with his typical withdrawal, totally ignoring her and staring at his BlackBerry. After fifteen minutes, Sally threw the potato she was peeling on the floor and screamed, "Screw this! We will never be able to live together, much less get married!" Dissolving in tears, she fled to her bedroom and slammed the door.

Needless to say, this is not the right way to set the stage for getting the commitment you want.

It would be much easier if you and your Beloved were ready for commitment at the same moment, like two buns that rise and connect, all set to pop out of the oven together. But it's usually the case that one of you is half-baked. By now, you've hopefully gotten yourself to the point where your commitment fears are not standing in the way, so that leaves your partner as the one still baking.

Maybe he is sending you both green and red light signals, or he's putting out blinking yellow lights that say *caution, caution, caution,* making you feel tense, tentative, anxious, and uncertain around him. Perhaps he's given the green light for living together, while you are ready for a bigger step: some serious ring shopping, for example, followed by the down-on-one-knee ritual. Situations like these all call for the same thing: The Talk. I know, just the thought of having The Talk can be enough to give you that jittery, queasy feeling in your gut, leave you immobilized like a deer in headlights, or even set off a panic attack where you can't breathe. It may seem impossible to get any words out of your mouth on this hot-button topic.

> One of the hardest things in life is having words in your heart that you can't utter.—*James Earl Jones*

Why Is It So Hard to Ask for What We Need?

To ask for what we really need: Why does this fill us with so much dread? We may be frightened that we will be disappointed, heartbroken, and wind up alone. We may fear that we are asking for too much or being too demanding. Our age-old role as caretakers has been impressed upon us from all kinds of external cultural forces. Hundreds of thousands of ads feature women busily cleaning the house, feeding their families, carpooling the kids, or counseling their girlfriends on birth control. For many years, popular Disney films have showcased the same story over and over—about a helpless princess needing a guy to get her out of a bad situation, ending up with the two falling in love and the woman giving up all to come and live his life at the castle. We are taught to ignore our own needs for the happiness of others.

Evolutionary psychologists believe that women may be genetically predisposed to develop traits such as nurturance. Nurturance, along with empathy, may have allowed our female ancestors to be in touch with the needs of their children before they could speak. And this may have increased the chances that their offspring would survive. From an evolutionary standpoint, this would be a highly desirable result, and therefore these caretaking traits became part of our genetic legacy.

If women are the "natural" caretakers of others, what does the research tell us about getting our own needs met? Here again we find that women often don't express themselves, say what they mean, or ask for what they want, even when it comes to salaries and money. Linda Babcock at Carnegie Mellon researched this and presented her findings in a book called *Women Don't Ask*. Even women with master's degrees from the university tended to not negotiate for higher starting salaries, and consequentially earned an average of $4,000 less than men. Only 7 percent of the women asked for more money than their initial offer versus 57 percent of the men. In another study, researchers asked students to play Boggle and told them they would receive between $3 and $10. After the game, the researcher gave the subject $3, saying "Is $3 okay?" Nine times more men than women asked for more money and, therefore, were given

$10, even though the women in the study rated their performance at Boggle as highly as the men did and *complained as much about the low $3 rate*. So here we see that the women seemed to be just as unhappy about the outcome as the men, yet did not speak up—and therefore *wound up with less*. Does this sound familiar?

I cannot even count the number of hours I have sat with women of all ages who struggle to speak the truth of their needs. So what do we do instead? We start thinking, *It's not so important. My needs don't really matter. He wouldn't understand. He doesn't want to listen to me. Anyway, this is not the right time.*

It is easy to assume that because you have been together a certain length of time, sleeping together or seeing each other frequently, you are exclusive or moving toward a commitment with a shared future. Because of this assumption, you let yourself off the hook in terms of the need to speak up. You reassure yourself that everything is moving along fine. You tell yourself, *I certainly don't want to rock the boat by speaking up and then driving him away.* Do you know what the result of this thinking is? The exact opposite of what we intend: We set our partners up to fail us. We don't speak our truths, and our partners are not mind readers. Then, to make things even worse, we pretend to ourselves that everything is just fine.

But muting yourself is a dangerous thing to do. Your boyfriend thinks very differently from you. Remember, men often view a committed relationship as a smothering noose or a heavy rack of burdens. A woman will refer to a guy she has been seeing as her boyfriend, while he may not even see her as remotely in the ballpark of being his girlfriend; she is just someone he is currently sleeping with. This kind of disconnect can go on for a year or more, until he drops the I'm-Not-in-Love-with-You bomb. You cannot afford to waste your super-precious time in these murky gray waters. Coming from a place of self-love and self-caretaking, when the time is right, you need to have a mature, straightforward discussion with your Beloved. *This is a key component of the Lasting Love Program.*

Love flows out of an open, honest dialogue where there is talking, listening, and sharing.

This is something you must do for yourself. Men can spend a lifetime burying their issues about not being able to provide, losing their freedom or their individual identities. With no pressing biological clock, they have little motivation to overcome these commitment fears other than a distant old age and infirmity and the desire to be able to play catch with the kid. It's *you* who feels the pressure of time ticking away and it's *you* who needs to know if he wants a future with you, if he loves you, if he wants a family or a baby with you. You need to know sooner rather than later. Not speaking up for your wants and needs leads to a gradual erosion of your own self-respect and self-love, and a smoldering resentment that over time you will not be able to cover up. The upset is bound to seep out and poison your relationship so that it will end badly.

As to your fear that any straight talk will drive him away: If a man is mature, just the opposite is true. An honest talk in which you are playful or casual, not bossy, needy, or bitchy, will draw him in and allow him to feel closer to you. Only immature men who are truly not ready for the real deal will be pushed away by a talk. The key is to communicate at the right time, in the right way, using the "real" laws of attraction to your advantage (especially the "No Drama" law) and thereby avoid the common mistakes women make in having The Talk. Let's start by setting the stage so that things can unfold smoothly in a mature win–win way.

Setting the Stage for the Commitment You Want: First Things First

First of all, you need to be grounded in self-love. You may consider yourself to be not so wonderful. You might have killer beliefs about lacking something, or being unhappy with your body. All of us struggle with negative judgments about ourselves and critical self-talk. We say things to ourselves we would never say to our friends or even strangers. Imagine saying "You look like a fat blob in that dress!" "You sound so stupid!" or "You are too boring," or "You look like an old hag!" to another woman. You wouldn't. But chances are, you have looked into a mirror and said some variation of these demeaning statements to yourself.

You may not feel very loving toward yourself right this minute. In fact, you may feel sick of your life and unhappy being you. You may feel like you don't really deserve to have your dreams and love goals come true. You may be carrying self-recriminating anger, bitterness, or guilt about how you have acted in the distant past or yesterday in this relationship—or even today. You may be feeling like you are no prize, or that you haven't met some condition of worthiness, such as a level of success in your job or being a certain dress size—which would automatically mean you are worthwhile in your mind.

So often we have these conditions in our heads, these if–then statements that stop us from fully accepting our wonderful selves. *If I get published, I am worthy. If I get engaged, I will be happy to be me. If I get married, then I will feel great about myself.*

Guess what? All of this negative self-talk is hindering your ability to have mature and successful conversations about the future with your Beloved. Conversations that open him up emotionally, bring him closer, and deepen your shared commitment. To set the stage for those conversations, you need powerful and positive self-talk.

To get there, I will teach you how to work on and develop your most lovable and self-loving identity, what I call your Diamond Self identity. We touched on this in Chapter 6, coming at it from a more sensual aspect. Now we will flesh out the Diamond Self definition.

It starts with self-love.

Self-love means having appreciative, warm, validating thoughts and feelings toward yourself, *unconditional* positive self-regard and *unconditional* self-acceptance—regardless of your circumstances, behavior, achievements, or conditions your mother, father, or others laid down to determine your worthiness. Self-love means feeling good and okay just the way you are. It is not dependent on what you do, accomplish, or have. It is not dependent on getting approval from others, from your partner, or from your family. It is not dependent on your being perfect and not making mistakes. You experience that you have value and worth. You are free to be yourself without fear of disapproval or rejection. While you take responsibility for actions that are mistakes or lacking in integrity, when they do occur, you do not collapse in a morass of self-doubt or punishing self-hate.

I am talking about believing and feeling that the bottom line is that you deserve to be happy; that you deserve to live, to admit your failings, to experience and enjoy your life fully. That you deserve a great man who appreciates you, a true partner who wants to fill your needs, make you happy, and grow into deepening love and an exciting future with you. You deserve the full and complete commitment of lasting love that fills in the holes in your heart and mends the tears, bitterness, and heartbreaks of the past. You, my precious one, deserve the care, the courting, prizing, and celebration of you that makes your heart sing. Intimate moments, passionate moments, touching moments that are filled with grace. Blessings that bring out your natural strength, clarity, steadiness, and integrity—plus your caring, devotional qualities so that you are the best you can be.

The Diamond Self: A Closer Look

To understand what I mean, let's revisit Queen Latifah. She was born as Dana Owens. Yet she found and focused on the Queen Latifah aspect of herself, an identity where she feels open, empowered, deserving, lovable, and loving toward others. This is what I call her Diamond Self.

In *Love in 90 Days*, I defined the Diamond Self as your most dynamic, most self-loving and passionate identity. It builds on all of your prior successes in life. It's the *you* that acts in ways you like, enjoy, respect, and admire, the best *you* that you can become. Personality psychologists refer to this identity as the "ideal self," because it contains our hopes and aspirations for the future along with various skills and behavior traits we would like to master.

Your Diamond Self comes from heartfelt intuition and constructive thinking when you relate to yourself and others. You affirm yourself and your needs as important, work through your fears, become more authentic, and ask for what you want and need. You help others to do the same.

This is not an all-or-none kind of thing. You are a work of art in progress, over time becoming and expressing more of who you really are, on the Diamond Self path. Understand this: Recent research shows that there is no such thing as a fixed structure in the brain that represents self! In other words, the self you think is permanent is actually a process in your neural network that is always in flux. Rich Hanson, a neuropsychologist, describes it like this:

> As different parts of self come forward and then give way to other parts, so do the momentary neural assemblies that enable them. If the energy flows of these assemblies could be seen as a play of light, an extraordinary show would move endlessly about your head. In the brain, every manifestation of self is impermanent. The self is continually constructed, deconstructed and constructed again.

So there is a constant play of brain structures that represent you. And as we've talked about throughout this book, your brain and its neural networks are very malleable. You can train and thereby change your brain's image of self, its physical representation of *you*, by adding a picture of that new *you*, your Diamond Self, into the constantly changing energy flow of identity. This is not a static process. And this is why I call it the Diamond Self path. On this path, you consciously influence the way your mind processes the very notion of who you are. You can:

- Become self-affirming.
- Become self-respecting.
- Be at home in your own body.
- Be confident and charismatic.
- Stop looking for the approval of others.
- Feel and express your real feelings.
- Become authentic in speaking your truth.
- Break through fear or self-doubt.
- Become self-forgiving and okay with making mistakes.
- Be creative and generative.
- Happily move toward being the better, more skilled, or accomplished person you would like to be.

Sounds good, you may be thinking, *but just how do I move forward on my Diamond Self path? And how is this going to help me have fruitful conversations about the commitment and love I need?* We will get to both of these questions. Just know for now that your Diamond Self has everything to do with having successful talks, thrilling talks that get you farther than you even dreamed! Because as you find and live from that empowered identity, you will naturally act in ways that are irresistibly attractive to your partner, ways that draw him closer, so that he feels at home around you and wants to be with you. And he will be able to see that his life is much better with you in it and would be much worse without you. This sets the stage for true commitment. The Diamond Self work will help you move your relationship forward to the commitment and love you want in five different ways.

How Being Your Diamond Self Moves You Forward in Your Relationship

1. CREATING A NET-PLUS EQUATION

Arthur Aron, a researcher at Stony Brook, found in his work that commitment varies depending on how much your partner enhances your life. He calls this "self-expansion." This is why women who are confident, independent, successful, and playful are the ones men find very special and attractive and want to be around. When you are being your Diamond Self and you are happy, your man will be uplifted by your positive energy and drawn into your orbit. Because it is a relationship without a lot of drama, he will want more and more. Being with someone who is genuinely self-loving and living a passionate life is a net plus for him. Simply, he will want more of the stimulating and uplifting emotional, physical, and social environments you create. You enhance his life, and that means he will be much more receptive to talking about a shared future.

2. AVOIDING THE *HELP I'M BEING SMOTHERED/RUN FOR THE HILLS* DYNAMIC

When you are on your Diamond Self path, you will naturally avoid acting in ways that kill attraction and actively push your partner away—like nagging, whining, or needling him for attention. He knows that he does not have to be "everything" to you; that you have your own meetings and events to go to. You have your own independent needs for space and time. With that he knows that he is not going to be smothered; thereby you've avoided one of the common male commitment fears we discussed in Chapter 5.

3. DRAWING HIM IN

As your Diamond Self, you act in appreciative ways that draw your man in. Projection does not simply operate in negative ways. It also works in the positive direction. If you have been together for a while, you will experience your partner as part of you on a psychological level. This means that as you appreciate and love yourself more, you experience more love for him. When you are more forgiving of your own faults, you will be more forgiving of his. You will be less harsh, critical, and judgmental toward him and more validating and prizing. This level of appreciation and ease will make it easier to have The Talk.

4. INSPIRING HIM TO BE HIS DIAMOND SELF

Actualizing your ideal self will make you a better role model and inspire your partner to follow suit. When you are on your Diamond Self path, you will access that place where you blossom as a relaxed, truthful, and loving person. You will then become the change that you would like to experience in your partner. Your clarity, strength, and warmth will help him rise to be more open, clear, thoughtful, and caring when you have conversations about a shared future.

5. CREATING THE POSSIBILITY OF PERMANENTLY LOSING YOU

Building self-love and a passionate life will allow you to have a true measure of emotional and financial independence from your man. If he does not step up to the plate and move things forward, you could walk out the door. Sensing this, your boyfriend or partner will have more respect and appreciation for you. Anything that can be lost usually has greater perceived value, so chances are that as you progress on the Diamond Self path, your Beloved will be begging for a commitment from you. He will not want a great woman like you to get away.

Now that I've shared the five benefits of being on the Diamond Self path, the next section will focus on six specific exercises to help you quickly and easily create that special identity. I guarantee that practicing these will help your conversations about having a future together go as well as possible.

✎ The Diamond Self Exercises_____

> Self-love allows you to be available to others in ways that lead to deeper connections. It allows you to be committed to yourself and your own happiness, which is necessary before you can really commit to being a part of somebody else's life and well-being
>
> —*Happily married Lasting Love survey participant*

EXERCISE 1: *YOUR DIAMOND SELF AFFIRMATIONS*

Make a list of Diamond Self affirmations. These are positive statements about yourself that start with *I* and are in the present tense. Make them bold and outrageously positive! As you write them out, imagine that you are your ideal self, the self you would like to become.

Unfortunately, Sally had neglected working on her Diamond Self before she had her outburst with Gary. She also had neglected to touch base with her Love Mentor, Beth, to help her set the stage for having mature conversations about a shared future with Gary. You saw how well that went! After the damage was done, Sally finally called Beth for guidance. Beth asked her to work on Diamond Self affirmations first, so that Sally would be emotionally grounded and ready to have a real and fruitful talk with Gary. Sally made the following affirmations list for herself:

- I am a fully lovable and loving person.
- I am a perfect child of God.
- I bring joy to my Beloved.
- I am the sexy Vivacious Vixen [her Diamond Self name].
- I am funny and fun to be with.
- Being with me brings out the best in my Beloved.
- I deserve a great family life with kids.
- I deserve miraculous, surprising, and lasting love.

Sally worked with these affirmations every day, putting her full attention on each one for a few minutes at a time. After several weeks, she felt confident enough to have straight talk with Gary about how she was envisioning giving herself an extraordinary relationship. He was intrigued.

When you make Diamond Self affirmations, you are creating the possibility of a future in which your life is richly fulfilling. Heartfelt affirmations don't typically work as quickly as you would like. *But they do work.* The more attention you put on a Diamond Self affirmation, the more quickly it will manifest. So put your list in a private place where you can look it over with full attention for a few minutes several times a day. Use the powerful process that you learned earlier for activating affirmations. If reading your affirmations leads to doubts or other thoughts, treat them as if you were in meditation: Observe them without judgment. Notice and accept them. The more you accept them without struggle, the faster they will go away. Always return to your affirmation, the way you go back to a mantra after a distracting series of thoughts. Following this method will speed up your progress in walking the Diamond Self path.

You can use these affirmations to construct a deliberate and more positive self-concept or identity. The wonderful thing is that you get to decide how you want to experience yourself. You get to decide who you are. The most powerful self-affirmation you can create is to give your Diamond Self a name. While it may feel strange or uncomfortable at first, taking on and using this name will become a playful and meaningful experience. Choose a great name, and when the time is right, share it with your boyfriend. You may even ask him to use your nickname when you are alone together. Sally chose the name Vivacious Vixen. Gary thought it was funny because it didn't "fit." But that Diamond Self name helped her to step out from behind the curtain of the numerous worries she had about being overweight and unattractive. Sally became more assertive, flirtatious, and sensual with Gary. He, in turn, was amazed and turned on.

Here are sample Diamond Self names to help you invent yours: Amazing Grace; Beloved Mighty Isis; Starbright Stacy.

EXERCISE 2: *ANCHORING IN YOUR DIAMOND SELF IDENTITY*

Read each section and then close your eyes, taking your time to do each step of the exercise. The whole process only takes about ten minutes to complete.

1. Remember a time when you felt incredible about yourself—alive, real, attractive, passionate, talented, connected, loving…lovable. Put yourself in the picture so that you are looking through your own eyes. Feel that completely.
2. Imagine yourself better, even better. Imagine yourself five times better.
3. Now take that image and bring it closer to you. Make it brighter, clearer. Give it a great soundtrack, magnify all those good feelings—make them stronger. This is your Diamond Self. If you have given yourself a Diamond Self name, say it to yourself. If not, give yourself one now—a grand name.

4. Shrink the Diamond Self and make it as small as a real diamond. Then put that image aside.

5. Get an image of yourself at a time when you felt rejected, abandoned, or unlovable. When you were overrun with negative self-talk, like, *It's hopeless for me. I'm too fat. He doesn't want me. I'm a loser.* This is your Disappointing Self.

6. Take the Diamond Self image, make it the size of a hand grenade, and imagine throwing it right into the center of your Disappointing Self, watching it explode and completely destroy the Disappointing Self.

7. Now, instant replay. Imagine your Disappointing Self, throw the Diamond Self grenade into the center, and blow up the Disappointing Self again.

8. Speed the whole thing up and do it several more times.

Do this until you cannot get a clear image of the Disappointing Self. You can do a quick version of this process whenever you need to be at your best or prepare for any difficult conversation.

EXERCISE 3: *YOUR DIAMOND SELF CLOTHES AND JEWELRY MAKEOVER*

Pull a new look together by thinking about your new-you name. Buy clothes that show your ideal self off. Get a haircut that speaks her name. Buy jewelry that symbolizes her radiant lovable and loving nature. Remember what I wrote about the potential healing power of gemstones in Chapter 3? Consider finding and wearing one or two gemstones that go along with both your Diamond Self name and your love intention. As I shared earlier, they may enhance your self-esteem and empower you to achieve your love goals.

One of my students from Omaha, who renamed herself Venus Rising, sent me this e-mail about discovering and strengthening her

Diamond Self identity through a makeover, new clothes, and new jewelry:

> *I used to go into stores in my sweats and the saleswoman would say, "Can I help you, sir?" Venus Rising is leaving that shell behind! It has been a year since I started on the Diamond Self path, threw out all the crappy clothes and started wearing fuchsia, rose or hot pink dresses and skirts. I bought a gorgeous Imperial Topaz ring with diamond chips for the new me! I even took dance lessons. My Italian boyfriend loves Venus Rising and so do I! We cook pasta primavera and make incredible love. He's started talking about where "we" are going to live. I cannot thank you enough.*

EXERCISE 4: *ACT LIKE YOUR DIAMOND SELF IN THE RELATIONSHIP*

Act in ways that your Diamond Self yearns to act. Be gorgeous and playful and flirt with your boyfriend. Feel with your intuition; get a gut sense of what interests you, what you need to say or do. Play full-out in your relationship in ways that you truly enjoy. If you are in the middle of a big fight or setback with your partner, take a moment to forgive yourself and your partner for any wrongdoing. Say something to yourself like, *We are doing the best we can. We're both hurting right now.* Your Diamond Self will always come from a place of appreciation and forgiveness. It seeks to resolve difficulties and arrive at win–win solutions.

EXERCISE 5: *DISCOVER AND FOLLOW YOUR PASSIONS*

Your self-esteem and feelings of worthiness will soar if you discover and follow your own unique passions in either your work or leisure. What truly calls to you? What do you enjoy doing the most? What activities give you the most pleasure? What would you like to study?

What career is truly right for you? Do you have a way of giving to others that is special and inspires you? When you are doing what you love, especially if it is helpful to others, you will feel great about yourself. You will be less dependent on your relationship to enliven your life.

I cannot stress this enough: Men ultimately want to be with women who have rich full lives, who are interesting and independent. Some men will wait to commit until the woman is fulfilled in this aspect of her life.

For example, Fran pressed her boyfriend, Peter, for a proposal. They were living together and she had moved to Seattle to be with him, which made her feel vulnerable. She refused to get a job and "commit" to living in Seattle until he proposed. Meanwhile, he didn't want to propose until she felt more comfortable with herself, because he felt tremendous pressure to make her happy. He was worried that she wouldn't be able to find work she enjoyed once they did get married, and that he might not be enough to fulfill her needs on his own. Eventually, Fran threatened to move out and told him about another man she had been spending time with, so Peter proposed. A few months later, Peter was offered a promotion, but it required him to transfer to the office in Phoenix. They decided to make the move and settled into their new place together. After four months in the hot desert city, Fran felt restless and terrified about getting married. She decided to leave Peter to find herself because she was so unhappy, bored, friendless, and dependent on him in a new city while he headed off to work every day. A few weeks after she left Peter, she met a new guy who lived in Los Angeles, and repeated this exact same cycle, moving to LA to be with him, pressing for a proposal, and ending the relationship a year later when it didn't happen. In both relationships, Fran's boyfriends were at first taken with the challenge of making her happy and found satisfaction succeeding with small things, like vacations or dinners out. But when it came down to proposing, they realized they wouldn't be able to succeed as the sole source of her happiness and strongly resisted giving her the commitment she wanted. Because of her lack of commitment to her own work path, Fran is still unable to have the lasting love she so desires.

On the other hand, Lola, a tattooed beauty, was able to find herself and save her relationship. She was living with Frank, a successful no-nonsense accountant. Frank and Lola came to therapy with me because they were at a crossroads: Lola had quit her bartending job a year earlier and was trying to reinvent herself. She had become confused and depressed, and had even started drinking. Frank was fed up with supporting Lola financially and emotionally and was on the verge of walking out. As we discussed in Chapter 5, men feel a strong self-imposed pressure to uplift a woman, and if she is in a downward spiral, they feel inept and frustrated in being unable to fix things. I asked Lola to do Diamond Self exercises and to dream about what career she would choose if she followed the passions of her Diamond Self path. Lola gave herself the Diamond name of Goddess Tara; what she wanted to do was to be of service by counseling people. There were only two problems: She had learning disabilities and was not good at schoolwork. So we got creative and helped find Goddess Tara a job as a director of recreation at a local retirement center. Lola had never been as thrilled about her job as she was working with the seniors at the center. With the help of her new passion and AA, Lola turned herself around. She proposed to Frank, and the couple became happily engaged.

If you are not doing what you love, consider going back to school, getting a new job, or creating a new and passionate purpose-driven involvement, like being a volunteer for a charity that is committed to ending world hunger, such as Heifer International, or mentoring disadvantaged kids by joining Big Brothers Big Sisters. You will then bring that excitement, energy, and aliveness back to enrich your relationship—which in turn will set the stage for coming together with your partner in the committed way you want.

EXERCISE 6: *PRACTICE THE LOVING MOTHER MEDITATION*

In Chapter 5, I described how our relationship with our mothers (or mothering figure) is our primary template for intimacy. In order to build on that, I've developed a guided imagery mediation that can help you gain self-love based on the archetype of an unconditionally loving mother (not your real mother, even if she was unconditionally caring). If the word *mother* brings negative associations to mind, you can substitute *angel* or *goddess*. The meditation is located in Appendix B. This meditation will soothe your fears and build a more peaceful and empowered sense of self that helps you move forward with your Beloved.

Practice these six easy-to-use Lasting Love Program exercises to bring out and polish your Diamond Self. If you do at least one of them daily, you will have done them all by the end of the week, getting yourself grounded in a powerful and generative way so that you are prepared to have intimate moments and inspiring conversations with your partner that draw him ever closer.

Your Commitment Goals Revisited

Now that you have done work on self-love and deservedness, I would like you to revisit your commitment goals from Chapter 1. The latter five from that list, having to do directly with the relationship, are below. Which one(s) do you want to focus on when you have commitment conversations or Talks with your Beloved?

- Agree that you and your boyfriend will be dating each other exclusively.
- Declare love for each other.

- Talk with your Beloved about what you both want in a shared future; lifestyle; finances; religious beliefs; fears, goals, dreams; and whether you want marriage and/or children.
- Commit to moving in together or getting engaged to your Beloved.
- Marry, make, or renew a lifetime commitment to live out your dreams together.

Write down your goal(s) and envision achieving it (them) with your boyfriend or partner in a beautiful win–win way.

I am right with you with these best wishes:

May today there be peace within.
May you trust that you are exactly where you are meant to be.
May you not forget the infinite possibilities that are born
of faith in yourself.
May you use those gifts that you have and take in the love
that flows to you.
May you be content with yourself just the way you are.
Let a healing presence settle into your bones, and allow your
soul the freedom to sing, dance, praise, and love.

—Adapted from St. Teresa of Avila's Prayer

How to Have The Talk So He Really Will Listen

Birds are entangled by their feet and [wo]men by their tongues.

—*Anonymous; at times attributed to Sir Thomas Fuller*

Shonda, a thirty-nine-year-old hairstylist with a radiant smile, had dated Darnell, a cocky music producer, for a year, and she was getting antsy. He said he was crazy about her, but his late-night work habits, recording with his twenty-something "discoveries," was unnerving. Shonda felt so in the groove with Darnell; going for walks, jamming with musical instruments, talking till all hours was great—not to mention their steamy sessions in bed. Shonda felt sure that Darnell was the great love of her life. She wanted to seal the deal and move in together, especially because his music studio was in his loft. Slowly she was leaving more and more of her stuff there, and Darnell seemed okay with it. Despite an occasional blowup, things were progressing well—Darnell was saying he loved her more frequently, they were spending more nights together at his loft, and he was introducing Shonda to his family as his girlfriend. Since things were moving along so well, Shonda decided to be patient and wait on having The Talk. She did not want to upset the nicely moving apple cart. Sure enough, eighteen months into the relationship, when she brought up the idea of living together, Darnell was fine with it.

Having The Talk: When's the Right Time?

The average time for a couple to move from dating to a committed relationship with a future that includes living together or getting married is from nine months to three years. A study of three thousand couples in the United Kingdom showed that the average length of courtship before a marriage proposal was two years, eleven months. So patience in having The Talk, up to a point, definitely pays.

Poorly timed or premature conversations can backfire. For example, Jorunn, a live-wire personal trainer, met Mike, a hunky real estate agent, online. After they had sex for the first time, Jorunn blurted out, "We should be exclusive now!" She never saw Mike again.

Timing for having The Talk varies considerably from couple to couple, especially when you have different goals (obviously dating exclusively occurs much earlier than getting engaged). So there's no exact time for it. But usually, if things drag on in an uncommitted state that does not improve much beyond a couple of years, the relationship will tend to go downhill, especially if one person is longing for a more permanent commitment like marriage and the other is dragging their feet.

Any relationship that moves from casual to committed will have a series of Talks, not just one. There are discussions that are appropriate for early stages and some that are for later in the relationship. But before you engage in any of them, let's look at the key Lasting Love Program Talk basics: common mistakes that backfire; how to develop self-discipline for these important Talks so that you are ready to go; and finally, how to have Talks in both the early and later stages of the relationship so that he really listens.

What *Not* to Do or Say: Thirteen Common Mistakes That Make The Talk Backfire

Are you replaying that Talk that spelled the end for you and your ex in your head? Or a relationship Talk in a movie that went down the wrong path? Wondering what *is* it that made your boyfriend break out in a cold sweat when you mentioned that you needed to chat? Chances are, in each of these cases errors were made. And, in honor of the unlucky number 13, here are thirteen of the most common mistakes women make that backfire and generally cause a man to become defensive, grow emotionally distant, and in the end run for the door.

Let's live and learn, ladies.

Here's what we tend to do naturally, which is what makes men completely freak out—totally different language we're speaking here! After reading this list a few times, you may see that you often use several of these (ahhh!). Bonus freak-out points if any of these are used in combination:

1. Holding things in for months, bending over backward to make things work, and then finally exploding in anger and blame.
2. Complaining about the relationship or saying critical things about him ("How dumb can you be!") and what he does wrong.
3. Pouring out all your frustration and upset feelings in an overwhelming gush.
4. Dissolving in tears and being the wounded bird who can't make it without him.
5. Collapsing into thoughts of your unworthiness, your lack of deservedness, or feeling bad about yourself—so that you are lost in a depressive funk.
6. Going mute and withdrawing so that he will pull the truth out of you.

7. Threatening to hurt or even kill yourself if he doesn't come through for you (the narcissistic or borderline approach to The Talk).

8. Overanalyzing him or the problems between you and telling him why he doesn't feel what you would like him to feel.

9. Making demands because it has been a certain number of months or years and he "should" be moving forward with you.

10. Begging, convincing, or talking him into liking or choosing you ("Your life is so much better with me because...").

11. Being overly focused on yourself and talking only about your own feelings.

12. Bringing up past issues, disappointments, or arguments.

13. Being entitled and bullying him ("You should!" "After all I've done, you'd better...").

When you use the thirteen backfiring maneuvers, a man will respond, depending on his personality, by withdrawing, throwing an angry jab at you, or even with pseudo-agreement. But in the end, these maneuvers will drive him right out of your life. One brilliant blond lawyer describes what happened when she angrily accused her boyfriend of being piggish (mistake 2).

> *How dumb was I! He nodded and listened intently, and even responded with "You're right, I am being selfish." After The Talk was done, I left, and didn't hear from him for weeks. I had no idea I'd violated these rules; he seemed to really be taking my serious "insights" to heart. Duh. I mean, I really had no idea that my approach was such a major mistake!*

Any of these rash maneuvers will tend to turn your man off and have the opposite effect of what you intend. (Unless your intention is for him to get lost—in which case you'll succeed admirably.) If your goal is for him to listen thoughtfully and engage with you in an open, honest, and loving conversation (even if you don't get an immediate positive outcome), you need to prepare yourself through self-discipline. And that's why in this chapter I'm giving you four exercises first, before I share all the secrets to successfully having The Talk, to ensure that when the time comes you will know how to be grounded, self-controlled, and focused on your love intention. In other words, you'll be on your strongest footing and fully empowered.

> Discipline is remembering what you want.
>
> —*David Campbell*

✎ Your Biggest Ally: Self-Discipline_____

Here's how to develop it:

EXERCISE 1: *IDENTIFY YOUR SELF-SABOTAGING TENDENCIES*

First, identify any tendencies you have to make any of the thirteen all-too-common mistakes in your normal conversations or fights with him.

EXERCISE 2: *STOP DESPERATION AND DRAMA*

Stop yourself the next time you open your mouth and desperation and drama threaten to take over—remember, they rarely have a place in healthy communication. When you are talking with your partner and emotions begin to overtake you, if you feel like you're about to lose control, close your mouth, take a deep breath, and visualize a big bold **Red Stop Sign**. When you've quieted down, immediately change the subject. Practicing the Stop technique will help you avoid running over him with your emotional outbursts. They won't get you anywhere good, I promise.

EXERCISE 3: *DISCUSS YOUR TALKS WITH YOUR LOVE MENTOR FIRST*

If you have a Love Mentor, she can help you avoid accidentally repelling your Beloved. Be sure to discuss having Talks with her beforehand so that you have an emotional ally and are more grounded and prepared to be constructive. It is much easier if you first air out your fears, own up to your drama, fire up your courage, gather your thoughts, and rehearse what you're planning to say with your mentor before you do it with your man.

EXERCISE 4: *DISCIPLINE YOURSELF TO FOCUS ON YOUR LOVE INTENTION*

Finally, it is of key importance for you to have the discipline to "keep your eye on the ball"—*that is, to be clear and focused on your own love intention*—so that you can have calm, optimistic, and open discussions with your boyfriend about what really matters to you. Here's a simple method:

Sit in a quiet place and listen to uplifting and inspirational music—music that really sends you—for five to ten minutes. Then shut off the music and have a little daydream about one or more scenes where you fulfill your love intention. It could be your wedding or honeymoon, having a first baby, or whatever you like. Imagine each scene in great detail. Enjoy the feelings, the sights; give it a soundtrack. Imagine your Beloved in the scene with you. Then superimpose several different faces on the guy in your fantasy.

Your love intention is a promise you make to yourself. If you are fully committed to actualizing your love intention, you will succeed.

Perhaps it will not be with your current love. But you will succeed. *You* are in charge of fulfilling yourself—*not* your boyfriend.

The self-discipline exercises are simple to do and together take only fifteen or twenty minutes. Many of us spend more time fussing with our hair! But I want you to feel at your best, and that includes doing your hair, your whole Diamond Self beauty routine, *and* these exercises. They will help you be less worried and less dependent on your boyfriend's reaction (what we psychologists call greater self-efficacy). They will foster feelings of greater relaxation and self-confidence so that you can speak in a casual, less emotional way. Remember, having a super-serious vibe or tone in your voice will not be helpful in creating the right atmosphere for a successful talk.

Common scenario: Suppose you're having a conversation with your man, you ask a question, get no response—and see that he's been surreptitiously reading his iPhone while you've been pouring your heart out. Well, I've got the secrets to prevent this from happening; secrets that get him to actually *hear* you when you have something important to say. I've developed them over the last twenty-five years by listening to what my many male clients have told me in the office.

Seven Tips on Helping a Man to Really Listen

Here are seven insights into men and how they process information. Knowing these facts will help you help him listen more effectively when you are bringing up a sticky subject.

1. Men have difficulty multitasking and having an emotionally laden dialogue. Do not speak to him when he is at the computer, watching a game, or working or playing on his iPhone. Talk at a time when you can have his full attention.

2. While you would never dream of taking your girlfriend out to a Yankees game for a heart-to-heart instead of to coffee, this is precisely what men do, because they tend to be more able to listen when they are side by side and not facing their partners. Try talking while walking or driving together.

3. A man's testosterone levels drop between 4 PM and 6 PM, which means that this is when they're able to listen best.

4. Men are more attentive when you start a touchy talk with a warm, affirming statement about them. By nature they are looking to win approval.

5. The male brain tends to hear men's voices as verbal speech but women's voices as music! So it may be hard for a guy to understand your point. Don't talk too much. Get to the bottom line quickly.

6. Men get physiologically flooded by upset and then have trouble self-soothing. Avoid a lot of emotionality and drama, which will result in your guy shutting you out. Speak to him nonchalantly and playfully about charged topics.

7. Use a light touch with humor that does not put your man down. Research on happy marriages reveals that the wife's use of humor was an important component of resolving difficult interactions.

As Mars/Venus maven John Gray and communication expert Deborah Tannen have described, men tend to listen and talk in ways that are quite different from women. I call this "Guy-Speak" versus "Woman-Speak."

Cheat Sheet on How Guys' Listening/ Talking Often Differs from Women's

"Guy-Speak"	"Woman-Speak"
• Focus on not being controlled, preserving independence, gaining approval and respect	• Focus on creating emotional closeness, connection, and rapport
• More connected when talking side by side	• More connected when looking into partner's eyes
• Need warmth and validation from their partners before starting a serious talk	• Start by sharing their own personal and emotional troubles in having a serious talk
• Like to quickly get to the bottom line and understand how they can solve a problem	• Like to analyze, talk about, and share troubles
• Get flooded by upset in the face of drama and emotionality	• Feel it is key to air strongly felt feelings in order to be heard and understood

Shonda, our hairstylist whom you met at the beginning of this chapter, used the seven tips and "Guy-Speak" in talking with Darnell about living together. She chose a time when they were driving together (side by side) to a concert in the late afternoon. Shonda started by stating how much she enjoyed hanging with Darnell, then cut quickly to the bottom line: how fabulous it would be to live together. Then she teased him about offering her cramped walk-up for their nest. He opened up and shared his fear that having her around would interfere with his recording schedule. Shonda was able to reassure him that he could still do his work. Darnell finally chuckled and said he would have to build an extra closet just for her shoe collection.

How to Have The Talk So He Really Will Listen

As your relationship moves along in the early stages, it is important to learn about each other's dreams and fears, goals, lifestyle preferences, outside passions and interests, finances, religious beliefs, and desires for marriage or children. You need to know whether the two of you are on the same page or not. *These discussions are different from having The Talk because they are not about whether he wants to do or share these activities with you.* They are just about getting to know each other as individuals. So ask questions of your boyfriend and share your own thoughts and feelings. These discussions prepare you to have intimate talks with him later in the relationship about a shared future.

HAVING A SUCCESSFUL TALK IN THE EARLY STAGES

If you have been with your boyfriend for three or more months of consistent dating and he has not yet expressed how he feels about you or his thoughts about the potential for the relationship, you could start by *nonchalantly or playfully* asking a few basic questions at a time when you are having fun or feeling close. Preface the question with a warm and validating statement. Perhaps use a Diamond Self nickname you have given him that he enjoys. This kind of "soft start-up" at the beginning of a tricky conversation helps men to relax and be more responsive.

A few soft start-ups:

- I'm really enjoying you. (Teasing) And I know you're enjoying me even more. What do you think of that?
- Honey, being with you is awesome! Are you enjoying being together?
- You are so much fun that I was thinking of taking my online dating profile down. Or not. What are your thoughts?

- Brilliant Dave (or whatever Diamond Self nickname he enjoys), if we could go into a time machine, what do you think our lives would be like in three years?
- Coach J (or whatever Diamond Self nickname he enjoys), you are so great with planning. What are our next steps?
- I'm so happy being with you. Are you happy being with me?
- (Teasing) It's been so fantastic being together you probably want to take down your online profile. What could you possibly say to make me take down mine?

If he opens up and shares his thoughts and feelings with you, listen with full attention and only reflect back to him what he is saying. For example, you might say, "You feel like you are not sure where we are heading, but something special is happening between us and you want to see where it goes." This will give him the feeling that he is being heard and understood by you. No commentary, reaction, or judgment is necessary at this time. All you want to get is a deeper understanding of whether your guy is (a) crazy about you, (b) willing to grow, and (c) meeting the basics. Good listening with full attention is the cornerstone of a successful talk.

Many guys, however, respond with ambiguous answers, like "I don't know. I'm not sure. I haven't figured out what I want." Or the all-time classic, "I haven't thought about it much." *Do not react to any of these responses.* Men, when they are caught off-guard, will often deflect to gain time so that they don't say something stupid. It doesn't mean anything. Just relax, breathe, and give him room. Then say something like, "That's okay. I understand." Let a week or so go by and try another soft start-up. Then you can say something like, "I would like you to think about it. Meanwhile let's just enjoy each other." All of your responses need to be patient and mature in the early stage.

It is important that after you listen to what he has to say, you, at some point, are clear in a light, breezy, nonchalant way about what your relationship goals are. *In the early stages, you are not saying that those goals have to be met through him.* You can still roll the bones, have several different conversations over time, and see how they pan out. But as time goes on, you will need to discover if this relationship is headed toward a shared future.

HAVING A SUCCESSFUL TALK IN THE LATER STAGES

You may have been with a guy for a solid nine months to a year or longer, sleeping together regularly and spending a great deal of time in each other's company, and yet things are still not clear in terms of your future. If you feel the need to move forward toward clarifying where you stand, use a soft conversational start-up—in a *lighthearted, playful, or casual way*—at some point when the two of you are having a great time or feeling very close. Here are some examples:

- Sometimes I feel like I love you. Do you love me?
- I am happy to be with you, honey. How do you feel about having me in your life?
- I love just lying in your arms. Do you feel ready for a committed relationship?
- Guitar Hero (or whatever Diamond Self nickname he enjoys), you have been the best karaoke partner this past year! Where do you see us in six months? A year from now?
- Big Bob (or whatever Diamond Self nickname he enjoys), the past year has been so great for both of us! Do you see us living together?
- You really helped me so much! Do you see us moving on together? Do you see me in your future years from now?
- I loved being with you these past two years! I can see us walking down the aisle at some point. What about you?
- Slow Hand (or whatever Diamond Self nickname he enjoys), when I think about last night and how great you are, I hear bells, as in chapel bells. What about you?

After you listen to what he says, repeat it back so that he feels understood. For example, if he says, "I need a few more months to know for sure," or the ever-popular "I need to get on my feet financially before I take a major step like marriage," echo his statement back to him. Afterward, be sure to clearly say what your goal is, in a nonpressured, light and casual or teasing way. Something like, "Well, I want to live with you, but only if you promise not to sing in the shower!" or, "Being married. Yup. That is what I want to work toward."

WHAT TO DO IF HE GIVES YOU AN AMBIGUOUS OR NEGATIVE ANSWER

All people can have ambivalent feelings in intimate relationships. There's love, hate, and every shade in between, not to mention times of complete disinterest. And that occurs in great marriages! So the question simply is: What do you focus on? If you let your fears take over and focus on his disinterest now that you asked the question and he responded ambiguously—that tends to grow. This becomes a self-fulfilling prophecy as it pushes a guy away. You experience being abandoned and act like it's all over, and then it is.

On the other hand, if you have patience and time, you can use Positive Paranoia to directly help your Beloved grow closer to his ideal self, which means he could become more loving and more able to commit. Here is a story about how one woman used affirming Positive Paranoia in having The Talk.

The Story of Rina and Justin

Rina, a twenty-eight-year-old sloe-eyed brunette, was a political science graduate student. She met Justin, a shy thirty-year-old Web site designer, on JDate.com, and they soon were like two peas in the proverbial pod. They were low-key, sweet-natured comedy club regulars who loved to go on cruises, take in plays, and simply hang out together. The sex was easy and great. However, nine months into their relationship, Justin had never said much about a future together. So Rina decided to initiate The Talk. She used a soft start-up and said, "Sometimes I feel like I love you. Do you love me?" He opened up and said, "I don't really think I know what love is." Justin's response caused a momentary reaction, but Rina calmed herself and moved herself into a state of Positive Paranoia. She laughed softly, shook her head, and answered. "I get that you feel that way, but I know you do love me." Justin chuckled in response.

Over the next few months, they had repeated interactions that went along the same lines and ended with Justin's grinning response to Rina's Positive Paranoia. Justin told Rina he wanted to be able to feel emotions like joy, happiness, or love more deeply (his version of an ideal self). Instead of judging him, she reassured Justin that he would be able to develop that capability and that she was committed to his goal. Six months later, while making love, Justin for the first time said, "I do love you."

After that breakthrough, Rina began to initiate talks about getting married and having kids. She definitely wanted them. Justin decided he wanted to get married and bought Rina an engagement ring. But he wasn't sure if he wanted kids with all the responsibilities, worries, and demands. Rina pointed out what a kind and wonderful dad Justin was to his dog, Mr. Bigs (a giant black Newfie whom Justin doted on), and occasionally mentioned what a great father he would be to his own children. Justin gave her big smiles when she validated him about his devotion and care of Mr. Bigs. After four years together, the couple were very happily married and planned to have children.

Notice that in this story, by chuckling and smiling, Justin was giving Rina signals that what she was saying was in line with his ideal or Diamond Self. He wanted to be a loving, caring, and mature man. She saw this and helped him to develop in that direction. If at a deeper level your man wants to learn to open his heart, to overcome his commitment fears, and to be a man who can choose committed love with you, you can put on your sculpting gloves and help him chisel his way out of the rock. This process is what researchers have called the Michelangelo Phenomenon.

The Michelangelo Phenomenon

As you may recall, the brilliant sculptor Michelangelo described his art of statue making as simply the process of releasing the ideal figure from the block of stone or marble. Like Michelangelo, partners in healthier relationships help each other grow and self-actualize. Each helps the other find hidden talents, develop skills and resources, refine values or ethical conduct, reach goals, and achieve dreams. In other words, they help each other actualize their Diamond Selves.

You can be a transformative agent who helps her man and her relationship evolve at the same time. Many studies have shown that in the Michelangelo process, the partners perceive each other more positively than each person perceives him- or herself, and their relationship is greatly enhanced. They see the loving and talented attributes that are in their mates, at times before their partners see them. And when these attributes are affirmed from one partner to the "target partner," it increases the "target's" belief that his Beloved understands and approves of him and genuinely cares about his well-being. This process has been shown to promote trust and *strengthen commitment*.

Let's be clear: Shaping your partner in the direction of his ideal self is not about nagging and imposing your insight and advice on your man. It's not about telling him what you think he should become or how he could be a better person. It is first and foremost about asking him about his dreams, about finding and then helping him become his own ideal self. And that takes listening carefully and seeing and delighting in his Diamond Self. What *he* considers to be his Diamond Self.

POSITIVE PARANOIA STATEMENTS TO JUMP-START
A STALLED RELATIONSHIP

If you have been together for six months or more, you can try making Positive Paranoia statements and see if they help a slow, stuck, or ambivalent relationship move forward. Do not make these statements when your man is opening up and expressing his fear or ambivalence. When this happens it is the time to simply listen. You don't want to invalidate him by saying, "No, you're wrong." This is a form of criticism that will just amplify his resistance and opposition to feeling connected and committed.

Instead, use your intuition and make affirming statements when you feel that they are true in any given moment. Make these Positive Paranoia statements in a *casual, teasing, light,* and *playful way*. You are not starting a debate. There is no convincing or presentation of evidence as to why what you are saying is true. It is simply the plain fact as you experience it in the moment.

For example, say you just had mind-blowing sex and are gazing into each other's eyes. At that moment, you might say, "You love me so much!" Or you're splashing each other and horsing around in the pool and as you try to dunk him, you say, "You're madly in love and are dying to get me to live with you!" Here are some other examples:

Positive Paranoia Statements
- You love me.
- You're madly in love with me.
- You want to know what deep love is.
- You are crazy about me.
- You want to live with me.
- You can't wait to get married.

- You would make a great father.
- You want kids.
- You're dying to say, *I love you*.
- You really want to make me happy.
- You know exactly how to make things great with us!
- You can easily handle a love relationship.
- You can't wait to have a family with me.

Here are signs that your Positive Paranoia statements are in line with your Beloved's ideal self and thus likely to help him stretch and grow as a man:

- He laughs.
- He teases you back.
- He makes more eye contact.
- He turns toward you or he moves closer physically.
- He acts affectionately, taking your hand, giving you a squeeze.
- He agrees with you in a playful way—for instance, he says, "Sometimes!" Or "I am crazy about you when you make this lasagna!"
- He starts making similar statements on his own.

There is some chance, on the other hand, that your boyfriend may be terrified when he hears your affirming statements. You will feel this because the vibes will go south as he becomes emotionally distant, upset, angry, or annoyed. Needless to say, these reactions are not good signs. But what he says and does will give you valuable data about his willingness to move forward with you.

He *must* show you that he is growing, whether with your help or someone else's, for you to continue in the relationship. That is, over time he is moving closer to you, saying the L-word and acting like he means it, and becoming more open and interested in living together or getting married (or having children). So pay careful attention to the trend over time in your relationship.

*   *   *

In sum, in having The Talk, summon your courage and don't be afraid to be honest in a way that helps him hear what you are saying. Follow any of the steps that I've described in this chapter and you will be more grounded and prepared. Ask questions and speak your truth in a calm, loving way. Chances are your Beloved will be more open, easier to talk to, and more deeply bonded with you. As you follow the Lasting Love Program, you will help your relationship move into a profound, living, transformational love like this one:

> *I love you*
> *For putting your hand*
> *Into my heaped-up heart*
> *And passing over*
> *All the foolish, weak things*
> *That you can't help*
> *Dimly seeing there,*
> *And for drawing out*
> *Into the light*
> *All the beautiful belongings*
> *That no one else had looked*
> *Quite far enough to find.*
>
> *I love you because you*
> *Are helping me to make*
> *Of the lumber of my life*
> *Not a tavern*
> *But a temple;*
> *Out of the works*
> *Of my every day*
> *Not a reproach*
> *But a song.*

I love you
Because you have done
More than any creed
Could have done
To make me good
And more than any fate
Could have done
To make me happy.
—Attributed to Elizabeth Barrett Browning,
among others

10

What to Do If He Won't Commit, Becomes Distant, or Cheats

> ...love in its fullest form is a series of deaths and rebirths. We let go of one phase, one aspect of love, and enter another. Passion dies and is brought back. Pain is chased away and surfaces another time. To love means to embrace and at the same time to withstand many many endings and many many beginnings—all in the same relationship.
>
> —*Clarissa Pinkola Estés*

Help, Dr. Diana!" started an e-mail I received on my Web site from Jennifer in Nashville. "All I did was bring up the idea of marriage a couple of times with Robert, my boyfriend of two years. Now he is MIA. What do I do now? I'm a mess and he doesn't seem to care. I even texted him that my grandmother died and all he did was text me 'sorry.' I have no clue what he's up to."

Maybe, like Jennifer, you've had The Talk—possibly even a few times—and your boyfriend or partner's reaction feels like your worst nightmare: He balked at committing, stonewalled, or broke away from your usual rhythm of contact. Maybe he told you he just wants to be friends, that he's "not ready," or the classic "It's not you, it's me" speech. Perhaps he went even farther, pulling back sexually or completely neglecting you for a week or more.

Your instinctive reaction, like Jennifer's, to his disappointing behavior may be to become saddled with upset, worry, and obsessive thoughts. You may feel a great deal of embarrassment or feel bad about yourself. You may have depressing, persistent thoughts like, *What is wrong with me? Why do I still love him after he treats me like this? Is he cheating on me?*

Passionate love can crown you with rapturous joy, only to then crucify you with hellish suffering. You might be facing the agony of loss now as you read these words. If you are feeling truly abandoned, your entire body chemistry is affected. Your serotonin levels drop and everything around you suddenly loses its color. You may lose your appetite (or overeat), have difficulty sleeping, or isolate yourself while spending hours obsessing about him. On top of that, feel-good endorphins drop, which can create physical aches and pains. Loss truly leads to a crucible of suffering.

But as the expression goes, "It ain't over until the fat lady sings." In this chapter, I will teach you some of the most effective tools in the Lasting Love Program, designed to empower you and optimize the possibility of getting the relationship back on track. You will learn how to be a powerful agent of change, so that he may be able to evolve into a new improved version of himself and take the lead in pursuing a love commitment from you. If the relationship is really over, you will also learn how to end things gracefully and quickly heal from heartbreak so that you can move on to create happiness in a new relationship.

Putting Your Relationship on Probation

If things have been dragging along in a stuck or uncertain state and your Beloved has not responded positively to The Talks, you may want to put the relationship on probation. This means you will let your partner know that you may be leaving him so that he has a chance to work on things. This is especially true if you still have hope for the relationship or you want to give him another chance. He is probably already feeling that things are off-kilter between you and that there are problems in the relationship. It may be time to have a caring yet honest talk with your partner that lets him know that for you, the relationship has entered a probationary period. If you have been seriously involved with your partner, it would not be fair to simply leave and pull the rug out from under him without warning.

There are five components of a probationary Talk:

1. Start in a mature, kind, and loving way.
2. Be specific about what is not working.
3. Be clear about your thoughts about the possible end of the relationship.
4. Touch on the losses you both will have if things end.
5. Suggest some actions or ask him for his thoughts on what actions he might suggest to turn things around.

Three of my Lasting Love Program mentees sent me the following e-mails describing what they said to their boyfriends in probation Talks:

I really care about you, but with what has been happening between us lately, I have begun to reconsider this relationship. I am not sure that it is best for us to stay together because we can't seem to work out our issues about the time we spend together and having a future together. Maybe if we get some help it might work out between us, but I am just not sure.—Stella, *twenty-nine*

It would be very sad and painful to lose all that we have built up, for one of us to have to move out, to lose our connection. And it would be so difficult to sort everything out. And I know how alone and lonely we will be feeling. But if it's not working, it is not working... Our fighting is just out of control and I can't live like this anymore, unless there is something you think we can do to get back on track. What do you think?—Marcie, thirty-five

It was so great in the beginning. But not now. We never talk like friends and rarely have sex. It's like we've become strangers. Maybe we should take a few days apart to think about it. I think going into couples counseling or taking a couples education course might give us a chance. What do you think?—Shakira, forty-seven

Don't throw this speech in his face as an idle threat during fights or as something you endlessly harass him about to gain power in the relationship. *If you turn it into an emotional ultimatum, you will lose personal power in the relationship.*

What to Avoid

- A lot of emotionality, tears, acting wounded or helpless.
- Making idle threats—for instance, saying over and over that you are going to leave if he doesn't shape up.
- Bringing it up in a fit of anger during an argument.
- Begging, pleading, convincing him to give you what you need.
- Emotional blackmail—"If you don't come through I am going to hurt or kill myself."
- Attacking or criticizing him for his inability to move forward with you.

Delivering the message in a kind and mature way shows you mean business and will optimize the chance that he will rise to the occasion and work with you so that your relationship can grow deeper. He may respond in a positive fashion or be willing to go into individual or couples counseling or get help through other growth or educational courses.

WHAT IF HE GETS ANGRY AND WITHDRAWS?

On the other hand, if you deliver the probation Talk and he becomes defensive, critical, or argumentative and withdraws even more and does not rebound, you have a serious problem. About 75 percent of the clients I have treated tend, after their own anger dies down, to text or call and pursue their boyfriends even though they reacted poorly and did not come around. And if you do this, he may respond in a lukewarm way but not wholeheartedly.

You want to hear him come to his senses. Admit he was wrong about pulling back and going radio silence. Promise that he will be a better man. That he wants you. That he must have you. Your heart, your gut are craving to get him back and for him to show that he's crazy about you—even though you are furious and are not sure you should give him another chance, and even though you may hate his guts. At the same time, you can't stop obsessing about him. Where you might catch a glimpse of him at a certain time of day. What you did wrong that drove him away. You can't imagine not talking to him at all and not ever seeing him again. Even though he acted very poorly and cut your heart to the quick.

Why do we do this to ourselves? Why do we listen to our emotions, instead of our more rational brains? Simple: Your heart wants more, much more; it wants to go back to being madly in love, to those floating-on-air days when you first met, to the feeling of being wanted by the one man you love being around. Even if things have gone very poorly, even if he has withdrawn, won't commit, or cheated. Our hearts want him back.

And the secret we all want to know more than anything else is: Can we come back together in that communion of souls, return to that lost wild ecstasy?

Can this be done?

The answer is yes. If you know how to do it. And if you know how not to do it. If you avoid the pitfalls and siren calls that lead you to approach him in exactly the *wrong* way, as so many women do—the way that backfires and kills things off!

This is the greatest news! Using the Lasting Love Program, you can get your Beloved back into a state of *I Gotta Have Her Love,* even after he says he won't commit, even if he becomes distant, even if he cheats. But you *must* pursue a certain course of action, one that doesn't include dramatic outbursts, playing the victim, whining, or wallowing in your grief. And although there are no guarantees, this course of action can work big-time.

So what is this secret strategy no one's told you about yet? A strategy that allows him to come back and fully and completely choose you? Get ready, because it's something *so* powerful, and I'm going to share it with you.

The Most Powerful Thing You Can Do Now: Show Him What Life Is Like Without You

The way to love anything is to realize that it might be lost.
—G. K. Chesterton

The Story of Jan and Blaze

Jan, a forty-something nurse and Love Mentee, was at a very stuck place with her boyfriend, Blaze, a forty-two-year-old real estate agent. Things had been working beautifully between them as Jan used Positive Paranoia to help them come together as a couple over the course of a few years. Although they were not living under one roof, they spent most of their free time together. But that made it all the more heartbreaking when she came up against Blaze's commitment fear (She'll Use or Screw Me Over!). Here's how she describes it:

> I would casually ask Blaze, "So where are we going with all this?" Often he would say, "I'm not sure." I would laugh and say, "Because you are dying to marry me sooner rather than later!" He thought that was funny. Meanwhile I was emotionally supportive to him as the housing market tanked and he went through one job crisis after another. When he made negative comments about marriage (because he had been burnt in one before), I pointed out that we had friends who had great marriages. I would call him on changing the game by saying, "When we first got together you told me you were open to getting married. Now you are talking anti-marriage. That hurts me."
>
> Meanwhile I had decided that I wanted the financial and emotional stability of being married. I was blessed to have a gifted Love Mentor and she taught me that I deserve to ask for what I want in a nice way. To be married. To receive. That I have the right to speak up and, with her support, I was willing to walk if it didn't happen.
>
> Things got to the point where I needed Blaze to step up but he was not proposing. My Love Mentor suggested that I show him what life would be like without me. It was very hard, but I called Blaze and told him I needed more and was backing away from our relationship, I would not be having sex with him (a biggie for Blaze) and I was taking a last minute cruise with my single girlfriend (whom he disliked because she was wild with the guys) to the Caribbean. He hung up the phone on me. We didn't see each other that week and the next one was the cruise. When I got back Blaze started seeing a counselor. We met for coffee but I kept my distance and told him I was thinking about seeing other guys. Blaze started sending me these romantic animated e-cards, asking me to be patient with him. I wrote back that I was out of time and patience.

Two months after I had first told him that I was backing away from our relationship Blaze came over with the biggest gift—it was a nested set of boxes. He said that he totally realized that I was the One he wanted. As I opened the last little gift box I found his mother's heirloom diamond. With tears in his eyes, Blaze asked me to marry him. I said, "Are you absolutely sure?" He said, "Yes. I want your father to know you will be taken care of." We had not just one, but two heartfelt wedding ceremonies. He's even happier than me!

Jan was willing to leave if she did not get the commitment she needed from Blaze. Her Love Mentor helped her build this independence and then, at a strategic point, take certain steps, pulling back from him in a way that would help her man stretch, grow, and truly want marriage. And although it took a couple of months, he was able to see that it was time to either choose her or lose her.

If your Beloved is not growing in his ability to love deeply and commit to you, you may find at some point that you want to leave. If he has stonewalled, been overly defensive, distant, or even cheated, you might get to the point where your heart is emptied and you feel you must do something. If you are in this position, there is a way to take a stand that both protects you from further pain and maximizes the possibility of his realizing how much you really mean to him—like Jan did with Blaze. This is the secret I am about to teach you. First a little background.

Research shows that healthy spouses are realistic in considering the costs of losing their relationship. First is the major cost of a broken heart: the emotional, psychological, and physical pain of loss. There's also the high stress, depressive spiral, aches and pains, sleeplessness, appetite problems, loss of motivation, and other negative changes in brain chemistry that separation or rejection create. Even the immune system goes downhill. Second for married couples, there are the economic and other real costs, including a lower standard of living and loss of time with the children. Many researchers believe that these exit costs serve as barriers to separation and therefore are major underpinnings of a couple's stability.

But healthy partners do not stay together simply out of fear or need. They have the emotional strength and self-confidence to leave each other, which creates mutual respect. These traits serve as reminders that loss could really occur, and that frightening possibility tends to keep the partners on their toes. Both know that they cannot get away with repeated disrespectful, thoughtless, mean, or cold treatment of the other. In short, they do not take each other for granted.

While research has focused on how *married* couples view and use the costs of loss to promote better conduct and stability, the same may also hold true for longer-term *unmarrieds*. Being able to assess the harsh realities a breakup would bring can help a couple to work through issues that inevitably erupt. Considering the *cost of loss* also helps them appreciate each other. I have seen this dynamic work beautifully in couples who have been together for a year or more who are not married. Susan Shapiro, author of *Secrets of a Fix-Up Fanatic*, got her own proposal only after she left her boyfriend. A Cost-of-Loss Stand that shows your Beloved what life will be like without you can be the most powerful step to take when your relationship is stuck in a way that is draining, painful, and unfulfilling. This stand can propel your partner forward and help him break through his commitment or other relationship fears.

When to Take a Cost-of-Loss Stand

The following thirteen markers indicate that it may be time to help your Beloved experience the cost of loss:

1. You have been seriously involved and in love with someone for a year or more, only to find that, while you are ready, he simply cannot or will not take that next step into living together or marriage.

2. Your partner does not respond to direct requests to fulfill your most important needs.

3. He does not change his behavior when you have The Talk, use Positive Paranoia, or put the relationship on probation.

4. You feel depressed or beaten down and your self-esteem has taken a hit from being with this man.

5. You are embarrassed about being with him when he has given you so little for so long.

6. He has become emotionally distant and/or stops having sex with you.

7. He says he "just wants to be friends."

8. **He says he doesn't love you.**

9. **You have "had it" and are ready to leave.**

10. **You fight all the time.**

11. **He is verbally abusive toward you.**

12. **He cheats (more on this later).**

13. **He says he's leaving you (you should seize control, protect yourself and any personal assets or credit cards, and do the leaving yourself).**

The last six (bold) markers are strong indicators that the relationship is in its last days. Therefore, it's time for you to take a stand because in reality *you have nothing to lose*, except your dignity, your self-respect, and your precious, precious time. I know that you are probably afraid to confront him. Maybe you even feel terror or dread. Facing loss is one of the hardest things we ever do. So it is important to lay the foundation emotionally to give yourself motivation, determination, and the courage to move forward.

One huge caveat: Do not take a Cost-of-Loss Stand if you are in a potentially violent or physically abusive relationship. It could be very dangerous, and your safety is of primary concern! For recommendations on how to handle this type of situation, see the Cautions Regarding a Violent Partner section on page 229.

✎ Show Him What Life Is Like Without You— Laying the Foundation_____

Laying the foundation for taking a Cost-of-Loss Stand involves four exercises or steps: looking into the bleak future you are currently facing with your partner; working on deservedness; facing your own fear; and using a Love Mentor for support.

EXERCISE 1: *LOOK INTO YOUR FUTURE*

First, decide if you are really committed to having real love in your life. That is, if you are truly committed to giving yourself what you want and need in your future. Here are two exercises that will help you face the loveless future you are headed into with this guy:

1. Look ten years into the future with this man. How old will you be? Will you have lost any chance for bearing biological children? Realistically, what will your life be like? Write a description. Write about what that life looks like, sounds like, and feels like.
2. Arrange for a close, loving friend who knows the situation to give you feedback about what you are not getting from this man— how awful or destructive the relationship is for you. Tell her not to worry about hurting your feelings—you want the brutal truth. Ask her what she sees in your probable future with your boy-friend or partner.

EXERCISE 2: *COMPLETE THE "I DESERVE COMMITMENT!" EXERCISE*

Once you come to terms with how much this relationship is costing you, you are ready to take the next step. It's important that you develop your sense of deservedness and self-worth if you expect your partner to respect and value you. Write the following five sentences down in your journal or tablet. Then finish each sentence with a different ending.

I deserve a commitment because:

_____

I deserve a commitment because:

_____

I deserve a commitment because:

_____

I deserve a commitment because:

_____

I deserve a commitment because:

_____

Keep writing different endings until you feel a shift in your mood and in your sense of deservedness. Keep at it; the shift in mood will happen.

EXERCISE 3: *FACE YOUR OWN FEAR*

You need to face and deal with your own demon first—that is, your own fear of being alone. I want you to come from a place where you are truly willing to walk away. Facing this basic fear of loss will make you a much stronger and braver person: someone who refuses to be treated poorly; who will not tolerate disrespect or abuse; who will not settle for crumbs; and who's proud of herself and of her inner strength. You will be a warrior who protects her own Beloved self. As Eleanor Roosevelt said,

> *You gain strength, courage, and confidence by every experience in which you really stop to look fear in the face. You must do the thing which you think you cannot do.*

In order to face and reduce your own fear of loss, do the following five-part exercise:

1. Write down a number of different endings to the following sentence with whatever comes to mind: If I lose my boyfriend (or partner), I will _____.

2. Now consider each sentence that you've written and ask yourself *Is this really true? Will it really be that bad?* Usually reality is nowhere near as bad as how we fear it will be. No matter how horrible you think the breakup will be, research shows that single women who have a strong, caring network of family and friends are just about as happy as women in good marriages!

3. Write down all the loving family and friends you have and what they provide for you—unwavering support, deep appreciation, validating your worth, having fun, and so on.

4. Write out ten reasons you will be okay or better off without your boyfriend in your life.

5. Close your eyes and think back to a time in your life where you were alone and more relaxed, happy, present, or peaceful. In your mind, see it, feel it, hear what it sounds like.

Repeat part 5 until you feel a positive shift in your mood.

EXERCISE 4: *USE A LOVE MENTOR*

Having a mentor can make all the difference in helping you overcome your own fear of loss so you can take a stand for yourself. If you don't have one, I strongly suggest you find one (see Chapter 4). If you can't find one, you can e-mail me at www.lovein90days.com/contact and I will help you find a professional Love Mentor. His or her support at such a delicate and difficult time can help you re-establish your relationship at a new level of commitment—or help you get out of this painful sinkhole and move on.

A Love Mentor's support is crucial if you find this whole process hard or even impossible. If you put up with BS and keep picking partners who won't choose you, *you'll be alone for the rest of your life.*

If you do have a Love Mentor and he or she agrees that the time is right, you can have the Facing Loss Talk. First make some notes (ideally with your mentor's help) about what you want to say. It could be the most important, life-changing discussion you have ever had. And one of the most difficult discussions you will ever have. But you can do it.

The Facing Loss Talk

If I am not for myself, who will be?—*Hillel*

The first step is to be mindful of your safety and that of your kids if you have them. Safety is always your first concern. If you are in a potentially violent or physically abusive situation, it is best not to have a Facing Loss Talk with your partner because it could cause him to escalate and attack you. In my opinion, there is no future for you in this type of relationship. Your only concern is to protect yourself and your children from danger. And for that you need a carefully thought-out plan. For my specific recommendations on how to proceed, go to the section called Cautions Regarding a Violent Partner on page 229.

Assuming you are not in a violent situation, it's time to take the first step in showing your partner what his life will be like without you in it. Start by calmly telling your partner that the two of you have to have an in-person talk that is very important. When you get together, the Facing Loss Talk will have three simple parts:

1. Say that you have decided to give yourself a committed lasting love relationship with one person. You would like that

relationship to be with him because he is so wonderful in so many ways, such as [fill in the blanks here].

2. State what the problem is without blaming him. Avoid starting a fight! For example, you can say, "We fight all the time" or "We're drifting apart" or "We are not moving toward a committed relationship.

3. Finally, explain that if he can't step up to the plate and work on himself, learn how to be close and committed, move in together, get engaged, [insert your goal here], and be your forever love, that is sad and unfortunate. Because you will be (moving on, dating others, cutting off all contact—choose one distancing action from the list of Facing Loss Action Steps below). Tell him this as a simple matter of fact, a decision you have made for yourself. Not as a threat. And again, without the dramatics.

Here are three examples of the Facing Loss Talk that follow these simple steps:

- My commitment to myself is that I will be married and have children. And it's time for me to take action. I would love to have that with you because we would make unbelievable teammates and parents together. You are a generous and kind person and would make the best father. But you said you don't want marriage. So if it can't be with you, I am going to do it with another man who can be a great teammate and father to my children. Even though I love you, if you simply cannot or will not do it, I am breaking up with you completely. I am taking all my things out of your apartment and you will not be seeing me again.

- You have grown in so many ways and so have I in this relationship. But we fight so much that I end up crying and depressed. I feel beaten down. So I have decided that I am giving myself a respectful and loving relationship. That's what I need from a lover. When you are kind, you fill that need better than anyone.

But there are too many moments that are just the opposite. I need someone with more self-control, which is not something you are working on. So, I'm sad to say, I will not be helping you with your business anymore. I will be sleeping in the other bedroom and will start looking for an apartment this weekend.

- I need to feel special, chosen, and you are saying that you are not sure you love me. I have decided I am giving myself a relationship with a man who is in a deep adventure of love with me. That is my intention for my life, and I am going to fulfill it. I would love it if you could be the One; we have had the best chemistry and you really helped me open up in bed in so many ways. But if you're still not sure about us as a couple, I totally accept that. I will find a man who is crazy about me, so I will be going back on eHarmony and dating other guys.

THIRTEEN FACING LOSS ACTION STEPS

Following through on the Facing Loss Talk is *imperative*. It's a matter of self-love, integrity, and self-protection. *Don't allow yourself to endure further disappointment or to waste more of your invaluable time. Follow-through shows your partner that you mean business.*

Below are thirteen steps you can take to back away from your partner. Don't make angry or idle threats, just solid moves in the direction of the impending breakup. This backing away falls along a continuum of possibilities from not texting to a total separation. You can start with the first steps or farther along as you see fit and the circumstances demand. For example, if he's distanced himself but still expects to see you Saturday night, cancel the date. Or maybe tell him you won't help him with his project or run his errand. If the relationship has deteriorated to the point where he's stopped being affectionate with you or stopped having sex with you, tell him you'll be dating other men. If you're living together, sleep in the other room, and so on. The point is that you *must* show him what he'll be losing when you're completely gone. And to show him, you must follow through.

Here are the steps on the fear-of-loss continuum:

1. Stop texting, e-mailing, or phoning him.
2. Cancel dates.
3. Spend time away from him that you would usually spend with him.
4. Be less available for help when he needs it.
5. Be less affectionate.
6. Stop having sex.
7. Tell him you will be dating others.
8. Stop sleepovers.
9. If living together, sleep in the next room.
10. If living together, leave and spend a night at a nice hotel.
11. If living together, start packing up your stuff or his stuff.
12. If living together, move out or ask him to move out.
13. Cut off all contact with him.

You need to follow your intuition in taking these actions. If it's extremely difficult, do it one day at a time. Think, *Just for today, I will have no contact with him.* Or, *Just for today, I will switch any thoughts I have of him to thoughts of appreciation for myself or my Love Mentor, or put my attention on appreciating other men.* Day by day, you will make progress. Each day you don't have contact, you're building a bridge. One day, you'll look back and see you've actually somehow crossed the river. And just maybe, he's coming across that bridge to find you.

If you find you are backtracking into obsessing about him, consider an e-mail or text purge so that you can't go back and over-analyze your communications with him. In general, avoid people, places, and things that remind you of your ex, because they, too, can weaken you so that you get back into pursuing him.

In addition, praying or working a spiritual program every day can help to fill the hole left by the relationship. This method is similar to the powerful process used for overcoming addictions. Exercise, meditation, spending time with close friends, and meeting new guys will also lift your mood and will give you positive stimulation at this critical time. If you keep busy, you are less likely to spend hours at home feeling lousy, depressed, and pining for him. Here is how one strong and clever woman handled it when she had to completely cut off her boyfriend:

> *I hit the gym—it gives you somewhere to go every night. I also found it helpful to make appointments for myself each night—Monday, yoga class, Tuesday, cocktails with the girls, Wednesday, aerobics, Thursday, phone call with my best friend on the West Coast, Friday, movie with Match.com guy.*

No matter where you start on the fear-of-loss continuum, I want you to ramp up the support from your Love Mentor. Have him or her soothe your fears, validate you, and urge you on. Maybe call every day. Ask for your mentor to be more available and closer to you in whatever way you need, to help you set appropriate limits with your partner, and to help you decide whether he is truly stepping up or falling away.

Remember that your actions are really guided by the decision that you made a while ago: your love intention coming true. Even if you have doubts or second-guess that it will manifest, continue to affirm that intention daily. If your partner wants to give that love to you, great; if not, you intend to find someone who will. This is a stand based on real self-love. Out of that self-love, you *will* eventually attract and create a lasting and committed relationship.

TWELVE SIGNS YOUR PARTNER IS RISING TO THE OCCASION

As you cut off from your man, he may respond—and if he does, you need to decide just how to proceed. He may suddenly resume his normal e-mails or texting with you. Or call and ask to spend more time with you. But before you rush back and pretend that everything is business as usual, ask yourself, *What's really changed?* You can give him some more contact, but do not make it too easy for him. For example, in the first few interactions, challenge him by asking if he has had any further thoughts about the breakdown in your relationship. If he wants to see you, just schedule a half-hour coffee date and make sure you have something planned that you must go to afterward. Please don't end up impulsively sleeping with him again when he hasn't demonstrated much transformation. This is the kiss of death, and I have seen it happen all too often.

Remember, you are taking a stand for change in the relationship. In order to have more and more contact with you, he has to show that he is sincere. Words are cheap. More important, watch for his follow-through on actions he promises you. To help you determine whether the fear of loss has helped your guy achieve a breakthrough in his commitment fears or self-doubts, look for one of these twelve signs, ranging from modest improvements in behavior to deep transformations.

1. He shows you that he's worried or upset (this is realistic if he really cares for you!).
2. You wind up having deep, open, and honest conversations with each other about your relationship, what was missing in it, and where you'd like to take it in the future.
3. He realizes what he did wrong and is sincerely apologetic (not defensive).
4. He wants to make things up to you.
5. He shows renewed devotion toward you—perhaps helping you with a work project or other tasks.
6. He courts you in novel romantic ways (poems, thoughtful gifts, or exciting dates).
7. He is suddenly saying all the things you used to say about the relationship being great.

8. He expresses his appreciation for you and all you bring to his life.

9. If he has cheated, he cuts off contact with his lover (see the next section for more).

10. He wants to enter therapy or take a growth course either individually or with you to understand his own dynamics and to make your relationship better. If he goes into therapy, suggest seeing someone who can see both of you as well as him individually. It'll work out better that way.

11. He actively pursues moving in together.

12. He proposes marriage.

If he shows these signs and does want to get back with you, make sure you are having serious conversations about your future and what it's going to take to get your relationship to a deeper level, like counseling, apartment hunting, and/or even ring shopping.

Here is how my now happily married forty-something client Ellen described drawing a line in the sand with her live-in boyfriend, who was being nasty and critical toward her.

The Story of Ellen and Jim

> *At times when I did wonder if Jim was right for me, you [Dr. Diana] let me know that if not, fine, we'll look to find someone else. I never would have believed that. But I trusted you because of your expertise and your own successful marriage. You empowered me and made me feel independent. One night when he said awful things to me and we had a big row I calmly left and stayed at a hotel. I took a bubble bath and ate a nice dinner. I was kind to myself instead of beating myself up like I usually did. I used to be so insecure. You helped me with that. Having a mentor meant I had an ally to support me, someone who could guide me and coach me through the next phase if this was not the right person for me. Luckily, because I was strong*

I found out that he was! Our wedding was simple, no-frills, but pro-found. I was so touched to see him tear up as he watched me come down the aisle.

The bottom line is courage. No guts, no glory. Instead of investing so much time and energy in a relationship that is dragging you down, you can choose to set a limit. After all, you could be much happier in a new relationship with someone who is appreciative and actively building a future with you. A relationship should make your life better, not worse.

When Sally Met Gary: The Finale

Remember how, in Chapter 8, Sally, after a year and a half, had a major meltdown with Gary, then reconnected with her Love Mentor and worked on her Diamond Self affirmations? She called Gary to apologize to him. He promptly invited her to a reading from his novel. Sally came and told him how great he was—helping him with his fear of not measuring up. Afterward they went out to a comedy club (the "Fun" law of attraction) and retired to her place, where she filled a tub with bubble bath and the "Vivacious Vixen" proceeded to ravage him (the "Having an Affair" law of attraction).

Sally worked her Diamond Self affirmations and knew she wanted an extraordinary love, a happy family life. She felt her clock ticking and needed more from Gary. She had a bit of wussy straight talk with him, which got her nowhere. After that, Sally started feeling tense and desperate around him. They had another knock-down drag-out, where Gary confessed he just didn't have the energy to write his novel, earn a living blogging, and build a relationship with Sally. It was all too much for him. "It's me, not you," he said lamely. Sally was devastated. Here's what she wrote to her Love Mentor, Beth:

Since then we haven't slept together in two weeks and the daily texts are history. I am at my wit's end. And still he had the nerve to ask me for help with editing another chapter of his freakin' novel! Sadly, I hate to say, I did it!

Beth told Sally that it was time for the big move, the Facing Loss Talk. Here's how Sally describes what happened next:

Beth and I worked on my love intention and did a journaling exercise about me deserving marriage and kids. She suggested that I sit Gary down, calmly and purposefully, and say that my commitment to myself is that I will be married and have children. And it's time for me to take action.

At first I refused to confront Gary and then canceled my next appointment with Beth. She called me and pointed out that my lack of self-worth and killer beliefs were taking over and that by rejecting her and taking Gary's meager crumbs I was wasting more precious time. Beth told me to stand up and face my demons before it was too late.

Then one night, I saw Gary out drinking with his friends and flirting with another woman. I was infuriated. I walked right up to him and told him we had to talk. He came outside and I delivered the bomb. For some reason I felt dreadfully calm as I said something like this to Gary: "I am done. I wanted a family life with you because I knew we would make great teammates and parents together. And you would make the best father. But you said you don't want marriage. So if it can't be with you, I am going to do it with another man who can be a great partner and father to my children. Even though I love you, if you simply cannot do it, I am breaking up with you completely. I am not going to be editing your work anymore. In fact, we are not going to be friends anymore."

By the time I was done, Gary was shaken. I was shaken. I left and called Beth on the way home. She was very proud of me. The next morning I went over to Gary's place and started collecting the few things I had left there. He was stone quiet. Then he asked for

*more time. I shook my head no. I didn't hear from him for a while,
but I kept busy with my friends, even went online and put my profile
back up. I got hits from some interesting-looking guys and went out
on a few coffee dates.*

*Three weeks later, Gary called me and told me that he loved me
and wanted to work on things. He came over and we made passionate love. Beth had me stay strong. But this was the turning point. A
few months later Gary proposed and I moved into his place.*

Sally and Gary are happily planning an intimate wedding at Cabo.
Such is the power of the Facing Loss Talk.

What If He Has Cheated?

If your partner has cheated on you, the Facing Loss Talk is the same,
but needs to be expanded to include reparations or symbolic acts
that you require in order to give him a second chance. These should
include promising not to see the other woman if she is still in the
picture. In fact, if she is, you may want him to call her in front of you
to end it. Other reparations may include:

- Confessing all the details of the affair.
- Listening quietly while you express all your disappointment and
  outrage.
- Making a sincere apology.
- Reassuring you that he will never cheat again.
- Courting you and showering you with attention, symbolic gifts,
  or helpful acts.
- Getting a new job if the woman he cheated with works at the
  same company.
- Going to couples counseling with you and/or getting individual
  therapy for himself.

- Taking the next step forward by showing that he chooses you and you alone. For example, he asks you to marry him and you get engaged and/or move in together.

Only you can decide what acts of reparation will help to make it right in your heart of hearts. But I've seen many couples get through the gut-wrenching firestorm of cheating and emerge stronger and better than ever.

ONCE A CHEATER, ALWAYS A CHEATER?

Let's say he is saying all the right things: He was an idiot for breaking your sweet trust; the fling he had was just a fluke, a colossal mistake; he wants you and only you. He is willing to make reparations, go to therapy, or even marry you. He seems like a new man. But you may be wondering, *How do I know if he will cheat again?*

You may feel torn, like you want to take your cheating partner back but feel like it is a point of pride not to. You think, *Maybe I should just dive into that online pool, start looking for some great profiles, and forget all about it.*

Well, before you do this, consider that infidelity, while not the norm, is still fairly commonplace. The National Research Opinion Center at the University of Chicago shows that among married couples, about 22 percent of men and 13 percent of women admit they've cheated at least once. Even spouses who describe themselves as "at least pretty happy" with their marriages have reported that they themselves had an affair. Yet according to research on divorcing couples, most people don't break up because of an affair; they separate because they've lost their feelings of closeness, appreciation, friendship, and connection. So despite the popular belief that to take him back is idiotic, many prominent couples therapists and researchers believe that you can get through his having an affair and build beyond it.

In my clinical experience, "Once a cheater, always a cheater" is just not true. There are many people who have learned painful lessons from previous mistakes and have gone on to become great husbands and wives. Couples that have decent chemistry and benefits for both partners *can* work through the crisis of an affair. Not only that, they can become closer and put an end to cheating once and for all.

Not everyone is worth your trust, though; there are players or sex addicts who will cheat and cheat again. These are the ones you truly have to watch out for. Here are thirteen red flags that may indicate he is cheating again:

1. He's less affectionate.
2. He's spending less time with you. He may be "working late," having "business dinners," or "going to the gym" more.
3. He's less interested in sex.
4. He's suddenly taking trips you can't go on.
5. He's got new hobbies that don't include you.
6. You get mysterious phone calls with hang-ups.
7. His cell is turned off at times you normally reach him.
8. You find credit card bills for unexplained hotel stays or gifts.
9. He's more distant, angry, or picky.
10. **He smells of perfume.**
11. **He has lipstick or a strange-colored strand of hair on his clothes.**
12. **He is defensive or lies if you ask him where he's been.**
13. **You find romantic texts or e-mail messages from another woman on his phone or computer.**

The last four signs in particular are very telling and require immediate action on your part by taking these three steps:

1. Ask your partner if he is having an affair and observe his reactions carefully. Be cool and watch his nonverbal and verbal behavior. Your partner may turn or look away, change the topic,

or bite his nails. He may give you strong defensive reactions: acting like a victim, saying something like, "How could you say that after I've been so good to you?" or getting angry and even accusing you of cheating. He may even laugh disdainfully and say, "Are you crazy? I love you!" Not good! Because all of these verbal and nonverbal reactions may be signs that he is guilty.

2. If things don't feel right, trust your gut and dig deeper. If you're living together, make sure you know where all the money is—check the various bank accounts and other assets that you have access to in order to protect yourself. See if there have been any unusual withdrawals. Go through the joint credit cards looking for hotel or other mysterious charges. Look at phone bills and check repeated numbers you don't recognize. Go where your partner is supposed to be—show up when he's "working late" or "playing poker." If you suspect a certain person, go to her house and look for your partner's car.

3. Assuming it is safe, get your courage up and present the evidence you find to your boyfriend.

If your partner has indeed started another affair or continued with the old one, it's time to protect yourself from any further heartbreak by ending the relationship. If he's a player or sex addict, *move on*. Let someone else deal with his recovery.

Cautions Regarding a Violent Partner

Domestic violence is the leading cause of injury to women in the United States and affects 1.3 million women per year. If your boyfriend or partner has a violent temper and/or subjects you or your children to physical abuse, I do not recommend taking a Cost-of-Loss Stand with him. In fact, if you act assertively and take a stand like this, he could easily lose control, escalate his violent behavior, and injure you or the kids. Therefore, you need to be smart about extricating yourself from danger. For that you have to develop a plan of action. And it is best not to do that on your own. Get help from trained professionals who deal with domestic violence situations every day. Here are a number of steps you can take to help ensure the safety of yourself (and your kids):

- Locate a safe and anonymous women's shelter or crisis center and work with staff there to extricate yourself safely from the situation.
- Consult with a seasoned therapist who specializes in abuse to help you shape a plan.
- See if you can move in with family members.
- If you are in the United States, call the National Domestic Violence hotline at 1-800-799-7233; if not, call the domestic violence hotline in your country.
- Take legal action, such as getting a restraining order.
- If you are in immediate danger, call 911 or the police.

Remember that, in my opinion, there is no future with a violent partner. But there is a future for you (and your children). So get professional help and move on with your life.

Ending Things Gracefully

Whether your boyfriend or partner has cheated repeatedly or just not come through for you, you may reach the point where you need to exit the relationship. Your days, months, and years are irreplaceable! Are you going to continue wasting them on a painful relationship? I hope not. Assuming you are dealing with a nonviolent partner, it's best if possible to end things with integrity in a win–win way so that both of you can feel complete and whole about it—like there has been a net gain. There is no benefit to holding on to the notion that you are right and he is wrong, to disappointment, blame, anger, or guilt. Those feelings will only poison you, resurrect your killer beliefs, and taint your future. Is that what you want to live in? A future of bitterness and cynicism?

So here's what I want you to say to yourself. *The relationship was what it was. It was a learning experience.* You have both learned important lessons. From this appreciative and mature place, meet with your partner, share what you have gained, and tell him that it's over.

Now begin to regroup. Follow the steps in my book *Love in 90 Days*. It has dozens of easy-to-follow and proven ways to meet and date lots of terrific men. You can work the program quickly or at your own pace and find someone who is committed to a shared future with you. Since that book was published, I've received thousands of e-mails from thankful readers who have used it to dramatically improve their dating and love life.

Healing from Heartbreak

...the selfsame well from which your laughter rises was oftentimes filled with your tears. And how else can it be? The deeper that sorrow carves into your being, the more joy you can contain.—*Khalil Gibran*

Ending a relationship is always hard, even if you are the one who pulls the plug. But this is the time for you to turn your mind away from your boyfriend or partner and toward yourself. Think about how much you have grown, worked on yourself, and given to others; what a well-intentioned, loving, and good person you are (even if you've had your bitchy moments—we all do).

You do not have to languish in pain. There are proven ways that will help you nip suffering in the bud so that it doesn't grow like an out-of-control weed and take over the garden that is your mind, body, and spirit. It is imperative that you get on this gardening project right away.

Here are five proven techniques to heal quickly from heartbreak. Use all five daily, if possible. If you do, you will radically cut short the amount of time you need to recover and be on your way to creating a new and happier love partnership.

1. GET MOVING!

Exercise has been shown to reduce feelings of loneliness, create uplifting endorphins, and reduce depression. Exercise can decrease depression as effectively as Prozac or behavioral therapy. I know you don't feel like it, but just get up and start with a few minutes at a time. Ask a girlfriend to be your workout buddy, so you are exercising and plugging into a support system. Assuming your doctor allows it, do a little more and more each day. That awful pain you are feeling will start to lift.

2. WATCH WHAT YOU PUT OR DON'T PUT IN YOUR MOUTH

Don't punish yourself by overeating, starving yourself, or drinking too much. As is well documented, these activities will wreak havoc on your brain chemistry and drag you down lower.

3. GET SLEEP

Sleep is very important in regulating mood, but it may be hard to come by. Consider starting a regular relaxation or meditation program—these have been shown to reduce stress, increase relaxation, and promote deep restfulness. Also, working out will help in the sleep department. Creating your own bedtime ritual with a long

hot bath and quiet activities (no late-night computer work) c
soothing. Read, listen to restful music, or watch something boring
on TV that puts you to sleep. Try to go to bed at the same time every
night.

4. TALK IT OUT WITH LOVING FRIENDS

In one UCLA study, talking about negative feelings lessened activity in the pain-feeling part of participants' brains. The researchers
concluded that a good remedy for heartache is to spend time sharing
with close friends, because this activity causes the brain to release
natural opioids, which are like the painkillers found in opium. So
make a beeline for your Love Mentor if you have one. And if you
don't, consider getting one. Also, call up your good friends—even
phone dates can be uplifting. Most important, don't isolate yourself
from your loved ones.

5. WORK ON YOUR THOUGHTS

Go back to Chapters 2 and 3 and work on any killer beliefs, like *All
men are jerks*; *There is something wrong with me*; or *True love doesn't exist.*
These beliefs may have popped up again and like weeds are threatening to take over your spiritual garden. Practice your Diamond Self
exercises (see Chapter 8) as needed to help you stop being down on
yourself. And then practice your love intention exercises from Chapter 3 to refocus your thoughts in a positive direction. Don't let the
weeds in your mind take root.

If you find that you cannot stop or slow down the depressive and
hopeless thoughts, consider therapy and/or medication. Take a
personal growth course. My students and clients have successfully
used the Landmark Forum (see www.landmarkeducation.com),
or The Work by Byron Katie (see www.thework.com) to alter their

"stinking thinking" and negative self-talk. Nothing, and I mean nothing, is more important than you getting control over your internal dialogue.

Choose Your Own Happiness

Taking a real stand for yourself and at the same time helping your partner to experience the cost of losing you is very courageous. No matter what happens, choose to create your own happiness.

Know that I am with you, brave one. And hold these inspiring words by Jennifer Welwood close to your heart:

> *Willing to experience aloneness,*
> *I discover connection everywhere;*
> *Turning to face my fear,*
> *I meet the warrior who lives within;*
> *Opening to my loss,*
> *I gain the embrace of the universe;*
> *Surrendering into emptiness,*
> *I find fullness without end.*

11

Should We Live Together First?

NEW RELATIONSHIP RESEARCH, SURPRISING ANSWERS

> Come live with me, and be my love,
> And we will some new pleasures prove
> Of golden sands, and crystal brooks,
> With silken lines, and silver hooks.
>
> —*John Donne, "The Bait"*

Living in sin. Shacking up. Playing house. A test drive. Cohabitation. No matter what you call it, it's become de rigueur as the next big step after The Talk or the trial phase before getting engaged or married. If it seems like all your friends are doing it, there's a reason: Since the 1960s, marriage rates have declined while the number of couples living together has gone up tenfold, and for the first time in U.S. history there are more couples living together than married. This trend is continuing. About a quarter of unmarried women ages twenty-five through thirty-nine are living with a partner. And about 53 percent of all first marriages were preceded by living together.

So is it really the best next step in your relationship? This is a key question to ask on the Lasting Love Program. If you want to get married, will it actually help you figure out if the marriage will last before you take the leap? How different is it from where you might be right now, spending many, or most, nights at each other's place? And what about the economics of it—is it really a fewer-strings-attached, safer, more economically sound alternative to tying the knot? Is there an answer, one way or the other, that predicts if this will make your relationship better, or worse?

Before you take the leap, I want you to have all the facts you need to make an informed decision. Believe it or not, this life-altering choice often happens without a great deal of planning or discussion. For younger women in their twenties or thirties, it is often perceived as a natural but unspoken step toward marriage. Guess what? For men the same age, the moving-in decision may have *little to do* with eventually saying "I do." So before you unpack your boxes (or let him unpack his), it's imperative that you get on the same page.

For many older couples who have already been through the family-children-divorce scenario, moving in together is the end-point companionship they seek—the relational Holy Grail. Still, that doesn't mean you can move right in without giving it some serious consideration. Why am I being so firm about this? Because moving in together is almost always a complicated and messy venture.

Angie and Jared's Home Sweet Home

Angie, a sparkly thirty-year-old graduate student in public health, ser-endipitously found Jared, her super-secret crush from high school, on Facebook. They wrote on each other's walls, chatted up a storm, and fell deeply into what seemed to be a magical connection. They used the L-word liberally with each other and called each other smoochie names. Cut to one year later. Angie's apartment lease was up. Jared, science teacher geek, had a roomy but knickknacked loft downtown, close to Angie's school. She was already spending so much time at his place...so they decided she would move in. There wasn't much discussion about it. Angie ensconced herself complete with Miffles the cat, right in the midst of Jared's clutter, and promptly began to reorganize and clean it all up. Angie had been through this before, when she lived with her ex, Jonathan. She was used to putting her touch on a guy's place.

Things had ended badly with Jonathan, when his drinking buddies took over the place one time too many, but this time Angie felt differently. She knew in every cell of her body, down to the tips of her toes, that Jared was the One. Angie was absolutely sure that they would have the whole white-picket-fence package, complete with two dogs, three kids, and, of course, Miffles II.

So, dear reader, do you think that this couple is likely to:

a.) Live together happily ever after?
b.) Get married and go through a yucky divorce?
c.) Live together unhappily ever after?
d.) Part ways after about a year and a half?
e.) Not enough information.

More Research Clues

Research on living together done over the last fifteen years sheds light on what might happen to our daring duo. Does living together really ensure a happy marriage? Well, most studies done from 1995 forward show that couples who lived together before marriage have higher divorce rates than couples who didn't. Other findings include poorer mental and physical health, including depression, especially for women.

More studies continue to show advantages for marrieds over cohabitors, especially if you're female. One explanation for these findings is that the burden placed on women is not compensated for in a living-together environment. Since women are known to do the lion's share of housework, the thinking is that a gal would go from taking care of her own place to having to do the housework and other domestic errands in the two-person apartment or house that she shared with her boyfriend. All this extra work occurs without the benefit of the financial and emotional security that comes with the commitment of marriage.

The most current research shows that if a person (like Angie) has lived with multiple partners, she or he will likely end up in a breakup or divorce. Other studies of living together show that after about a year and a half, cohabitors either marry or break up, with a 50 percent breakup rate. Given all this, we can say that living together for many couples is a coin toss with no guarantees.

But that's not the whole story. The age of the cohabitors seems to matter quite a bit in terms of outcomes. Older partners (over fifty) who live together report more favorable psychological and physical well-being than their younger counterparts. And longer, more stable relationships. We'll get into this later in the chapter.

Taking all this research into consideration, what do you think happened to Angie and Jared? Have you changed your guess? Here are your choices once again:

a.) Live together happily ever after?
b.) Get married and go through a yucky divorce?
c.) Live together unhappily ever after?
d.) Part ways after about a year and a half?

If you answered *(d) They parted ways after about a year and a half,* you are correct! They broke up and are still both single, although Angie thinks she may be getting engaged to her new guy.

So is there anything to be gained by living together? Actually...yes!

The Plus Side of Playing House

Come live with me and be my love,
And we will all the pleasures prove
That valleys, groves, hills, and fields,
Woods or steepy mountain yields.

And we will sit upon the rocks,
Seeing the shepherds feed their flocks,
By shallow rivers, to whose falls
Melodious birds sing madrigals.

And I will make thee beds of roses
And a thousand fragrant posies...
                              —Christopher Marlowe

A bed of roses and posies? Sort of. Living together means more physical closeness, and that simple fact alone bonds the two of you together biologically. Sleeping together, cuddling, spooning, and even simple hugs and kisses release the bonding hormone oxytocin. If you have sex more often, you will also release more oxytocin. Throughout the whole sexual act, you will experience increases in this hormone—and your oxytocin levels stay high afterward. Meantime, he gets a blast of oxytocin during his orgasm.

Another plus is to be able to experience the joy of putting together a household with a mate who can team well with you, especially if you have never done it before. There is a nesting instinct that makes it very pleasurable to set up house together. The planning, the sorties to Bed Bath & Beyond, the picking out of colors for the living room, the setting aside of a potential nursery space, the creation of a cozy and romantic hideaway bedroom all create a great shared feeling of accomplishment, of moving forward as adults and the fulfillment of the dream of living happily ever after, once and for all.

But Will It Last?

Here's where recent research and my own clinical work point. The critical success factor for couples who live together and manage to create a more lasting relationship is their commitment to persevering and staying together. Two prominent studies based on broad samples of couples living together confirm this finding. Both studies found that when a woman lived with her future husband—that is, when there was a commitment—there was not an elevated risk of divorce as compared with noncohabitors who simply got married. In my book *Love in 90 Days,* I show that commitment is one of the eight habits of lasting love relationships. That same element of *mutual investment in a shared future* needs to be developed during the living-together phase if the couple is to make it. This means they are more willing to work on the inevitable differences, disappointments, and setbacks that occur in that most complicated of arrangements, a love relationship.

Without commitment, unmarried couples end up splitting apart as soon as the problems of everyday life confront them. For younger couples, that commitment often includes engagement and marriage. For older ones it means being life partners. In Angie and Jared's case there was no commitment to a shared future. Living together was a convenience and an experiment. We now know how that went.

What About After Fifty?

In less than ten years, the number of people over fifty who are living together has just about doubled, to more than 2.2 million. As I mentioned earlier, for older singles who have already had children or been through a divorce—or the death of a spouse—moving in together is often their final goal. Only about 10 percent of these cohabitors have never been married. They are interested in companionship and not in building a whole new family life. Is sharing digs a good move for these singles? Will it help or hurt the development of a deeper dedication and caring in the couple?

Before we answer that, let me share a story: My client Janeen, a fifty-one-year-old glam event planner, met Julio at her local AA meeting in Greenwich Village. Julio was a fifty-three-year-old dead ringer for the singer Marc Anthony, definitely not the Nordic type she usually went for. But Julio glowed with born-again energy when he presented his AA qualification, the story of losing it all and finding a Higher Power. Julio had destroyed his marriage through heavy drinking with his broker buddies and their clients. Then he lost his job when his firm was taken over. Julio realized that he had messed up his life and reconnected with his church, AA, and finally a new career. Now reborn as a yoga teacher and clean for five years, he radiated hope and compassion to the members of his 12-step group. Janeen herself had been in recovery for three years.

Janeen and Julio had much in common as they both went about their mission of sponsoring the newly sober group members. It was inevitable that they would start dating, and with their sponsors' blessings they eventually became exclusive. Then Janeen's company went under in the wake of the recession and she lost her job. Finances were tight, and she could no longer afford her pricey Village digs. Julio sprang into action and found a tiny but decent one-bedroom apartment in Brooklyn. He jokingly got down on one knee and presented Janeen with a cigar band, asking her to live soberly and spiritually forever after with him.

Janeen wasn't sure. But they discussed all the ramifications—how they would handle his visitation with his fifteen-year-old, where she would get to smoke her cigs (outside). They talked about dividing up household chores and finances. They shared their dreams, fears, and visions of a future together. They even talked about which one of them, if things tanked, would move out. And finally Janeen said yes.

They rolled up their sleeves, gave the place a good painting, and moved in. The question for you, dear reader, is this: Is there likely to be a great *Moonstruck* ending here? More specifically, based on the latest research on cohabitation, are Janeen and Julio likely to:

a.) Live together happily for at least five years?
b.) Get married and go through a yucky divorce?
c.) Live together unhappily ever after?
d.) Part ways after about a year and a half?
e.) Get married and live happily ever after?

Well, as I mentioned earlier, the latest research on living together shows that older cohabitors form happier and more stable relationships than younger couples. They have fewer arguments, less conflict, and spend more quality time together than younger couples. They also stay together longer, five years versus less than two for their younger counterparts. And as I said earlier, marriage plans don't seem to be a big factor for older couples any longer. So if you picked *(a) They lived together happily for at least five years*, for Janeen and Julio you are probably right: They've already lasted three years, and Janeen tells me she's never been happier!

In addition, even when older partners are compared with married couples, while marrieds often are happier than their cohabitating counterparts, there is no significant difference in general satisfaction or well-being. In a 2010 study, cohabitors and marrieds reported similar levels of relationship quality in terms of emotional satisfaction, pleasure, time together, and openness. While marrieds were far more likely to rate their union as "very happy" than cohabitors, they were also more likely to report that their partners made "unreasonable demands" on them.

There may be several reasons that explain this dramatic shift in living together for older couples becoming more acceptable. First, women don't want the additional burden of care (both financial and physical) for older men who will probably get sick and die before they do. No less an authority than my own mother gave this reason for not remarrying after my dad died. Second, she, like so many other women, wanted to maintain her own financial independence and not mix her money with anyone else's. Finally, she wanted to ensure that her money passed to her five daughters after her death.

Ironically, my mother's best friend started living with a man when she was seventy-five in order to save on living expenses. This same woman literally had fainted many years earlier upon learning that her own daughter was living "in sin."

All this research is great, but what does it mean for your relationship? How do you apply it to make living together work, you might be wondering? Well, there are certain preconditions that set you up for success. What we know from studying healthy long-term couples is that when there is planning, discussion, and a clear commitment to a lasting relationship where differences will be worked out—lasting love is more likely.

The Preconditions

While it might feel tempting to just jump into living with your Beloved, there are certain preconditions that you should establish before you take the plunge:

- **You feel comfortable and have a value system that does not prohibit unmarrieds living together.** Just because "everyone" is doing it doesn't mean that it's right for you. Don't be coerced into anything that does not fit with your spiritual or religious path. If he wants to and you don't because of your value system, stand your ground and, if need be, have a Facing Loss Talk with him about how you see marriage as a special covenant with God. If he is crazy about you and a partner who can live a life with you that honors your values, it may be tense for a while, but you will work things out.

- **Your love intention, and even more important, his love intention, is to create a lasting relationship together.** Remember, especially among younger singles, moving in often is simply an experiment for a guy, while it carries the promise of lasting love in a woman's mind.

- **You have worked on your killer beliefs and fears.** If you have negative thinking or a great deal of fear, chances are the arrangement will not work out. You will tend to worry, whine, sulk, or attack when the inevitable breakdowns and disappointments occur. In order to move forward in a relationship, your own self-sabotaging beliefs have to be observed and managed so that they do not tank things.

- **You have developed your Diamond Self and a real sense of deservedness when it comes to love.** This means you will be able to express your needs and wants clearly and help your partner to fulfill them. And you will be able to be at your best and fulfill his as well—so things will work out.

- **You have determined that he is the One.** (Review Chapter 7.) This is a guy who is, for the most part:

  a.) crazy about you,
  b.) willing to grow, and
  c.) meeting the basics in terms of being a best friend and teammate in life.

This means he truly appreciates how special you are and is in love with you. He is not perfect, but he is self-reflective, knows he's flawed, and is willing to work on himself. He's generally a good person who has integrity and a work ethic. You have chemistry with him. You can have straight, honest talk with him, where both of you are clear, and you can come to a win–win understanding with each other (even if you agree to disagree). Most important, he is invested in a future with you.

- **The overall trend is that the relationship is getting better.** You are getting closer, understanding each other better, more devoted to each other, and sharing more time and space in a happy way. Even though there are disappointments and fights, you tend to come together and work things through. When you step back and look at the relationship, you see that over the months or years it has gotten better and better.

- **You understand that there are other alternatives.** You can learn almost as much about a partner by spending a great deal of time together or sleeping over at each other's places as you can by living together. You may be able to maintain two places and spend almost all your time together in order to get a sense of whether you want this person to be your life partner.

- **You know there is a downside to work through.** Moving in will make some things easier, but it will also make other things harder. The toilet seat will always be up. The track-smeared underwear will constantly be in the laundry. The trash will be piling up in the kitchen and smelly to boot, even if he was supposed to take it out yesterday. And there is no place of your own to escape to. This will tend to bring up commitment fears, smothering fears, grass-is-greener fears, and more anxieties that may be lurking in both your heads. Chances are you will fight. Even if you had planned and discussed how things will work out, they never work out exactly as you planned.

- **You realize that once you move in, it is hard to get out.** That means you could be wasting a great deal of your time with this guy. Remember that bonding hormone, oxytocin? Well, it will lure you to stay with him, even if it turns out that he's an alcoholic, even if he starts acting like a slacker or an a**hole. Your body will still long for his touch, long to sleep with him. The oxytocin will tend to keep you tethered to living with him, even if it's not good for you. Then there are the hard logistics of separation. There is a wad of cash to put together to secure a new place, and a whole bunch of stuff that has to be moved. This is true whether it's him or you that is vacating. Finally, there are all those cozy day-to-day habits of hanging out—the comfort and companionship—that will be lost forever. In sum, there is tremendous inertia that occurs when you shack up together. All of these things will hold you like superglue, even though you may be throwing away your never-to-be-recovered childbearing years with him, even though you're miserable together. Please remember: Once you move in, it's hard to move out.

So think it all through carefully before you sign that lease!

Let's say you and your partner have met most of the preconditions. You are taking the plunge. How do you make sure you have a happily-ever-after?

The Rules: Seven Conditions That Make Living Together Work

Following my seven rules for living together will guarantee that you optimize the chances for lasting love:

Rule 1: You make it a point to keep having fun together.

Rule 2: You and your partner have clearly agreed about the financial arrangements. (You pay half the rent; he covers the car and insurance.)

Rule 3: You have an agreement with your Beloved about housekeeping responsibilities that feels fair. (Remember, most women wind up doing the lion's share of the laundry, cleaning, and cooking—and by the way, they tend to get fatter doing it. Probably less time at the gym!)

Rule 4: You have win–win household living rules. (He has the man cave in the garage; you get the den for your artwork.)

Rule 5: You have a clear commitment from him to the shared future you really want.

Rule 6: If your goal is marriage, you are engaged.

Rule 7: You have discussed what happens if things go south and you split up. You know who will move out. You get the puppy; he gets the flat screen.

I am very proud of you for getting to this point in your love relationship. Congratulations! It is truly an exciting time for you to be considering the union of living together. This may be one of your final goals in working with this book. Or you may be thinking not only of moving in, but also about getting engaged. In either case, be sure to read the last two chapters, which cover the surprising benefits of marriage and the latest research on how to make passionate love last.

Whatever you decide to do (and for all those who are simply reading along to learn), I am wishing you tremendous success at this time on your greatest adventure, the adventure of lasting love.

> Some think that love is all flowers and good times, but I think that love is more than just that. Love is the bad, as well as the better, not lived alone, but a journey together. Something that only the closest can share...
>
> —*Anonymous*

12

Thinking of Getting Married?

WHAT YOU NEED TO KNOW NOW

Why Marriage? Because to the depths of me, I long to
love one person,
With all my heart, my soul, my mind, my body...

Because I need a forever friend to trust with the
intimacies of me,
Who won't hold them against me,
Who loves me when I'm unlikable,
Who sees the small child in me, and
Who looks for the divine potential of me...

Because I need to lie in the warmth of the night
With someone who thanks God for me,
With someone I feel blessed to hold...

Because marriage means opportunity
To grow in love in friendship...

Because marriage is a discipline
To be added to a list of achievements...
—*Mari Nichols-Haining*

L et's say you have worked things through and come together in a marvelous way with your Beloved, with or without the aid of a few Cost-of-Loss skirmishes. You've even gone so far in the commitment process that marriage looks like the next step, and he's willing, if not eager, to go for it. All systems are go, right?

But what about all the skeptics who claim that marriage is a bad deal for women today? My many friends (especially women) from around the world on my dating and relationship advice YouTube channel, www.youtube.com/lovein90days, are constantly posting comments like "marriage is dying," and living together is "so much better." In her best seller *Committed: A Skeptic Makes Peace with Marriage*, Elizabeth Gilbert quotes research showing that married women are less successful, more depressed, less healthy, and more likely to die a violent death than single women. Citing what she calls the "Marriage Benefit Imbalance," Gilbert points out that, while women fare poorly, men actually benefit physically and psychologically from marriage. Nonetheless, she winds up, like many other women, getting married herself by the end of her book. Hmm.

In response to this controversy, I decided to look at the hundreds of studies conducted around the world on the impact of marriage on women's mental health, longevity, lifestyle, general well-being, and finances. We'll look at these key areas one by one and see what the latest research shows. Here's a secret I learned when I got my Ph.D. in clinical psychology: To find more of the whole truth, don't rely on one study or one author's work, especially if there are others that contradict it. So while I admire Gilbert as a writer, I have to say I'm disappointed that she relied on the work of one sociologist who did her research way back in the 1970s.

The "Marriage Benefit Imbalance" was first popularized by Jessie Bernard in her book *The Future of Marriage*. This work created a lasting myth that women do not profit from marriage. Bernard argued that there are two marriages: his and hers. She tried to prove this by showing: that women were unpaid for their parenting and domestic responsibilities as housewives and were not as valued as men are for their work; that men, by controlling the finances, had power over women in marriage; and that married men lived longer than single men. Bernard also claimed that married women, on the other hand, did not live longer than single gals. In her comparison studies, she said that married men reported they were happier than single men but also that they were happier than married women.

And the list of the supposedly toxic effects of marriage continued. Bernard claimed that more women than men are unhappy in marriage; so unhappy, in fact, that they are depressed and have poorer mental health than single women. In short, Bernard believed that marriage was a good deal for men and not so kind to women.

Well, a lot has changed since the 1970s. Marriage is no longer the hallowed institution it once was. Greater numbers of unmarried couples are living together; the age at first marriage is higher; more women are participating in higher education, have better-paying jobs, and enjoy brighter career opportunities; and greater numbers of women are choosing to become single mothers, through either adoption or insemination with donor sperm. Women are more independent all the way around. So they need marriage less. And yet, despite all of these advances, *many women still want to get married.*

Let's face it: We all would agree that nothing is worse than an abusive marriage and that for many women single life works just fine, thank you. But I think it's worth understanding, while you are working the Lasting Love Program, whether marriage really *is* a bad deal for women and what marriage can and can't do for you. And that's exactly what we'll do together in this chapter as we look at women, marriage, mental health, longevity, general health, money, and the overall impact of marital satisfaction.

Marriage and Mental Health

Ah, yes. Marriage and mental health. What image does that conjure up for you? Happiness? Stress? Your depressed mom? Depression affects about twenty million adults in the United States alone and is therefore one of the most common diseases. The bad news here is that women are twice as likely as men to suffer from it. Depression has been widely studied and has been found to correlate very highly with other markers of mental health. Research done in the 1970s claimed that married women were more depressed than single women or married men. Is that still true today? The short answer is no.

In 2007, using data from the largest national studies ever done, researchers found that marriage *reduces* the blues in both men and women. Here's the skinny:

- In studies of those continuously married versus those single or living together, researchers found that entry into marriage significantly reduces depressive symptoms in women (and men).
- Those who were single and stable reported increases in depression over a five-year period, while the married women did not.
- These findings are not due to the fact that those who got married were already less depressed. Depression doesn't seem to be a factor in who gets married.
- A stable marriage helps women ward off the blues. Other studies show that when we look at overall mental health, married women may be happier and emotionally healthier than singles.

What about the argument that marriage is better for men than it is for women? We know that married men are far better off than single men. Granted, men may benefit from marriage even more than women, but those differences can be accounted for by the nature of male single life: The bachelor tends to have more unhealthy habits and is less likely to have emotional and social support than the bachelorette. So when he marries, he steps away from the beer and pizza to a much healthier lifestyle. Single women, on the other hand, are not significantly different in lifestyle from their married counterparts.

So where do married women suffer relative to singles? In two areas: when they are in bad marriages and when they have kids. It's as simple as that. Women in bad marriages report having trouble sleeping, not feeling okay, and being more stressed than those who say they are in a satisfying marriage. This is true even in studies that control for being prone to depression or having kids. In other words, a good marriage may contribute a lot more to a woman's well-being than we previously thought.

As to having kids, women with young kids have more stress than women without kids. Duh! Oh, and they feel they have no time for themselves, for self-caretaking, so they report even more stress. Duh, duh! Let's not get confused and blame it on those vows. If you're looking to have kids, be prepared for a heck of a lot more responsibility and a more stressful life than being single without kids. If you are married and one of those lucky few who have a househusband, you'll have more responsibility outside the home and have the privilege of feeling guilty about being a "bad mom." There's no winning here, ladies—stress comes along with young kids and teenagers. Of course, if you're a single mother with kids, countless studies have shown that your stress level is much higher than marrieds with kids or singles with no kids.

Bottom line: Contrary to myth, a stable marriage tends to be emotionally uplifting for women. It can reduce depression and improve overall mental health. Does it help men even more? Yeah, but what woman didn't know that?

Marriage and Longevity, Lifestyle, and General Health and Well-Being

Gilbert cites research that married women are more likely to suffer a violent death than singles and are also more likely to die younger. Let me get these two out of the way quickly. No way!

Let me put my doctor's hat back on.

For more than a hundred years, researchers around the world have found that married people, both men and women, live longer than singles.

- In a recent review of fifty-three studies of the effect of marriage on longevity, researchers found that mortality rates are about 18 percent lower for marrieds in comparison with singles, and *there was no significant difference in that effect between guys and gals.*
- Another U.S. study conducted over an eight-year period showed that the odds of mortality are 39 percent higher for widows, 27 percent higher for the divorced, and a whopping 58 percent higher for never-married singles in comparison with marrieds.
- Controlling for age, the longevity effect held true at older ages for both sexes and was greater for younger men than younger women.

In other words, married women tend to live longer than single, divorced, or widowed gals. Period.

As to the claim that violence is greater for married women, that's just plain not so. For example, some of the top researchers in the field, in their original studies and in their reviews of the literature, have concluded that for young women marriage is a much less dangerous place than living with someone, and (depending on the study) is either as safe as or safer than being single.

Bottom line: A Mrs. who still has her Mr. lives longer.

LIFESTYLE

When it comes to lifestyle, we find a mixed bag of results. For younger women (and men) who get married, booze consumption and binge drinking go way down in the first few years of marriage and stay down in comparison with singles. There is also some reduction in pot smoking, but more for guys than gals.

On the other hand, recent studies show that marriage probably has no impact on that killer vice, smoking cigarettes. Plus, getting married is likely to lead to slowly packing on extra pounds. In comparisons with singles, married women and men gained about five pounds over a ten-year period. Much of that gain may come from the fact that marrieds exercise about 15 percent less per week than their single friends.

Bottom line: For women, marriage tends to be beneficial in some lifestyle areas like drinking, yet problematic when it comes to hitting the gym and keeping your waistline from expanding.

GENERAL HEALTH AND WELL-BEING

Many studies conducted around the world show that married people are more likely to reach the Holy Grail of a longer, healthier life. While the longevity issue is beyond doubt, the better-physical-health claims...well, it depends. Many of the studies have been flawed with design errors. More recent work has concluded that marriage has more of a beneficial impact on the health of men than that of women.

On the other hand, divorce has been shown to negatively impact women's health in comparison with marrieds. For example, risk of cardiovascular disease is much higher (60 percent) in divorced women over fifty than in their still-married counterparts.

Bottom line: It's very clear that marriage is beneficial to men's health and that divorce (or being widowed) is bad for women's health. It's not so clear that marriage is good for women's health.

Yet we know for sure that married women live longer. So what's the special sauce of this fountain of youth? We've already seen that it's not exercise or diet. Is it money and better healthcare? Let's see.

Marriage and Money

Having gone through the benefits and risks of marriage, we come at last to the "root of all evil." How does marriage impact men's and women's economic circumstances?

Well, for about thirty years researchers have found that married men enjoy a "marriage premium" in earnings over singles—that is, they earn more money and also have a higher earning potential. One of the most frequent reasons given for this finding is that in most households, women do more of the domestic work, including child rearing—thus freeing their husbands to work harder outside the home. Even today, with women enjoying higher-paying and better jobs than ever, this inequality in household work persists.

So what about women? Do they enjoy an "earnings premium"? Nope. A series of national Australian studies has confirmed that no matter how you slice it, married women don't get the same earnings advantages as their hubbies. But there's more to this story. Common sense would tell us that having access to a husband's earnings must give some kind of advantage. In fact, some researchers believe that a married woman's standard of living is higher because of that access.

There is indirect evidence to support this claim. For example, married women are more likely to have health insurance partly because they can get coverage through their spouse. This benefit becomes especially significant if the woman has her own coverage and either loses her job or quits the job market because of a major life event, like having a baby. And the health insurance benefit alone may explain some of the better health that researchers, especially in the United States, find when comparing married women with singles.

Another way to look at the financial picture is to review some of the work on divorce and its consequences. We know that divorce is devastating for all parties and for women and children in particular. For example, research shows that:

- Women's standard of living drops by about 20 percent after a divorce, and homeownership by more than 10 percent.
- Divorced mothers have much lower incomes than marrieds.
- Three-quarters of all women who apply for welfare benefits do so because their marriages or living-together arrangements have broken up.

Bottom line: Being married is no guarantee that you'll be richer. But if you have access to your husband's earnings and earning potential, you probably will enjoy a higher standard of living, including better healthcare for you and your kids.

Marital Satisfaction, Health, and Happiness

The key to understanding the conflicting research on marriage, health, and happiness is the variable of marital satisfaction. Many studies simply did not measure marital happiness as part of their experiments or surveys. Of those that did, here's the overview: Bad or unsatisfactory marriages may contribute to health and psychological problems, while a good marriage may protect a woman from certain diseases or help her to recover faster if she does get ill.

We can't go into all of the studies, but here are a few. Studies of long-term marriages in which the partners were unhappy showed that:

- Women more than men were likely to suffer from high blood pressure and obesity.

- Poor marital quality was associated with depression, worsened physical health, poor sleep, and metabolic problems.
- As we've already seen, once a woman is divorced her economic circumstances, health, and general well-being are all adversely affected.

In other words, there is a severe marriage penalty for being in a bad marriage or getting divorced that never-married singles don't pay. In an earlier chapter, we've already discussed that singles with strong social support have been found to be nearly as well off as married women in good relationships. That's because social support and love are probably the key drivers behind many of the positive findings in comparison studies of single, married, living-together, and divorced gals.

So what about women in satisfying marriages? In comparison studies with their single, divorced, or widowed counterparts, women in good marriages had:

- The least amount of atherosclerosis in their arteries. They also lived much longer if they did have heart disease.
- Fewer doctor visits.
- Lower blood pressure than singles or women in unhappy marriages.
- Fewer headaches and back pain.

Women in happy marriages also had better immune systems than marrieds who demonstrated hostility toward each other. They healed twice as fast from flesh wounds!

Two final brain studies show some of the more amazing benefits of a high-quality relationship. In the first, neuroscientists did fMRI scans of married women while they received a very mild electric shock. They were put in three groups: having their hands held by their husbands; by a stranger; and by no one at all. Quality of marriage determined the women's brain responses to the threat, with the strongest decrease in brain activity occurring with those who reported the highest marital satisfaction. It was as if they had taken a tranquilizer. In another fMRI study, men and women in long-term healthy marriages who viewed their spouse's photo showed activation in the areas of the brain associated with dopamine—that is, the passion centers—as if they were newlyweds. Not only were they madly in love, but their scans showed another bonus: less anxiety than newlyweds. Passion without the craziness: Sounds good to me.

Bottom line: There is no question that the social support of a loving partner contributes to having a healthier, longer, and happier life. But marriage by itself is not an answer to all of life's problems. Being single today, coupled with a strong loving network of family and friends, is a very viable alternative to even a healthy marriage. So relax. You have a lot of great alternatives to choose from.

In sum, if you do decide to tie the knot, choose a man who is a good match, devoted to you, and committed to handling the inevitable bumps and potholes that you will face on your journey. Because if it does not go well and you divorce, the research suggests that you will be worse off all the way around than if you had never been married.

On the other hand, a good marriage is worth creating and working on because it can have many positive effects on your health and well-being. In the next chapter, we'll look at one of those surprising benefits, which has been recently confirmed in research: the Michelangelo Phenomenon. In this process, great couples, like great sculptors, shape each other so that both move toward their own individual goals and dreams.

Marriage and Men

(You may want to show this section to your boyfriend!)

Study after study has showed that marriage is a tremendous boon to men. Here is a partial list of the benefits:

- Married guys earn more than single men and have a higher earning potential.
- Married men are healthier and live longer than single men.
- Married men are less likely to die than their single counterparts.
- Entry into marriage significantly reduces depression for men.
- Men who marry step up to a healthier lifestyle with more social support.
- Alcohol consumption, binge drinking, and pot smoking go down when guys say "I do."

On top of all this, if a man is in a good marriage with a woman who is devoted to his growth and the realization of his goals and dreams, he can also reap the tremendous benefits of becoming his ideal or Diamond Self, becoming happier, more fulfilled, and more successful at whatever he does.

Now that you are armed with research-based evidence about what marriage can and can't do, you can make a more informed decision about your own Lasting Love Program goals. I am proud of you for delving into all this critical information.

Maybe you are getting engaged. What a cornucopia of gifts and delights you have chosen! My biggest congratulations and best wishes to you! Next, in Part IV, we will look at how to make the music of passionate love play on and get fuller, richer, and more rapturous over time.

> A happy marriage perhaps represents the ideal of human relationship—a setting in which each partner, while acknowledging the need of the other, feels free to be what he or she by nature is; a relationship in which instinct as well as intellect can find expression; in which giving and taking are equal; in which each accepts the other, and I confronts Thou.—*Anthony Storr*

PART IV

How to Be Happily
in Love Together Forever

13

Secrets That Make Passionate Love Last—No Matter How Long You've Been Together.

This is how a love relationship is meant to work, each partner transforming the other. The strength and power of each is untangled, shared. He gives her heart drum. She gives him knowledge of the most complicated rhythms and emotions imaginable. Who knows what they will hunt together? We only know that they will be nourished to the end of their days.—*Clarissa Pinkola Estés*

The other day I asked Sam, my husband of more than twenty-five years, why he stays with me. He said, "Because I feel good around you." Feeling good and at home with a woman is one of the drivers for a man to be in a long-term relationship. But is that all there is? No, there's a lot more. In our marriage, we are having more laughter and high jinks, deeper talks, more exotic adventures (think Amazonian rain forest), plus bigger fireworks in bed than ever before. (Apologies to my kids who have to read this.)

Trust me, we are not the only couple in the world whose love has not only lasted but also deepened over time. Studies of long-term marriages going back almost fifty years have been able to separate out three distinct types of couples: unhappy; normal or generally satisfied; and happily married, passionate couples. Of course, we live in a cynical age when the conventional view is that most long-term couples are either unhappy or bored out of their minds. We often hear or read about couples whose passion and romance have been totally eclipsed by diaper duty, tuition bills, hated jobs, and the stress of paying the monthly nut.

Readers ask me, "Dr. Diana, where are these so-called still-passionately-in-love couples? Is finding them some kind of treasure hunt that requires Indiana Jones?"

Hmmm. Sam did like wearing that hat when I first met him...

Okay. I have good news. You don't have to go to Outer Mongolia or a remote cave in India. All you have to do is look at the treasures brought to us by the pioneer researchers who have confirmed the existence of these romantically in-love-forever couples. First, researchers in the 1960s and 1970s discovered what they termed "vital" and "total" marriages, or couples who were intensely in love after ten, twenty, or more years. Then studies in the 1980s found more evidence of these treasures. One researcher interviewed and tested women aged fifty through eighty-two who had been married an average of thirty-three years. Some of these women reported *that they were still passionately in love and very turned on to their spouses.* Then researchers developed a highly reliable and valid rating scale, the Passionate Love Scale (PLS), which measured passionate love in both men and women of all ages and in a variety of cultures. The PLS asks questions about feelings of infatuation for "the person you love or have loved most *passionately.*" And over the next twenty-five years, many other studies by different researchers using the PLS confirmed the existence of romantic love in long-term marriages. A recent review of twenty-five relevant studies in different countries once again showed that, in the words of the authors, "a long-term relationship does not kill off romantic love."

Over the last ten years, researchers have also studied the brain scans of passionate couples. First, studies have shown that high scores on the PLS were correlated with the fMRI scans typical of people in love. In other words, finding couples who claimed they were still madly in love wasn't just some weird result on a survey. Then, in a compelling study, Arthur Aron and his colleagues found that fMRI studies of couples who had been together an average of twenty-one years showed the same dopamine reactions in their brains as younger lovers when they were shown photographs of their Beloved. But there's more! Not only did these older couples display the passionate "limerence" of newlyweds, but they did so without the newlyweds' chemical roller coaster of anxiety and obsession.

So now you're probably thinking, *What is the percentage of long-term couples that are really still madly in love? Are there others besides the Obamas and the one couple I met in the Bahamas who were holding hands and smooching at the beach at age eighty-something?* In my experience and based on the research on long-term couples, I believe one out of ten couples can keep the fireworks of romantic love going for many, many years. That estimate was confirmed in Aron's fMRI study, which found that 10 percent of long-term couples had brain scans that showed they were *intensely* in love. The researchers nicknamed these couples "swans," because, as you may know, swans are mated for life.

How many couples would that make in the United States? Well, according to the 2001 Census Bureau's data, there were almost twelve million couples who had reached their thirty-fifth wedding anniversary, about the same number that the previous (1996) census had found. By my estimate, the number of long-term couples who are still madly in love is well over a million. Just in the U.S. And we're talking about intensely in love. The number of couples *in love* may be much higher! So when I talk to you about role models (and potential Love Mentors who can help you on your Lasting Love Program), please pay attention. These folks are all around you.

The Michelangelo Phenomenon
and the Diamond Self

I love you not only for what you have made of yourself,
but for what you are making of me.
I love you for the part of me that you bring out.
—Attributed to Elizabeth Barrett Browning

So now that we know there are plenty of couples who've achieved the happily-ever-after, how in the world do they do it? Twenty-five years ago, my husband and I published a book for marriage and family therapists. In that book, we described the process by which healthy couples assist each other to grow as marital partners, as parents, and as individuals. We suggested that in passionate marriages, the partners help each other fill their deepest emotional (TTLC) needs while promoting each other's skills and personal goals. In other words, like good mentors, they help each other become their ideal selves. Over the last ten years, research-ers have confirmed the existence of one critical aspect of the process: the Michelangelo Phenomenon that I touched on previously.

Let's take a deeper look at how the Michelangelo Phenomenon works. Healthy spouses sculpt each other's behaviors, values, atti-tudes, skills, and achievements. They perceive, affirm, help, and develop each other's ideal self, or what I call the Diamond Self. Diamond Self affirmation from one partner to the target partner increases the target's belief that his partner understands and approves of him and genuinely cares about his growth and fulfillment. It has been shown to promote couple and individual well-being so that the partners enjoy greater vitality, happiness, trust, and commitment. In other words, the Michelangelo Phenomenon rocks!

This type of interaction is quite different from the Pygmalion effect. Named for the play by George Bernard Shaw, where a pho-neticist, Henry Higgins, decides to make over a Cockney girl with a strong accent named Eliza Doolittle, in the Pygmalion effect one partner decides that he or she knows better about what is "good for" the other and tries to impose his or her will. Pushy know-it-all Pygmalion advice and nagging is destructive to both personal and couple well-being. It is this squelching process that leads to urban legends like *You can't change your partner.*

In fact you can—through the Michelangelo process, but only if your partner's own concept of his or her Diamond Self leads the way. Here is a real-life illustration:

When Nathaniel Hawthorne was fired from his job at a customs house, he went home to his wife, Sophia, in a brokenhearted state. He confessed that he felt like a total failure. She said (in modern English), "Are you kidding? This is great, honey—now you can write your book!"

"What? And what will we live on?" he asked.

She pulled out a huge wad of money.

Nathaniel asked, "Where on earth did you get that?"

"I always knew that you had genius in you and that someday you would write a masterpiece. So I saved a little each week over many years," Sophia slyly responded.

And thus was born one of the greatest American novels, *The Scarlet Letter.*

Hawthorne, in turn, had this to say about Sophia, whom he referred to as his "dove": "She is in the strictest sense, my sole companion and I need no other—there is no vacancy in my mind any more than in my heart. Thank God that I suffice for her boundless heart."

Extraordinary love comes from the Michelangelo dynamic! Now a contemporary example:

The Story of Dan and Carole

I met Dan and Carole at a couples resort in the Caribbean. What attracted me to them was that they were laughing and horsing around in a pool like kids, but they seemed to be in their late forties. They were kind enough to let me interview them. Dan and Carole had been married for twenty-five years. They disclosed that from the beginning they wanted a real partnership built on sharing intimately and a deep understanding of each other's hopes and dreams. In other words, they both wanted to understand all the different aspects of each other's Diamond Selves. And after some confusion and rough patches in the early days, they got into a rhythm of actively promoting and helping each other. That's what they'd been doing ever since. For example, it was a stretch for him, but Dan wanted his own business. Carole never wavered in believing he could do it, even though he was very introverted and had learning disabilities.

Carole, in turn, wanted to have kids. But she had difficulty conceiving and went through a long road of hopelessness. Dan insisted it would happen and went with her to just about every doctor's visit. Eventually they were able to have a daughter, and Carole fulfilled her dream. Dan was interested in practicing Transcendental Meditation because he thought it could help him de-stress at work. Knowing this, Carole found the local TM center in town and put the schedule on their refrigerator. She encouraged Dan in his daily morning practice by offering to make breakfast. "He was the shyest guy when I met him, but the meditation has changed all that," Carole said with a grin. "Dan is now CEO of his own computer consulting company!"

Now that their daughter was going to college, Carole resurrected an old dream of becoming a social worker. To do that, she applied and was accepted into a top master's degree program in social work. Dan encouraged her, found the money to pay for it, and even helped edit her papers. As they described it, "We're in the second half of our lives, and it's much better than the first. And the first wasn't shabby, either."

There are many stories of couples like Dan and Carole. Probably at least a million in the United States alone (remember?). What's striking about them is how aware they are of the dance in their couple. Dan said that he felt tremendously supported by Carole, appreciative of her help, and wanted to give back to her. Carole, in turn, felt more empowered and successful. Her latest victory: scoring her ideal internship working with the homeless. Because Dan had helped make it happen for her, she was more committed than ever to him and their relationship.

INSIDE THE MICHELANGELO PHENOMENON

In healthy couples, the partners alternate roles in helping each other and the relationship develop. Many great results can grow out of the process of focusing on and supporting each other's Diamond Self:

- An ever-increasing cycle of giving and receiving true understanding
- Tailored care and perfectly crafted support
- Deeper intimacy and heightened sexual fulfillment
- More effective teamwork in family life, parenting, and careers
- Greater individual success and self-actualization

In addition, partners who are sculpting each other and growing through their relationship are automatically regenerating passionate feelings and chemistry over and over again. As they evolve, their behavior becomes more novel and spontaneous—and novelty leads to more dopamine, that exciting neurotransmitter that produces infatuation. The ongoing transformation of each person means they say and do unexpected things; funny, creative, thoughtful, or intimate openings occur and create the opportunity to fall in love all over again. In this way, romantic love is rekindled continuously.

The Michelangelo process gives us an idea of the overall process by which passionate long-term married couples keep love alive. Now I'm going to share the secrets that these happy couples know, secrets that researchers have discovered in the course of interviewing tens of thousands of these couples. Secrets that my husband, Sam, and I have taught to many therapists around the world and to thousands of couples. And more important, that we've used in our own lab, our marriage. I call them the Eight Habits of Living Love.

The Eight Habits of Living Love

It was not always easy. We used to be conflict avoiders. We learned to express emotions, to fight, to trust, to listen, to learn from each other. We speak of marriage as the "gymnasium of the soul."

—*Survey participant, reflecting on his fifty-one-year marriage*

Because a soul mate doesn't come to you as a perfectly fitting puzzle piece or twin personality, because there are no perfect princes (or princesses), if we hope to make love and passion last we all need to develop ourselves, our partners, and our relationships by practicing certain all-important skills. It is these skills that are embodied by the Eight Habits of Living Love. Here are the habits along with simple suggestions to enable you to start practicing them immediately with your Beloved.

The eight habits are:

1. Cultivating Intimacy

2. Enlightened Self-Interest

3. Dedication and Service

4. Considering the Cost of Loss

5. Showing Appreciation and Gratitude

6. Practicing Care-full Communication

7. Following Fight Club Rules

8. Collaborating as Teammates

I. THE HABIT OF CULTIVATING INTIMACY

> We lie in each other's arms, eyes shut and fingers open
> and all the colors of the world pass through our bodies like
> strings of fire.—*Marge Piercy*

In cultivating intimacy, spouses turn toward each other to share thoughts, feelings, affection, and sexual pleasuring. They know each other well. They spend time alone together, talking, listening, and sharing authentically. They are genuinely interested in each other's past, present, and future. They spend time discovering each other's deeper needs, wants, goals, and dreams. Each tries to understand the other's ideal or Diamond Self, which sets the preconditions to help each other grow. Part of cultivating intimacy is having little rituals, signals, and signs that set the stage for sex, dates, and romance. They may routinely say silly endearing things to each other that signify their special bond and connection.

Healthy couples keep passion alive, kindling and rekindling their chemistry and fulfilling each other's sexual needs regularly. Activating a commitment to shared passion that gets progressively richer and sexier instead of devitalizing with time, they create novel and exciting ways to flirt with, romance, and bed each other. They treat each other as if they were having an affair, fulfilling each other sexually in new, more intimate, and satisfying ways over time. Here are seven steps you can take to develop the Habit of Cultivating Intimacy in your relationship:

1. Spend time alone as a couple (no friends, no kids, no texting).
2. Know each other's daily routines and habits.
3. Take turns having formal ten-minute listening sessions where one of you talks while the other listens with full attention, like a validating therapist.
4. Share hugs, kisses, and affection in ways both of you enjoy.

5. Start a sweet bedtime or greeting ritual with silly or endearing phrases or nicknames.

6. Create win–win sexual fulfillment. In Chapter 6, I described three different categories of sexual play that these couples enjoy: sexual trance, partner engagement, and role play. Reread that section of the chapter and practice these regularly. You and your partner will both thank me.

7. Act like you are having an affair with each other.

EXERCISE 1: *BUILD THE HABIT OF CULTIVATING INTIMACY*

Read over the seven steps. Take out your calendar for the next month. Make notes on which of these steps you would like to focus and work on, indicating the day and time for each. Preferably do this planning with your Beloved. Or if he is not yet on board, start initiating a couple of these activities in a loving way.

II. THE HABIT OF ENLIGHTENED SELF-INTEREST

> When you love someone, all your saved-up wishes start coming out.—*Elizabeth Bowen*

The habit of acting from enlightened self-interest means revealing those saved-up wishes and TTLC needs and seeing that they are granted and fulfilled by your Beloved. This is the balancing habit that goes hand in glove with the next habit, that of dedication and service to the Beloved. Often, this habit of receiving and having needs met is hard for women, since they are used to being the nurturers. Nonetheless, this habit must be followed. If the giving only flows one way, the relationship becomes boring, predictable, and stagnant. Under those conditions, dopamine falls off a cliff, which in turn means that passion and feelings of being in love also disappear. That's when people start having affairs. And not with each other.

Enlightened self-interest means making sure your needs are fulfilled, and one of the most important is your need to grow as a person. Abe Maslow, the great psychologist, called it the need to self-actualize, a need that is so powerful that it informs the choices we make in mate selection, careers, and in our most passionate pursuits. The drive to self-actualize creates a· deep need to transform and become our ideal self, our Diamond Self. And it is a lifelong drive. Fulfilling that need is accomplished in part by asking our Beloved to help us get there—in other words, practicing the Habit of Enlightened Self-Interest.

By practicing this habit, you are getting the encouragement, support, and dedication you need to become who you want to be, which means you are reinventing yourself over and over again. You are perennially new, at times becoming more intimate and connected, at other times becoming more sexually open, and at still other times more empowered, creative, and generative in the world. The self-actualizing process brings freshness, novelty, and excitement to the relationship, which stimulates in-love feelings over and over again.

We now know through understanding the Michelangelo Phenomenon that having your partner's help in becoming your ideal or Diamond Self also improves the quality of the whole relationship. In passionate couples, there is a rhythmic give-and-take where the partners fluidly play out enlightened self-interest in novel ways that create mutual interest, fun, and excitement. They may function as best friends, teammates, lovers, mentors, mentees, parents, or children with each other. Fulfilling each other's needs and wants in the many roles helps them to develop all the different sides of themselves.

In other words, by coming from healthy self-interest, you are giving your partner a great opportunity. For example, you might be furthering his sense of competence and personal success. Also, as your needs and wants are fulfilled, you can give more back to him. Because you are content, soothed, recharged, and in a state of appreciation and gratitude, you are able and want to give back in a whole, real way, with your full attention. Here are four steps to help you develop the Habit of Enlightened Self-Interest in your relationship:

1. Pay close attention to what you need or want, and lovingly ask your Beloved to get it for you. Attention, compliments, a cool drink, a long slow kiss, fulfilling a sexual wish, a romantic dinner out—or as the commitment deepens, an adventurous or exotic trip, a new home, or having a child are all okay. Down deep your partner wants to make you happy, even though he might not be able to take full action right now.
2. Accept and appreciate what your Beloved gives to you. Thank him.
3. Ask your partner to fulfill your Tough and Tender Loving Care (TTLC) needs (see Chapter 4).
4. Ask your partner to help you actualize your ideal goals and dreams.

EXERCISE 2: *BUILD THE HABIT OF ENLIGHTENED SELF-INTEREST*

Read over the four steps. On your calendar for the next month, make notes on which of these steps you would like to focus and work on, indicating the day and time for each.

III. THE HABIT OF DEDICATION AND SERVICE

> My bounty is as boundless as the sea,
> My love as deep;
> The more I give to thee
> The more I have,
> For both are infinite.
>
> —*William Shakespeare*

The Habit of Dedication and Service starts and ends with commitment. Both spouses completely commit to each other and the relationship for the long-term future. They speak and act in ways that show they have made a decision to maintain a love relationship solely with each other. This habit allows a healthy couple to work through the unavoidable disappointments, conflict, and hard times of family life so that they can heal and move on together. Many studies have shown that commitment is the most important element in a relationship and determines a couple's long-term success. It's been found to be related to better relationship quality, greater happiness, better communication, and less abusive behavior.

Dedication and commitment imply that the partners do not have physical or emotional affairs with outsiders. When you practice this habit, you are showing that the needs of the couple or the other partner often come before your own personal needs or wants. Each member is willing to sacrifice and invest time and energy for the sake of the relationship. The partners view the relationship as bigger than the sum of their individual parts. When couples truly "get" that, they can experience the infinite bounty of romantic love that the Bard's quote describes.

It is this habit of service, together with enlightened self-interest, that organizes each spouse to help the other actualize his Diamond Self. When one falls, the other is there to hold him as needed, providing a safe haven of care, listening, reassurance, and emotional communion. When it comes time to go back out there, a loving partner gives encouragement, advice, prizing, and, at the moment of success, heartfelt celebration. A loving partner co-creates a vision of success for her Beloved, often seeing the real potential unnoticed by the Beloved himself. Then she encourages her Beloved to dream big in the direction of his ideal self and go for it. Here are six steps you can take to develop the Habit of Dedication and Service in your relationship:

1. Think of ways you can more deeply understand your partner and his life.
2. Think through the Tough and Tender Loving Care (see Chapter 4) needs of your partner based on his past wounds and disappointments—for example, he had a critical, withholding mother or ex-wife. Or his father was verbally abusive or absent.
3. Informed by your understanding, fill your partner's TTLC needs (you are validating, but setting limits as needed).
4. Find ways you can support your partner's goals and dreams.
5. Give more than 100 percent to your partner.
6. Keep emotional entanglements in check (overly close relationships with family or friends that interfere with the needs of your partner or couple).

EXERCISE 3: *BUILD THE HABIT OF DEDICATION AND SERVICE*

Read over the six steps. In your calendar, make notes on which of these steps you would like to focus and work on, in the next month, indicating the day and time for each.

IV. THE HABIT OF CONSIDERING THE COST OF LOSS

> Ever has it been that love knows not its own depth until the hour of separation.—*Khalil Gibran*

Healthy spouses are realistic in thinking about and considering the costs of losing their relationship. Since we covered what this means in depth previously, let's look at this habit from the perspective of long-term intensely-in-love couples.

First, healthy partners do not stay together simply out of fear or need. They are independent enough to actually be able to leave each other and be happily on their own if circumstances demand it. In fact, in healthy couples it is fairly common for one partner to use a facing loss maneuver when the other steps too far out of line. This kind of limit-setting can help the offender grow and pull the couple back together through the processes of reparation and forgiveness. The fear of loss fuels the desire to treat each other well because the partners know they cannot get away with disrespectful, thoughtless, cruel, or cold treatment.

Second, this habit prepares the partners for the ultimate loss, death. I've seen death come to these couples after fifty years of love, and the survivor—despite the terrible and almost unimaginable loss—resurrects herself. Other partners choose not to live and suddenly die when they lose their soul mate. In both cases, the partners have exercised choice and they've done it with fierce determination.

With these two goals in mind, here are four steps you can use to develop the Habit of Considering the Cost of Loss in your relationship:

1. When your Beloved does something that offends you, where you might normally distance yourself or cut off from the relationship, consider the cost of losing him. How would you feel? What would your life be like without him in it? What would you miss? How valuable are these things to you?

2. Instead of dumping your partner because of his problematic behavior, consider the cost of loss and use Positive Paranoia to shape a loving straight talk where you simply ask for what you need.

3. When you find yourself acting in bitchy, diva-like, moody, cold, out-of-control, or overly demanding ways, consider the cost to the relationship and how such behavior might kill it off entirely.

4. If you feel your relationship has become painfully stagnant and that you absolutely need to move forward into greater closeness and a deeper commitment, help your Beloved consider the cost of loss by showing him what life would be like without you (see Chapter 10).

EXERCISE 4: *BUILD THE HABIT OF CONSIDERING THE COST OF LOSS*

Read over the four steps. In your calendar, make notes on which of these steps you would like to focus on, journal about, or work on in the next month, indicating the day and time for each.

V. THE HABIT OF SHOWING APPRECIATION AND GRATITUDE

> The deepest principle in human nature is the craving to be appreciated.—*William James*

The gift of knowing that loss can occur helps partners appreciate and be grateful for each other. Each one appreciates who the Beloved is, who he or she can be—the Beloved's Diamond Self—and what is received from the Beloved. Both live in a state of gratitude. This habit enhances self-esteem, leading to great personal and shared happiness. It sets up the cycle of giving and receiving that is the hallmark of long-term passionate love. In a study of sixty-five happy couples, one person's feelings of gratitude increased emotional connection and relationship satisfaction for both members. And this positive effect was reported even on the day following the expression of gratefulness. A little goes a long way!

Everyone has flaws; there is no perfect person. In the practice of this habit, the partner's flaws are not the focus. The focus is on what is right with the Beloved the majority of the time. Partners give each other the benefit of the doubt when they do something that is disappointing or hurtful. They often see good or simply uninformed intentions underlying what their partners do or say instead of seeing meanness, criticism, rejection, or a right–wrong attack. Sound familiar? It is the powerful Positive Paranoia process at play.

Because healthy couples are naturally focused on blessings and feel grateful in their relationship, they are happier. Research clearly shows that appreciation and gratitude are the royal roads to happiness. Here are eight steps to help you develop the Habit of Showing Appreciation and Gratitude in your relationship:

1. Every day write down three things you are grateful for in your relationship.
2. Notice all the wonderful qualities, large and small, that your Beloved possesses.
3. Appreciate the Diamond Self that your partner is actualizing.
4. Express unconditional acceptance and appreciation of your Beloved as he is right now.
5. Give thanks to your partner for what he brings or gives to you.
6. Write appreciative and thankful texts, e-mails, notes, and cards.
7. Give your Beloved thank-you gifts.
8. Build your Positive Paranoia skills. When your Beloved seems unsupportive or negative, or he ignores you, practice deliberately thinking thoughts like, *I bet he is proud that I gave that presentation even though he hasn't called.* Or, *He does want to make love, even though he is so involved in that game.*

EXERCISE 5: *BUILD THE HABIT OF SHOWING APPRECIATION AND GRATITUDE*

Read over the eight steps. In your calendar, make notes on which of these steps you would like to focus on, journal about, or do in the next month, indicating the day and time for each.

VI. THE HABIT OF PRACTICING CARE-FULL COMMUNICATION

> Before we got engaged there were many conversations about what we both envisioned for the future. We both were honest about where we were in the process, even when it meant admitting we weren't on the same page.

> Also, we were both vocal about what we wanted/needed
> to see from the other person in order to keep moving for-
> ward and to remain happy, comfortable and satisfied with
> the relationship.—*Happily married survey participant*

This is the habit of caring, positive, and straightforward verbal and nonverbal communication. The partners share affection, humor, benevolence, and praise along with straight talk and truthfulness. When there are disagreements, the partners agree to talk about them, appreciate each other's point of view, and may agree to disagree.

Listening with full attention is a key component of care-full communication. Couples who are making it listen and know each other's fears, problems, wishes, and dreams. This also sets the stage for the Michelangelo sculpting process. The spouses warmly and clearly explain what they want and need so that they help each other win and come through for each other. They make statements like, "Honey, I need you to hold me," or "Sweetheart, I would really love it if you took out the trash!" In other words, in practicing this Habit, the partners avoid relying on mind reading, where it is assumed that your significant other should just understand what you need and provide it without you having to ask. This negative pattern sets your partner up to fail, which creates disappointment, anger, and emotional alienation.

Healthy couples fight, and fighting is an important way to air anger and be authentic, but they follow Fight Club Rules (see the next Habit). Most of the time, however, they maintain a more kind and loving way of communicating. Studies show that healthy couples maintain a ratio of five positive interactions to each negative one they have. In general, they avoid or minimize nitpicking, harsh judgments, belittling, abusing, defensiveness, or freezing each other out. When such incidents do occur, they repair them as soon as they can. In great measure, loving couples speak and act out of honor, respect, and appreciation; they speak as the best of best friends.

Here are three steps you can take to help you develop the Habit of Practicing Care-full Communication in your relationship:

1. Practice listening with your full, undivided attention. If you are distracted, tell your partner that you will give him your undivided attention and energy at a certain time.
2. Notice whether you tend to be negative, pessimistic, critical, defensive, or withholding of positive prizing statements or gestures with your Beloved.
3. Notice how many positive interactions you create for each negative one. Try giving your boyfriend or partner five positives for every negative comment or act you make and see what happens.

EXERCISE 6: *BUILD THE HABIT OF PRACTICING CARE-FULL COMMUNICATION*

Read over the three steps. In your calendar, make notes on which of these steps you would like to focus on, journal about, or do in the next month, indicating the day and time for each.

VII. THE HABIT OF FOLLOWING FIGHT CLUB RULES

> All married couples should learn the art of battle as they should learn the art of making love. Good battle is objective and honest, never vicious or cruel. Good battle is healthy and constructive, and brings to a marriage the principle of equal partnership.—*Ann Landers*

Almost all couples belong to what I call the Fight Club, because they fight. Couples that don't fight are the ones that therapists worry most about. In fact, couples who do not fight have twice the mortality rate of those who do. Loving couples are straight with each other and air their differences. But over time, they learn self-control and generally do not let anger escalate and explode.

Criticism and anger lead to "flooding," a stress explosion in which the heart beats more rapidly, blood pressure soars, and adrenaline surges. Reason goes out the window. In studies of conflict, when couples are asked to calm down, men simply aren't able to while women can more easily. Biologically speaking, men are wired to react more quickly and for a longer time period, probably for vigilance and safety reasons. So that's why it's best to start an interaction that could become a fight in a soft, loving, or affectionate way. Then your man will not feel like he has to shut down or distance himself in order to self-soothe. Here are five steps you can take to help you develop the Habit of Following Fight Club Rules in your relationship so you can air differences in a more constructive way:

1. Use breathing, gentle touch, time-out, or humor to defuse the situation.
2. Practice doing whatever it takes to come out of your anger and create a dialogue.
3. Agree to disagree. Try on his point of view.
4. Apologize. Go for closeness instead of being right. Deep down it's the loving feelings you really want, so insisting on being right is just shooting yourself in the foot.
5. Use the "Take Two" technique: Agree that either of you can call out "Take Two" when a fight erupts and you will redo your "scene" all over again, *but from a loving place.*

EXERCISE 7: *BUILD THE HABIT OF FOLLOWING FIGHT CLUB RULES*

Read over the five steps. In your calendar, make notes on which of these steps you would like to focus on, journal about, do, or discuss with your partner in the next month, indicating the day and time for each.

VIII. THE HABIT OF COLLABORATING AS TEAMMATES

A house divided against itself cannot stand.
—*Abraham Lincoln*

Partners in a romantic loving relationship team together with mutual support and respect. This habit of effectively teaming and coordinating activities is a key factor in their happiness. Each partner takes into account the other's thoughts, feelings, and opinions before making a major decision. In other words, there is shared power where both members of the couple influence each other. There is also a fair distribution of household chores, child care, and management of the couple's intimate time together.

In happy couples, teamwork is often shaped and informed by the desire to help the other self-actualize. The great existential philosopher Rollo May called this form of caring a "state composed of identification of oneself with the pain or joy of the other." Mutual identification helps build marital trust and openness. It also fuels dedication and devotion to each other, so that teamwork is enhanced. As an example, if a woman needs to finish a paper to complete her advanced degree, her Beloved might encourage her, bring her food, and proofread the document if he can. When she gets her degree, which is a milestone in the blossoming of her Diamond Self, they celebrate the win together, which brings them even closer.

My experience of teamwork in passionate couples is that it actually gets better and better over time. The partners work out any issues of control or needing to be right. Instead they come to realize that their individual and shared goals are more easily achieved when they team together. Much like the teamwork on a great basketball team or superb orchestra, the partners mesh together in highly nuanced ways to produce almost amazing results. They come to know, respect, honor, and utilize each other's strengths and gifts more and more as they work together, making their dreams come true on the home front and in their careers. Here are three steps to help you develop the Habit of Collaborating as Teammates in your relationship:

1. When you plan outings, dates, and vacations with your Beloved, share your thoughts and opinions about the experience and ask for his.
2. If you tend to be the one running the show, practice stepping back so that you can become more flexible. If you tend to be more passive, practice taking a leadership role.
3. Plan a trip or activity that requires a lot of coordination and practice dividing up responsibilities. Aim to work well together to create a positive experience for both of you.

EXERCISE 8: *BUILD THE HABIT OF COLLABORATING AS TEAMMATES*

Read over the three steps. In your calendar, make notes on which of these steps you would like to focus on, journal about, discuss with your partner, or do in the next month, indicating the day and time for each.

These are the Eight Habits of Living Love. Remember, happy couples are not practicing the habits all the time, just most of the time. And through the Michelangelo process, healthy partners hone their skills and get more and more competent at loving as the years go by. This is the very best news! No matter what, if you and your Beloved practice these habits and are patient and persistent, you, too, can join the ranks of these passionately-in-love-forever couples.

Final Words

Now you have the whole Lasting Love Program and we are almost ready to say good-bye. But at this point we have spent a good deal of time together and, chances are, I will be in your head, even if at times you disagree with me. Know that you are very special to me and I wrote this for you. I cannot express how proud I am of you for inquiring into this deepest of subjects, and for any and all work you have done, the goals you have met, the riches of love you will create now and in the future. Of course, the Lasting Love Program is never ending; it is a forever thing.

My wish is that you digest this book like a good meal. May it nourish and guide you along the path you have chosen. You and only you can determine the right way. Choose your love intention and then act with one-pointed determination. Be open to your deepest intuition, listening carefully for the faint voice in your heart. When you are willing to follow that whisper and be as flexible as the reed without compromising your integrity, the great and lasting love that is your heart's calling will unfold perfectly.

> There is a light that shines beyond all things on earth, beyond the highest, the very highest heavens. This is the light that shines in your heart.—*Chandogya Upanishad*

APPENDIX A

Lasting Love Online

WWW.LOVEIN90DAYS.COM AND

WWW.DATING-ADVICE.TV

You are invited to join me at my Web sites, www.lovein90days.com and www.dating-advice.tv. The sites are designed with one goal in mind: helping you create exactly the lasting love you want. On both sites there are unique resources and the freshest information on dating and relationship success. Lovein90days.com features my blog and a daily love affirmation. Dating-advice.tv showcases funny and educational videos on overcoming shyness, winning flirting tips, and dealing with challenging love difficulties like being in long-distance relationships and being in love with two people.

Make sure you subscribe to my free *Dating Tips and Relationship Advice Newsletter*, which you can find on either site. The weekly newsletter will give you timely support and up-to-date articles on commitment, relieving heartbreak, rekindling passion, and much, much more, delivered to you for free by e-mail.

Your Love Mentoring Consult by Phone or Skype for Free

Both sites also describe my professional Love Mentoring coaching service. Study after study has shown that adults who are mentored are more successful in their careers and in school. Women, in particular, have greatly benefited from mentoring, with reports of greater self-esteem and a heightened ability to break through the "glass ceiling."

And love is no different.

In fact, what is the most important thing you can do to truly amp up your dating and love life? Get coaching from Love Mentors! These are people who give deep emotional support, guide you, boost your self-esteem, and assist you in becoming your most beautiful self. Love Mentors help you in developing self-love and positive self-talk, along with busting through shyness, creating irresistible attractiveness, and getting the closeness and commitment from the One you want. *So ultimately you can form a lasting and great love relationship.*

I got to thinking, *Why is there no service like this for dating and relationships?*

Well, now there is. I just started a highly personalized Love Mentor coaching service. Now you can have coaching from an expert Love Mentor who has used Love in 90 Days and Lasting Love principles to get or stay happily married. So they walk the talk. Each one has a long background in powerful transformational work and is closely supervised by me. Most important, each mentor is gifted and can help you move forward to the love relationship you really want.

The best news is we can give you an introductory one-on-one session for free by phone or Skype. Just go to www.lovein90days.com/coaching or www.dating-advice.tv/coaching to let me know you want your free personalized session ASAP, because the time slots are filling up very fast.

> Some people come into our lives and quickly go. Some stay for a while and leave footprints on our heart and we are never, ever the same.—*Anonymous*

The Love Mentoring program can help you do a 180 in your love life! Here are a few topics you could discuss in your session:

- How to handle a problem you are having with the One you really want.
- How to quickly get out of heartbreak.
- How to win him back.
- How to deepen your relationship.
- How to succeed in having The Talk so he becomes closer and more committed.
- How to determine if he is the One.
- How to get the commitment you want.
- How to rekindle connection and passion in your marriage

So now you can have your very own caring, devoted, and knowledgeable Love Mentor who gives you love inspiration and support, as well as powerful dating tips and relationship advice to help you make your dreams come true. And right now, we can give you an introductory one-on-one session by phone or Skype for free.

So go to www.lovein90days.com/coaching or www.dating-advice.tv/coaching now. See you soon!

Wishing you lasting love,
Dr. Diana

APPENDIX B

The Loving Mother Meditation

Start by sitting in a comfortable private place. Put on uplifting or inspirational music and then close your eyes and take some deep breaths to relax. Listen for about five minutes. After the music ends, read each paragraph of the guided meditation to yourself and then take a few seconds to close your eyes and imagine it happening. This is like feeding yourself extremely nutritious food—but food you can use to build your mind instead of your body. It can help you develop positive associations about yourself and your relationship. Feel free to go with any other loving images that might come to mind as you do the meditation. This exercise only takes about fifteen minutes but is truly powerful.

If you want an even more powerful experience, make a recording of this meditation so you can simply listen to it with eyes closed as you sit in a private place.

Loving Mother (Angel, Goddess) Meditation

Imagine a special place, a place that is just right for you. Your own special place. It may be on a beach, in a meadow, or on a mountaintop. It's a place where you feel safe, you can feel the ground underneath you, see the sky above, feel the air brush against your cheek, hear the wonderful sounds. You know that you are in a place that is just right for you—all the right feelings, all the right sights, all the right sounds. Feeling safe, secure, content, happy. Go there right now.

Imagine a loving maternal presence, the Great Earth Mother or Angel or Goddess, holding you in the tenderest way. A comfortable way that is just right for you. She may remind you of a very loving person you once saw, or of a saint or goddess figure. And as you feel her tender touch, see her beaming open smile, feel her eyes looking deeply into yours, catch her lightly perfumed scent—it is remarkably easy and effortless to take in her great appreciation and delight in you.

She knows your perfection, the perfection of the Divine. As she looks deep into you, her gaze melts away your fears, your walls, your need to protect. You feel so good and know that all is right.

Imagine gently floating out of your body and into hers—so that you can see what she sees and feel what she feels, hear your voice the way she hears it. And looking through her eyes, you can't help but be struck by the fact of your real innocence, your special beauty and radiance.

Now imagine floating back into your body, and feel her love coming to you. And you know that it is the love that is meant just for you. It may be like a flowing light that changes colors—now purple, now blue, now golden. The love is filling you with warmth and such a good, good feeling. The love may come as a melody, a love song that you hear coming from her heart to yours.

Become one with the Great Mother. Now you have absolute trust in yourself, your own intuition, your own strength, and your ability to speak truth. Fully empowered and loving, you feel so good about yourself, so very good—better than you've ever felt before.

Park the feeling of being love permanently in the deepest part of your heart, so that it can be with you 24/7. Take love's feeling, love's light, love's melody with you, wherever and whenever. While you are sleeping, while you are walking down the street, while you work.

Now focus that love into a golden beam of light coming forth from your heart and flowing into your Beloved's heart. So that any pains or heartbreak in his heart fall away like dark chips. Send him the healing light.

Imagine purifying golden beams of light pouring forth from his heart to yours, cleaning out your pain and heartbreak, which fall away like dark chips.

Expand the light of love so that it surrounds both of you. Face each other and feel the oneness of your being and know that your joy is his joy and his joy is yours.

Remember that this meditation only takes about fifteen minutes to complete. You can do part of it or the whole thing. Use it to center yourself before you have The Talk, to calm yourself down after a fight, or to stop from binge eating or drinking. Use it to prevent yourself from making a phone call or sending an e-mail or text that you'll regret later. Nourishing yourself with a loving meditation will restore you to sanity and bring out your Diamond Self. Believe me, all will be brighter.

NOTES

Introduction

xv. "The mystery of love" Oscar Wilde, *Salome* (Mineola, NY: Dover Publications, 1893), 66.

xvii. "O that you and I escape" Walt Whitman, "Pent-Up Aching Rivers," *Leaves of Grass* (New York: Random House, 1900), 76.

Chapter 1: The Lasting Love Program

3. "The fountains mingle" Percy Bysshe Shelley, "Love's Philosophy," *Selected Poems* (Boston: Houghton Mifflin, 1907), 34.

4. Love Mentor™ and Love Mentoring™ have been trademarked by the author.

4. "Somewhere there waiteth" Sir Edwin Arnold, "Somewhere," *Random House Treasury of Favorite Love Poems* (New York: Random House, 2000).

8. "93 percent of the females" R. F. Baumeister, S. R. Wotman, and A. M. Stillwell, "Unrequited love: on heartbreak, anger, guilt, scriptlessness and humiliation," *Journal of Personality and Social Psychology* 64, 1993, 377–94.

12. "Oxytocin, the 'tend and befriend' hormone" Helen Fisher, *Why We Love* (New York: Henry Holt, 2004), 89.

18. "The latest research shows" For a thorough review of the literature on brain neuroplasticity, see Chapter 6 in Joe Dispenza, *Evolve Your Brain* (Deerfield Beach, FL: Health Communications, 2007).

18. "Hebb's law" D. O. Hebb, *The Organization of Behavior* (New York: John Wiley & Sons, 1949).

20. "Love feels no burden" Thomas à Kempis, *Of the Imitation of Christ: Four Books by Thomas à Kempis,* The World's Classics, vol. 49, translated by Anthony Hoskin (London: Oxford University Press, 1903), bk. 3, ch. 5.

Chapter 2: Killer Beliefs: How Hidden Thoughts About Love Sabotage Your Relationship

22. "The greatest barrier" Sven-Göran Eriksson (www.thinkexist.com).

23. "Psychologists point out" See, for example, the extensive research by L. Hasher and R. T. Zacks, "Automatic processing of fundamental information: the case of frequency of occurrence," *American Psychologist* 39, 1984, 1372–88.

24. "recent brain research" B. P. Acevedo and A. Aron, "Does a long-term relationship kill romantic love?" *Review of General Psychology* 13, 2009, 59–65.

25. "Traumatic events" Rick Hanson, *Buddha's Brain* (Oakland, CA: New Harbinger, 2009), 41.

27. "Deal honestly" Brian Tracy, *Excerpts from the Treasury of Quotes* (www.yoursuccessstore.com, 1998).

29. "women can be picky" L. Gottlieb, *Marry Him: The Case for Settling for Mr. Good Enough* (New York: Dutton, 2010).

30. "Study after study" See D. H. Olson and A. Olson, *Empowering Couples: Building on Your Strengths* (Minneapolis: Life Innovations, 2000).

30. "it is contempt" J. M. Gottman, *The Marriage Clinic* (New York: W. W. Norton, 1999), 45.

43. "If I believe" Mahatma Gandhi (www.thinkexist.com).

Chapter 3: Overcoming Fears That Destroy Any Chance of Lasting Love

44. "The experience of overcoming fear" Bertrand Russell (www.heartquotes.net).

45. "Those who reported being unhappy" E. A. Robinson and M. G. Price, "Pleasurable behavior in marital interaction: an observational study," *Journal of Consulting and Clinical Psychology* 48, 1980, 117–18.

45. "even in unhappy relationships" Gottman, *Marriage Clinic*, 181.

49. "O to speed" Walt Whitman, "One Hour to Madness and Joy," *Leaves of Grass,* 87–88.

50. "our brains are incredibly plastic" Norman Doidge, *The Brain That Changes Itself* (New York: Penguin Books, 2007), provides an excellent and eye-opening review of recent research on how the brain rewires and transforms itself until the moment of death.

50. "To have an intention" *Oxford Dictionary of Philosophy* (Oxford, UK: Oxford University Press, 2007).

51. "power of positive self-talk" See a thorough review of the literature in D. Sherman and G. L. Cohen, "The psychology of self-defense: self-affirmation theory," in M. P. Zanna, editor, *Advances in Experimental Social Psychology* 38, 2006, 183–242.

51. "Positive affirmations" S. Spence, S. Fein, and C. Lomore, "Maintaining one's self-image vis-à-vis others: the role of self-affirmation in the social evaluation of the self," *Motivation and Emotion* 25, 2001, 41–65.

52. "When we firmly resolve" J. Dispenza, *Evolve Your Brain,* 358.

58. "practicing Positive Paranoia" D. H. Baucom, N. Epstein, L. A. Rankin, and C. K. Burnett, "Assessing relationship standards: the inventory of specific relationship standards," *Journal of Marriage and the Family* 10, 1996, 72–88.

59. "Gemstones have been studied" For a review, see Swami Shiva Tirtha, *The Ayurveda Encyclopedia* (New York: Ayurveda Holistic Center Press, 1998).

60. "six separate experiments" L. Damisch, *Keep Your Fingers Crossed* (doctoral dissertation, Universität zu Köln, May 2008), 36–69.

61. "improve actual performance" Ibid., 69.

61. "Eastern and Western lore" A good overall source besides Tirtha, *Ayurveda Encyclopedia,* is J. Hall, *The Encyclopedia of Crystals* (London: Octopus Publishing Group, 2006).

62. "The time will come" Derek Walcott, "Love After Love," *Collected Poems: 1948–1984* (New York: Farrar, Straus & Giroux, 1987).

Chapter 4: The Single Most Important Thing You Can Do for Yourself and Your Relationship: Getting a Love Mentor

65. "Four Horsemen of the Apocalypse" Gottman, *Marriage Clinic,* 68.

68. "a physiological process called flooding" Ibid., 82.

68. "more successful in their careers" S. Seibert and M. L. Kraimer, "A social capital theory of career success," *Academy of Management Journal* 44, 2001, 219–37.

68. "and in school" M. Jacobi, "Mentoring and undergraduate academic success: a literature review," *Review of Educational Research* 61, 1991, 505–32.

69. "Women, in particular" R. A. Noe, "Women and mentoring: a review and research agenda," *The Academy of Management Review* 13, 1988, 65–78.

69. "greater self-esteem" M. Davidson and R. J. Burke, *Women in Management: Current Research Issues* (New York: P. Chapman Publishing, 1994).

69. "multiple mentors" Seibert and Kraimer, "Social capital theory."

69. "For one human being to love another" Rainer Maria Rilke, *Love and Other Difficulties* (New York: W. W. Norton, 1975), 31.

69. "we tend to revisit these negative scenarios" Duane Harvey, *Imago Relationship Manual* (www.imagomatch.com), 22.

78. "When we talk about understanding" J. Krishnamurti (www.thinkexist.com).

79. "a mirror can actually work its magic" A. Jansen, et al., "Mirror exposure reduces body dissatisfaction and anxiety in obese adolescents," *Appetite* 51, 2008, 214–17.

80. "shifting to more positive self-talk" S. Spencer, S. Fein, and C. Lomore, "Maintaining one's self-image vis-à-vis others," *Motivation and Emotion* 25, 2001, 41–65.

81. "The good life" Bertrand Russell, *Why I Am Not a Christian and Other Essays* (London: Barlow Press, 2008).

Chapter 5: Inside His Head: Men and Commitment

87. "All relations are with M(others)" Henrietta L. Moore, *The Subject of Anthropology: Gender, Symbolism and Psychoanalysis* (Malden, MA: Polity Press, 2007), 63.

88. "a man may have various unconscious fantasies" Daniel Levinson, *The Seasons of a Man's Life* (New York: Ballantine Books, 1978), 107.

91. "Bob won't be in to work tomorrow" Web video at www.liveleak.com/view?i=a96_1256201352&c=1.

94. "This battle for a separate identity" See, for example, Irene Fast, *Gender Identity: A Differentiation Model* (London: Lawrence Erlbaum Publishers, 1984), 67–69.

109. "To defend oneself against a fear" James Baldwin, *The Fire Next Time* (New York: Vintage Books, 1993), 27.

Chapter 6: The Seven "Real" Laws of Attraction: The Litmus Test for Your Relationship

115. "I love thee" Thomas Hood, "I Love Thee," *Poems of Thomas Hood*, vol. 1 (London: Macmillan, 1897), 44.

116. "serotonin levels fall" D. Marazziti, H. Akiskal, A. Rossi, and G. B. Cassano, "Alteration of the platelet serotonin transporter in romantic love," *Psychological Medicine* 29, 1999, 741–45.

116. "biologically timed to fade out" Daniel G. Amen, *The Brain in Love* (New York: Three Rivers Press, 2007), 63.

120. "Laughter is the closest distance" Victor Borge (www.thinkexist.com).

121. "shared humor" Gottman, *Marriage Clinic,* 91.

121. "people who are emotionally aroused" D. G. Dutton and P. Aron, "Some evidence of heightened sexual attraction under conditions of high anxiety," *Journal of Personality and Social Psychology* 30, 1974, 510–17; A. Aron, D. G. Dutton, E. N. Aron, and A. Iverson, "Experiences of falling in love," *Journal of Social and Personal Relationships* 6, 1989, 243–57; E. Hatfield and S. Sprecher, "Measuring passionate love in intimate relationships," *Journal of Adolescence* 9, 1986, 383–410; E. Hatfield and R. Rapson, "Passionate love/sexual desire: can the same paradigm explain both?" *Archives of Sexual Behavior* 16, 1987, 259–78.

121. "Adrenaline makes the heart grow fonder" E. Walster and E. Berscheid, "Adrenaline makes the heart grow fonder," *Psychology Today,* June 1971, 47–62.

121. "Novelty has been shown" G. Berns, *Satisfaction: The Science of Finding True Fulfillment* (New York: Henry Holt, 2005).

122. "Love is a gift" Kurt Langner (www.thinkexist.com).

126. "There is more hunger for love" Mother Teresa (www.maryvilledailyforum. org).

127. "state of appreciation" R. A. Emmons and M. McCullough, "Counting blessings vs. burdens: an experimental investigation of gratitude and subjective well-being in daily life," *Journal of Personality and Social Psychology* 84, 2003, 377–89.

127. "a five-to-one ratio" Gottman, *Marriage Clinic,* 35.

128. "Beauty is truth's smile" Rabindranath Tagore, *Fireflies* (New York: Collier Books, 1975).

129. "This is the female form" Whitman, *Leaves of Grass,* 79.

130. "Sexual love" Amy Lowell (www.thinkexist.com).

131. "playful novelty and uncertainty" H. Fisher, *Why We Love: The Nature and Chemistry of Romantic Love* (New York: Henry Holt, 2004), 205.

132. "physical nonsexual contact" See a review of the literature in M. Kosfeld, M. Heinrichs, P. J. Zak, and E. Fehr, "Oxytocin increases trust in humans," *Nature* 435, 2005, 673–76.

132. "strangers shared intimate details" A. Aron, et al., "Reward, motivation, and emotion systems associated with early-stage intense romantic love," *Journal of Neurophysiology* 94, 327–37.

134. "only about 95 percent" D. H. Hockenbury and S. E. Hockenbury, *Psychology,* 4th ed. (New York: Worth Publishers, 2005), 448.

134. "feeling intimate and close" Kosfeld, Heinrichs, Zak, and Fehr, "Oxytocin increases trust."

135. "physical and mental health" Amen, *The Brain in Love*, 16–20.

135. "three primary ways" D. Mosher, "Three psychological dimensions of depth of involvement in human sexual responses," *Journal of Sex Research* 16, 1980, 1–42.

135. "sensate focus" Procedure described in H. S. Kaplan, *The New Sex Therapy* (New York: Brunner/Mazel, 1974).

138. "Once the realization is accepted" Rilke, *Love and Other Difficulties*, 28.

140. "Wise [wo]men, when in doubt" Napoleon Hill (www.brainyquote.com/quotes/quotes/n/napoleonhi138094.html).

Chapter 7: Is He *Really* the One? How to Know for Sure

157. "A soulmate is someone" Richard Bach (www.thinkexist.com).

157. "more than 90 percent of young adults" Barbara Dafoe Whitehead and David Popenoe, *The State of Our Unions* (New Brunswick, NJ: The National Marriage Project, Rutgers University, 2006).

159. "those who are of similar educational levels" H. Domanski and D. Przybysz, "Educational homogamy in 22 European countries." *European Societies* 9, 2007, 495–526.

161. "The most wonderful" Hugh Walpole (www.thinkexist.com).

Chapter 8: Setting the Stage for the Commitment You Want

165. "Yes, your desperation has its place" Michele Ritterman, *The Tao of a Woman* (Berkeley: Skipping Stones, 2009), 62.

166. "One of the hardest things" James Earl Jones (www.wisdomquotes.com).

167. "part of our genetic legacy" J. S. Nevid, *Psychology: Concepts and Applications,* 3rd ed. (New York: Houghton Mifflin, 2008), 408–09.

167. "women often don't express themselves" L. Babcock and S. Laschever, *Women Don't Ask* (New York: Bantam, 2007).

172. "the 'ideal self'" See E. T. Higgins, "Beyond pleasure and pain," *American Psychologist* 52, 1997, 1280–1300.

172. "As different parts of self" R. Hanson, *Buddha's Brain* (Oakland, CA: New Harbinger), 212.

174. "'self expansion'" Acevedo and Aron, "Does a long-term relationship."

176. "Self-love allows you" The author conducted a national survey of couples in committed relationships through her Web site www.lovein90days.com, the press newsletter *HARO*, and Dan Poynter's newsletter, *Publishing Poynters*.

177. "use these affirmations" D. H. Meichenbaum, *Cognitive Behavior Modification: An Integrative Approach* (New York: Plenum Press, 1977).

184. "May you be content" Available at www.poeticexpressions.co.uk/StTheresasPrayer.htm.

Chapter 9: How to Have The Talk So He Really Will Listen

185. "Birds are entangled" E. Strauss, *Concise Dictionary of European Proverbs* (New York: Routledge, 1998), 119, Proverb 463.

186. "average length of courtship" See www.marieclaire.co.uk/news/world/181134/average-man-proposes-after-three-years.html and www.metro.co.uk/lifestyle/99603-average-man-takes-3-years-to-propose.

189. "Discipline is remembering" D. Campbell. Available at http://quotations.about.com/cs/inspirationquotes/a/SelfDiscipli1.htm.

192. "The male brain" M. Hunter, Dilraj S. Sokhi, et al., "Men hear women's melodies: male and female voices activate distinct regions in the male brain," *NeuroImage* 27, 2005, 572–78.

192. "wife's use of humor" Gottman, *Marriage Clinic*, 85.

193. "Cheat Sheet" D. Tannen, *You Just Don't Understand* (New York: Ballantine Books, 1990).

194. "'Soft start-up'" Gottman, *Marriage Clinic*, 224.

199. "partners in healthier relationships" C. E. Rusbult, E. J. Finkel, and M. Kumashiro, "The Michelangelo Phenomenon," *Current Directions in Psychological Science* 18, 2009, 305–09.

199. "their relationship is greatly enhanced" S. L. Murray, J. G. Holmes, and D. W. Griffin, "The benefits of positive illusions: idealization and the construction of satisfaction in close relationships," *Journal of Personality and Social Psychology* 70, 1996, 79–98.

199. "promote trust and *strengthen commitment*" E. T. Higgins, "Self-discrepancy: a theory relating to self and affect," *Psychological Review* 94, 1987, 319–40.

202. "To make me good" This poem is attributed to both Elizabeth Barrett Browning and the American poet Roy Croft (www.foreverwed2.com/Religious_Ceremonies/poems/other4.html).

Chapter 10: What to Do If He Won't Commit, Becomes Distant, or Cheats

204. "love in its fullest form" Clarissa Pinkola Estés, *Women Who Run with the Wolves* (New York: Ballantine Books, 1992), 162.

209. "The way to love anything" G. K. Chesterton, *On Lying in Bed and Other Essays* (Calgary: Bayeux Arts, Inc., 2000), 32.

212. "the same may also hold true" This is what I have found in more than twenty-five years of clinical and supervisory experience with thousands of cases.

215. "You gain strength" Eleanor Roosevelt (www.thinkexist.com).

216. "single women who have a strong, caring network" See Chapter 12 for a review of the literature.

217. "If I am not for myself" Hillel, *Pirkei Avot (Ethics of the Fathers),* 1:14.

227. "cheated at least once" Since 1988, the National Opinion Research Center at University of Chicago has been asking couples about infidelity as part of their General Population Survey. The last full analysis is Tom W. Smith, "American Sexual Behavior: Trends, Socio-Demographic Differences, and Risk Behavior," March 2006, 55 (www.norc.org).

227. "had an affair" Ibid.

227. "lost their feelings of closeness" Gottman, *Marriage Clinic,* 23.

227. "you can get through" Gottman, *Marriage Clinic,* 24.

229. "Domestic violence is the leading cause of injury" Available at http://www.ncadv.org/files/DomesticViolenceFactSheet(National).pdf.

231. "the selfsame well" Khalil Gibran, *The Prophet* (New York: Knopf, 1983), 29.

232. "Exercise can decrease depression" American College of Sports Medicine, cited in *Wall Street Journal,* January 5, 2010, D1.

232. "these activities will wreak havoc" Amen, *The Brain in Love.*

232. "a regular relaxation or meditation program" Robert K. Wallace, *The Physiology of Consciousness.* (Fairfield, IA: Maharishi International University Press, 1993), 59–62.

233. "spend time sharing" N. Eisenberger, J. Jarcho, M. Lieberman, and B. D. Naliboff, "An Experimental Study of Shared Sensitivity to Physical Pain and Social Rejection," *Pain,* 126, 2006, 132–138.

234. "Willing to experience aloneness" Jennifer Paine Welwood, "Unconditional," in *Poems for the Path* (Mill Valley, CA: Jennifer Welwood, 2001), 21.

Chapter 11: Should We Live Together First?
New Relationship Research, Surprising Answers

235. "Come live with me" John Donne, "The Bait," *The Songs and Sonets of John Donne* (Cambridge, MA: Harvard University Press, 2009), 160.

235. "more couples living together" *The 2005 Current Population Survey* (www.census.gov).

235. "about 53 percent of all first marriages" Larry Bumpass and Hsien-Hen Lu, "Trends in cohabitation and implications for children's family contexts in the U.S.," *Population Studies* 54, 2000, 29–41.

236. "the moving-in decision" G. K. Rhoades, S. M. Stanley, and H. J. Markman, "Pre-engagement cohabitation and gender asymmetry in marital commitment," *Journal of Family Psychology* 20, 2006, 553–60.

237. "poorer mental and physical health" Popenoe and Whitehead, *The State of Our Unions*.

237. "advantages for marrieds" See R. Parker, "Researching married and cohabiting couples," *Family Matters* 74, 2006, 52–55.

238. "a 50 percent breakup rate" Bumpass and Lu, "Trends in cohabitation."

238. "longer, more stable relationships" V. King and M. E. Scott, "A comparison of cohabiting relationships among older and younger adults," *Journal of Marriage and the Family* 67, 2005, 271–85.

239. "Come live with me" Christopher Marlowe, "The Passionate Shepherd to His Love," *The Works of Christopher Marlowe* (London: George Routledge, 1876), 381.

239. "release the bonding hormone oxytocin" See a review of the literature in M. Kosfeld, M. Heinrichs, P. Zak, and G. Fehr, 2005, "Oxytocin increases trust in humans," *Nature* 435, 673–676.

239. "a blast of oxytocin" Many studies, but see early work by M. R. Murphy, J. R. Seckl, S. Burton, S. A. Checkley, and S. L. Lightman, "Changes in oxytocin and vasopressin secretion during sexual activity in men," *Journal of Clinical Endocrinology and Metabolism* 65, 1987, 738–41.

240. "not an elevated risk of divorce" Jay Teachman, "Premarital sex, premarital cohabitation, and the risk of subsequent marital disruption among women," *Journal of Marriage and the Family* 65, 2003, 444–55; D. Lichter and Z. Qian, "Serial cohabitation and the marital life course," *Journal of Marriage and the Family* 70, 2008, 861–78.

240. "people over fifty" S. L. Brown and S. Kawamura, "Relationship quality among cohabitors and marrieds in older adulthood," National Center for Family and Marriage Research, Working Paper Series, WP-10-01, 2010, 1–30.

241. "only about 10 percent" S. L. Brown, J. R. Bulanda, and G. R. Lee, "Cohabitation among older adults," *Journal of Gerontology: Social Sciences* 60B, 2006, 21–29.

242. "older cohabitors" King and Scott, "A comparison of cohabiting relation-ships."

242. "their partners made 'unreasonable demands'" Brown and Kawamura, "Relationship quality."

Chapter 12: Thinking of Getting Married?
What You Need to Know Now

248. "Because I need a forever friend" Mari Nichols-Haining, "Why Mar-riage?" www.marinichols.com and on many wedding vow Web sites.

249. "married women are less successful" Elizabeth Gilbert, *Committed: A Skeptic Makes Peace with Marriage* (New York: Viking Adult, 2010).

249. "'Marriage Benefit Imbalance'" Jessie Bernard, *The Future of Marriage* (New Haven, CT: Yale University Press, 1983).

251. "marriage *reduces* the blues" See R. G. Wood, B. Goesling, and S. Avel-lar, "The effects of marriage on health: a synthesis of recent research evidence" (Princeton, NJ: Mathematica Policy Research, 2007). This is a review of seventy studies. Available at www.mathematica-mpr.com.

251. "married women may be happier" See the review by J. K. Kiecolt-Glaser and T. Newton, "Marriage and health: his and hers," *Psychological Bulletin* 127, 2001, 472–503.

253. "effect of marriage on longevity" Manzoli, et al., "Marital status and mortality in the elderly: a systematic review and meta-analysis," *Social Science & Medicine* 64, 2007, 77–94.

253. "odds of mortality" Kaplan and Kronick, "Marital Status and Longevity in the U.S. Population," *Journal of Epidemiology and Community Health* 60, 2006, 760–65.

253. "marriage is a much less dangerous place" See review by Patti How-ell, *Healthy Marriages, Healthy Women and Girls* (2009), available at www.camarriage.com/content/resources/aa49b2c4-af4d-43e7-9765-edbd80321fc4.pdf.

254. "reduction in pot smoking" Wood, Goesling, and Avellar, "Effects of marriage on health," 13–14.

254. "smoking cigarettes" Ibid., 14.

254. "marrieds exercise about 15 percent less" Ibid., 15–17.

254. "a longer, healthier life" Kiecolt-Glaser and Newton, "Marriage and health."

254. "more of a beneficial impact" Wood, Goesling, and Avellar, "Effects of marriage on health," 41.

255. "inequality in household work" J. Baxter, "Marital status and the division of household labor: cohabitation vs. marriage," *Family Matters* 58, 2001, 6–21.

255. "married women don't get the same earnings advantages" J. Baxter and E. Gray, "For richer or poorer: women, men and marriage," paper presented at the 8th Australian Institute of Family Studies Conference, Melbourne, 2003.

255. "standard of living is higher" Ibid.

256. "after a divorce" Howell, *Healthy Marriages.*

256. "a good marriage may protect a woman" Wood, Goesling, and Avellar, "Effects of marriage on health."

257. "depression, worsened physical health" Kiecolt-Glaser and Newton, "Marriage and health."

257. "least amount of atherosclerosis" Howell, *Healthy Marriages.*

257. "Fewer doctor visits" Wood, Goesling, and Avellar, "Effects of marriage on health."

257. "Lower blood pressure" J. Holt-Lunstad, W. Birmingham, and B. Q. Jones, "Is there something unique about marriage? the relative impact of marital status, relationship quality, and network support on ambulatory blood pressure and mental health," *Annals of Behavioral Medicine* 35, 2008, 239–44.

257. "Fewer headaches" Centers for Disease Control study of 128,000 adults: "Marital status and health: United States, 1999–2002." Available at cdc.gov.

257. "Better immune systems" Janice K. Kiecolt-Glaser, Ph.D., Timothy J. Loving, Ph.D., Jeffrey R. Stowell, Ph.D., William B. Malarkey, M.D., Stanley Lemeshow, Ph.D., Stephanie L. Dickinson, M.A.S., Ronald Glaser, Ph.D., "Hostile marital interactions, proinflammatory cytokine production, and wound healing," *Archives of General Psychiatry* 62, 2005, 1377–84.

258. "taken a tranquilizer" J. A. Coan, et al. "Lending a hand: social regulation of the neural response to threat," *Psychological Science* 17, 2006, 1032–39.

258. "less anxiety than newlyweds" B. P. Acevedo, A. Aron, H. Fisher, and L. L. Brown, "Neural correlates of long-term pair-bonding in a sample of intensely in-love humans," paper presented at the Annual Conference of the Society for Neuroscience, November 16, 2008.

258. "a tremendous boon to men" See major reviews by Wood, Goesling, and Avellar, "Effects of marriage on health," and Kiecolt-Glaser and Newton, "Marriage and health."

259. "A happy marriage" Anthony Storr, *The Integrity of the Personality* (New York: Ballantine Books, 1992).

Chapter 13: Secrets That Make Passionate Love Last—
No Matter How Long You've Been Together

263. "This is how a love relationship is meant to work" Estés, *Women Who Run with the Wolves,* 165.

263. "Studies of long-term marriages" J. F. Cuber and P. B. Haroff, *The Significant Americans* (New York: Appleton-Century, 1965).

264. "couples who were intensely in love" P. Ammons and N. Stinnet, "The vital marriage: a closer look," *Family Relations* 29, 1980, 37–42.

264. "women aged fifty through eighty-two" E. Hatfield, J. Traupman, and S. Sprecher, "Older women's perception of their intimate relationships," *Journal of Social and Clinical Psychology* 2, 1984, 108–24.

264. "Passionate Love Scale" E. Hatfield and S. Sprecher, "Measuring passionate love in intimate relationships," *Journal of Adolescence* 6, 1986, 383–410.

264. "a long-term relationship" Acevedo and Aron, "Does a long-term relationship."

265. "correlated with the fMRI scans" First reported by A. Bartels and S. Zeki, "The neural correlates of maternal and romantic love," *Neuroimage* 21, 2004, 1155–66.

265. "same dopamine reactions" Acevedo, Aron, Fisher, and Brown, "Neural correlates."

265. "twelve million couples" "Number, timing, and duration of marriages and divorces: 2001," U.S. Census Bureau (February 2005). Available at www.census.gov.

266. "I love you" This poem is attributed to both Elizabeth Barrett Browning and the American poet Roy Croft.

266. "help each other become their ideal selves" D. A. Kirschner and S. Kirschner, *Comprehensive Family Therapy* (New York: Brunner-Mazel, 1986).

266. "Healthy spouses sculpt" C. E. Rusbult, E. J. Finkel, and M. Kumashiro, "The Michelangelo Phenomenon," *Current Directions in Psychological Science* 18, 2009, 305–09.

266. "promote couple and individual well-being" E. T. Higgins, "Self-discrepancy: a theory relating to self and affect," *Psychological Review* 94, 1987, 319–40.

267. "Pygmalion advice and nagging" C. E. Rusbult, M. Kumashiro, K. Kubacka, and E. Finkel, "The part of me that you bring out: ideal similarity and the Michelangelo Phenomenon," *Journal of Personality and Social Psychology* 96, 2009, 61–82.

267. "When Nathaniel Hawthorne was fired" J. Griffith, *Speaker's Library of Business* (Englewood Cliffs, NJ: Prentice-Hall, 1990), 102.

267. "She is in the strictest sense, my sole companion" P. McFarland, *Hawthorne in Concord* (New York: Grove Press, 2004), 87–88.

271. "We lie in each other's arms" Marge Piercy, *Colors Passing Through Us* (New York: Alfred A. Knopf, 2003).

272. "When you love someone" Elizabeth Bowen, *Death of the Heart,* 10th ed. (New York: Anchor, 2000).

274. "My bounty is as boundless as the sea" William Shakespeare, *Complete Works of William Shakespeare: Romeo and Juliet* (New York: Wordsworth Edition, 1997), 2.2.133–35.

275. "better relationship quality" See S. M. Stanley and H. J. Markman, "Assessing commitment in personal relationships," *Journal of Marriage and the Family* 54, 1992, 595–608.

276. "Ever has it been" Khalil Gibran, *The Prophet* (New York: Alfred A. Knopf, 1983), 8.

278. "The deepest principle in human nature" William James (www.thinkexist .com).

278. "this positive effect was reported" S. B. Algoe, S. L. Gable, and N. C. Maisel, "It's the little things: everyday gratitude as a booster shot for romantic relationships," *Personal Relationships* 17, 2010, 217–33.

280. "ratio of five positive interactions" Gottman, *Marriage Clinic,* 68.

281. "All married couples" Ann Landers (http://quotations.about.com/od/ relationships/a/marriage2.htm).

282. "In studies of conflict" Gottman, *Marriage Clinic,* 73.

283. "A house divided" Abraham Lincoln, House Divided Speech, June 16, 1858. Full text available at http://showcase.netins.net/web/creative/lincoln/ speeches/house.htm.

283. "identification of oneself" Rollo May, *Love and Will* (New York: W. W. Norton, 1969), 289.

285. "There is a light" *The Upanishads,* translated by Swami Nikhilananda (New York: Harper, 1949).

INDEX

Index